The Educator's Guide to
EMOTIONAL INTELLIGENCE
and
ACADEMIC ACHIEVEMENT

*To the many educators with whom we have collaborated, and
those kindred spirits we have not met, who see students as children and understand
that nurturing their social-emotional learning skills and emotional intelligence is the only way
to ensure that all children are moved closer to realizing their potential for success in school and life.*

The Educator's Guide to
EMOTIONAL INTELLIGENCE
and
ACADEMIC ACHIEVEMENT

Social-Emotional Learning in the Classroom

MAURICE J. ELIAS • HARRIETT ARNOLD • Editors

CORWIN PRESS
A SAGE Publications Company
Thousand Oaks, California

For information:

Corwin Press
A Sage Publications Company
2455 Teller Road
Thousand Oaks, California 91320
E-mail: order@corwinpress.com

Sage Publications Ltd.
1 Oliver's Yard
55 City Road
London EC1Y 1SP
United Kingdom

Sage Publications India Pvt. Ltd.
B-42, Panchsheel Enclave
Post Box 4109
New Delhi 110 017 India

Printed in the United States of America.

Library of Congress Cataloging-in-Publication Data

The educator's guide to emotional intelligence and academic achievement: social-emotional learning in the classroom / Maurice J. Elias and Harriett Arnold, editors.
　　p. cm.
Includes bibliographical references and index.
ISBN 1-4129-1480-9 (cloth) — ISBN 1-4129-1481-7 (pbk.)
　　1. Emotional intelligence—Study and teaching (Elementary) I. Elias, Maurice J.
II. Arnold, Harriett.
BF576.E38 2006
370.15′23—dc22

　　　　　　　　　　　　　　　　　　　2005025359

This book is printed on acid-free paper.

06　07　08　09　10　11　9　8　7　6　5　4　3　2　1

Acquisitions Editor:	Faye Zucker
Editorial Assistant:	Gem Rabanera
Project Editor:	Tracy Alpern
Copy Editor:	Julie Gwin
Proofreader:	Richard Moore
Typesetter:	C&M Digitals (P) Ltd.
Indexer:	Sylvia Coates
Cover Designer:	Michael Dubowe
Graphic Designer:	Anthony Paular

Contents

Preface

This book is for educators. Just about every educator we know is wondering, in this climate of No Child Left Behind (NCLB), how do we bring all children forward academically, socially, and emotionally? What kinds of teaching approaches and what methods of organizing and structuring of classroom environments are necessary so that no professional is left behind the advances in relevant knowledge and practice that have occurred in recent years?

This book is designed to provide answers based on existing best feasible practices. We use the word *feasible* because our emphasis has been on selecting approaches that have been used successfully in many places for a long time, both before and after NCLB. We show readers how to bring emotional intelligence (EI) or social-emotional learning (SEL) into classrooms in ways that enhance academic achievement, from elementary grades through Grade 12. The book is designed to illuminate the connection between soul, heart, and mind.

SEL/EI restores and reaffirms the value of teachers as creators of learning momentum and links education with the larger social world and set of social responsibilities that children will encounter as adults. Most chapters begin with stories . . . the words of master educators who have used SEL to improve both the character and the academic achievement of their students, designed to animate the enterprise of bringing SEL into classrooms. As you read, you will see how relatively small changes in classroom and school practices now can renew your sense of education as an inspirational profession.

After reading this book, you will be familiar with the field of SEL, its rationale, how it supports and enhances academic achievement and other areas of school improvement, and best practices in the field as exemplified through acclaimed SEL programs and approaches. Through the discussion of different forms of teacher preparation to carry out SEL, you will be able to identify areas in which your own SEL-related skills or those of colleagues might be further developed. Finally, you will have ample raw materials in sample activities provided to allow for the opportunity to bring what you are reading into practice "Monday morning," and you should be well on your way to selecting an SEL/EI approach to bring into your classroom and school.

Acknowledgments

This book is the product of three decades of collective work by the authors; the contributors to this volume; the contributors to our first book, *EQ + IQ = Best Leadership Practices for Caring and Successful Schools* (Corwin Press, 2003); our colleagues at the Collaborative for Academic, Social, and Emotional Learning (CASEL; www.CASEL.org); and the many, many people who have worked with and supported all of these people. I am acutely aware of standing on many, many shoulders, and I only hope that the contents in this book will be a credit to all those who have contributed through their efforts in the schools and via research, writing, and policy making and will be an inspiration to our readers to climb on all of our shoulders and improve on what we have done.

I want to give special thanks to my parents, Agnes and Sol; my in-laws, Myra and Lou Rosen; and my wife Ellen and daughters, Sara Elizabeth and Samara Alexandra. Their support for my work has been unwavering, and each in his or her own way has gone to great efforts to keep me grounded. I hope you will see that groundedness reflected throughout this book.

Finally, thanks to Faye Zucker, Gem Rabanera, Tracy Alpern, Julie Gwin, and the fantastic team at Corwin Press. Not only are they terrific for authors, they are great friends to readers and for the field of education. This book is far, far better for their input, insights, and attentive care.

—Maurice J. Elias

I am most grateful to Maurice Elias, my colleague and friend, for his vision, tenacity, and encouragement. I thank my colleagues at CASEL for their leadership in the field of social and emotional development and each of the contributors to this publication. I extend my thanks to John, my husband, for his support and thoughtful listening, and to Laura Frey, Central Michigan University, and Thomas Nelson, University of the Pacific, for their suggestions and recommendations.

—Harriett Arnold

Corwin Press thanks the following reviewers for their contributions to this book:

Robert DiGiulio, Professor of Education, Johnson State College, VT

Beverly Eidmann, Principal, Arvada Middle School, Arvada, CO

Steven Reifman, Teacher, Santa Monica-Malibu Unified School District, Santa Monica, CA

David A. Squires, Associate Professor, Southern Connecticut State University

About the Editors

Maurice J. Elias, PhD, is Professor, Department of Psychology, Rutgers University, and directs the Rutgers Social-Emotional Learning Lab. He is Vice Chair of the Leadership Team of the Collaborative for Academic, Social, and Emotional Learning (CASEL; www.CASEL .org) and Senior Advisor for Research, Policy, and Practice to the New Jersey Center for Character Education. He devotes his research and writing to the area of emotional intelligence in children, schools, and families. His books for parents include *Emotionally Intelligent Parenting: How to Raise a Self-Disciplined, Responsible, Socially Skilled Child* (Three Rivers Press, 2000) and *Raising Emotionally Intelligent Teenagers: Guiding the Way for Compassionate, Committed, Courageous Adults* (Three Rivers Press, 2002), both published in several languages. Recent releases are *Engaging the Resistant Child Through Computers: A Manual for Social-Emotional Learning* (available through www.nprinc.com), *Building Learning Communities with Character: How to Integrate Academic, Social, and Emotional Learning* (ASCD, 2002) and *EQ + IQ = Best Leadership Practices for Caring and Successful Schools* (Corwin Press, 2003), *Bullying, Peer Harassment, and Victimization in the Schools: The Next Generation of Prevention* (Haworth, 2004), and updated versions of his research-validated school-based social-emotional learning (SEL) curricula: *Social Decision Making/Social Problem Solving: A Curriculum for Academic, Social, and Emotional Learning, Grades 2–3; Social Decision Making/Social Problem Solving: A Curriculum for Academic, Social, and Emotional Learning, Grades 4–5;* and *Social Decision Making/Social Problem Solving for Middle School Students: Skills and Activities for Academic, Social, and Emotional Success* (www.researchpress.com). He is married and the father of two children. He can be reached at RutgersMJE@aol.com.

 **Harriett Arnold** serves as Associate Professor in the Gladys L. Benerd School of Education, Department of Curriculum and Instruction, at the University of the Pacific, Stockton, California. A veteran educator, she has served as an elementary school teacher, a middle school administrator, an elementary school principal, an international consultant, and director of personnel and staff development. Her higher education experience includes serving as a coordinator of the Stanford Teacher Education Program, Stanford University, Stanford, California. Her professional associations include Executive Board, California Association of Supervision and Curriculum Development; Constituency Board of the Association for Supervision and Curriculum Development (ASCD), Issues Committee; Association of California School Administrators; California Council on the Education of Teachers; Phi Delta Kappa; Board of Directors, Project 30 Alliance; and other educational organizations. Her teacher training projects have involved teacher training for the Ministry of Education in the Bahamas, where she trained elementary teachers in the area of reading, and training in Japan, England, Trinidad, St. Maarten, Germany, and Curacao in the area of SEL. She serves as the cofacilitator of the Network for Research on Affective Factors in Learning, a special interest group of educators interested in the role of emotions and learning funded by ASCD. Her publications include professional journal articles and reviews; the chronicles of an African American church, *Antioch: A Place of Christians* (Western Book Journal Press, 1993); *Succeeding in the Secondary Classroom: Strategies for Middle and High School Teachers* (Corwin Press, 2001); and, as coeditor with Maurice Elias and Cynthia Steiger Hussey, *EQ + IQ = Best Leadership Practices for Caring and Successful Schools* (Corwin Press, 2003).

About the Contributors

Kathy Beland, **MEd**, is author of *Second Step, A Violence Prevention Curriculum* (PreK–Grade 9) (Committee for Children, 1992, 1997) and *The Eleven Principles of Effective Character Education Sourcebook* (Character Education Partnership, 2003) and is writer/executive producer of 12 award-winning, educational videos on the prevention of child abuse and youth violence. Currently she is developing School-Connect, a social and emotional learning curriculum for high school students released in 2005.

Sheldon Berman, **EdD**, has been the Superintendent of the Hudson, Massachusetts, public schools since 1993. Before coming to Hudson, he was a founder and president of Educators for Social Responsibility. He is editor of *Promising Practices in Teaching Social Responsibility* (SUNY Press, 1993) and author of *Children's Social Consciousness* (SUNY Press, 1997), as well as numerous articles and book chapters, and he holds leadership roles in the Character Education Partnership and the Collaborative for Academic, Social, and Emotional Learning.

Christine Blaber, **EdM**, is Associate Director of the Center for School and Community Health at Education Development Center, Inc. (EDC). Since 1993, she has served as project director for Teenage Health Teaching Modules (THTM), EDC's comprehensive health curriculum. Her role includes overseeing and contributing to curriculum development, designing and implementing a train-the-trainers system, and marketing products. THTM addresses such issues as adolescent mental and emotional health, substance abuse, violence prevention, sexuality education, and life skills.

Linda Bruene Butler, **MEd**, has worked for more than two decades in the area of school-based programs in social and emotional learning (SEL). She is currently the Director of the Social Decision Making/Problem Solving Program at the Behavioral Research and Training Institute of University Medicine & Dentistry of New Jersey–University Behavioral HealthCare. Her current area of interest is developing technology to help to institutionalize SEL programming in school districts.

Cary Cherniss, **PhD**, is Professor and Director of Organizational Psychology at the Graduate School of Applied and Professional Psychology, Rutgers University. He co-chairs (with Daniel Goleman) the Consortium for Research on Emotional Intelligence in Organizations. Among many publications related to emotional intelligence, work stress, management training, and organizational change are *Promoting Emotional Intelligence in the Workplace: Guidelines for Practitioners* (American Society for Training and Development, with Mitchel Adler) and *Professional Burnout in Human Service Organizations* (Praeger, 1980).

Carol Cummings, **PhD**, conducts workshops for parents and teachers throughout the world on social skills, reading and writing strategies, classroom management, and motivation. She has worked on three research projects at the University of Washington and with teachers at the Seattle Pacific University. She is the author of 16 books for teachers and children.

Steven J. Danish is Director of the Life Skills Center and Professor of Psychology, Preventive Medicine and Community Health, at Virginia Commonwealth University. He is a registered sport psychologist, U.S. Olympic Committee's Sports Medicine Division. His Going for the GOAL program won the National Mental Health Association's Lela Rowland Prevention Award, was honored by the U.S. Department of Health and Human Services as part of its Freedom from Fear Campaign, and received an honorable mention by the Points of Light Foundation.

Ellen Dietz, **MS**, has been the staff writer and resource developer for Project Oz since 1990. She has raised more than $9 million in grant money and has expertise in technical and public relations writing. She has taught university science courses and has led grant writing seminars for colleges and community agencies. She also has written several nonfiction articles and has had her writing and photographs published in *Intervention in School and Clinic, Illinois Magazine, Their World,* and *International Wolf.*

Mike Dobbins, **MFA**, is the lead trainer for Project Oz. He joined the staff in 1990, coming from a background in theater and teaching. He is part of many organizations in the prevention field. He is a Certified Senior Alcohol and Drug Abuse Preventionist, as well as a certified K–12 teacher. He is former Chair of the Prevention Steering Committee and Subcommittee on People with Disabilities, both part of the Illinois Alcohol and Drug Dependence Association.

Joan Cole Duffell is Director of Marketing and Community Education at the Committee for Children, an international nonprofit organization dedicated to the safety, well-being, and social development of children. Since 1983, she has been a leading advocate for social-emotional learning programs in schools. More recently, she has developed partnerships with education systems in Northern Europe and Asia, bringing the award-winning Second Step violence prevention program to educators, schoolchildren, and families across the globe.

Gloria S. Elder, **MA**, is the Deputy Director of Training, co-developer and Project Director of the Pre-School Stress Relief Project, and developer of the ParentWise Parenting Program at the Wholistic Stress Control Institute, Inc. She has extensive expertise and experience in early childhood education, administration, prevention, and health and wellness issues, with a particular focus on curriculum development and implementation and program replication. She received her master's degree in Early Childhood Education from Atlanta University.

Tanya Forneris, **MS**, obtained her bachelor of arts and master's of science from the University of New Brunswick in New Brunswick, Canada. She is currently pursuing her doctoral degree in counseling psychology at Virginia Commonwealth University. Her interests include life skill development, at-risk youth, and research methods and analysis. She is a recipient of a doctoral fellowship from the Social Sciences and Humanities Research Council of Canada.

Karin Frey, PhD, is a Research Associate Professor at the University of Washington. Her work on children's social and academic motivation has been published in leading journals of child development. Current research examines the effect of school programs on children's aggression, moral engagement, and positive social behavior. She has developed social competence programs for special-needs children and led the development of the Steps to Respect bullying prevention program at the Committee for Children.

Joanne Glancy, BS, has been a Preventionist and Curriculum Specialist for Project Oz since 1986. She has coauthored several drug, life skills, and violence prevention curricula for Project Oz that are sold nationally. She has trained school administrators, teachers, and social service personnel. Joanne uses the materials she has coauthored to teach prevention to adolescents. She is a member of ASCD and is a certified Alcohol, Tobacco and Other Drug Abuse Preventionist.

Daniel Goleman, PhD, is co-director of the Consortium for Research on Emotional Intelligence in Organizations, in the Graduate School of Professional and Applied Psychology at Rutgers University. As a science journalist, he covered the brain and behavioral sciences for the New York Times for many years, before writing *Emotional Intelligence: Why It Can Matter More Than IQ* (Bantam Books, 1995), which has been translated into more than 30 languages. His most recent book is as coauthor of *Primal Leadership: Learning to Lead with Emotional Intelligence* (2002).

Mark T. Greenberg, PhD, holds the Bennett Chair in Prevention Research in Penn State's College of Health and Human Development and is the Director of the Prevention Research Center for the Promotion of Human Development. He has been examining the effectiveness of both universal school-based curricula (the Promoting Alternative Thinking Strategies [PATHS] curriculum) and comprehensive programs (Fast Track) to improve the social, emotional, and cognitive competence of elementary-aged children. He is a member of the Leadership Team of CASEL.

Kevin Haggerty, MSW, is a faculty member at the Social Development Research Group, University of Washington, School of Social Work. He is the Co-Principal Investigator of the National Institute on Drug Abuse–funded Raising Healthy Children project. He has specialized in the development and testing of prevention programs at the community, school, and family levels. He is an international trainer and speaker in the areas of substance abuse and delinquency prevention and has written extensively in the field.

Thomas Hatch is Co-Director of the National Center for Restructuring Education, Schools and Teaching at Teachers College, Columbia University. His research focuses on key issues in large-scale school reform, and he is also involved in creating new methods and resources that support the documentation of teaching and teacher learning at all levels. He previously served as a senior scholar at the Carnegie Foundation for the Advancement of Teaching, where he co-directed the K–12 Program of the Carnegie Academy for the Scholarship of Teaching and Learning and the Knowledge Media Laboratory.

Susan Carroll Keister is an educational consultant for the Service-Learning Life Skills Network and the Senior Consultant and International Training Coordinator for the Lions Clubs International Foundation. Since 1983, she has led the development of the acclaimed Lions-Quest K–12 positive youth development programs, including Skills for Growing, Skills for Adolescence (Center for Substance Abuse Prevention Model Program), and Skills for Action, all of which were awarded the CASEL SELECT designation for curriculum and training excellence in social and emotional learning, character development, positive prevention, and service learning. She collaborates with leaders from more than 22 countries, advises several major educational organizations, and is a Fellow of the Fetzer Institute in Kalamazoo, Michigan.

Rachael Kessler is the Director of The PassageWays Institute, where she conducts professional and curriculum development for schools, districts, individual educators, and youth development professionals. Author of *The Soul of Education: Helping Students Find Connect, Compassion and Character at School* (ACSD, 2000), as well as coauthor of *Promoting Social and Emotional Learning: Guidelines for Educators* (ASCD, 1997), she is a frequent contributor to journals and to books that address social, emotional, and spiritual development in schools. For more information, see www .passageways.org.

Mindy L. Kornhaber is an Assistant Professor in the College of Education at the Pennsylvania State University. Her research addresses two questions: How do institutions and the policies surrounding them enhance or impede individual potential? How can potential be realized both on a high level and on an equitable basis? She has recently contributed a chapter on assessment and equity to *The Handbook of Research on Multicultural Education*, edited by James Banks and Cheryl A. McGee Banks, and coauthored a new book, with Edward Fierros and Shirley Veenema, entitled *Multiple Intelligences: Best Ideas from Research and Practice* (Allyn & Bacon, 2003).

Beverly J. Koteff, MA, a consultant for Open Circle, has edited the Open Circle Curriculum and newsletter, *Open Circle Newsline*. She has been an active parent volunteer in her children's schools for 25 years. She received her MA in English from East Carolina University.

Roxann Kriete is the Executive Director of Northeast Foundation for Children (NEFC), a nonprofit organization whose mission is to help K–8 educators create safe, challenging, and joyful classrooms and schools. She is a former classroom teacher and author of *The Morning Meeting Book* (Northeast Foundation for Children, 2002) and *The First Six Weeks of School* (Educational Media Corporation, 2000). *Morning Meeting* is part of the Responsive Classroom approach to teaching, an approach developed by NEFC.

Carol A. Kusché, PhD, is a Graduate Psychoanalyst and Clinical Psychologist in private practice in Seattle, Washington, where she treats children, adolescents, and adults. She is also a faculty member at the Seattle Psychoanalytic Society & Institute and the Northwest Center for Psychoanalysis, and she is a Clinical Associate Professor in the Department of Psychology at the University of Washington. She is co-developer and coauthor of the PATHS curriculum, as well as other research articles and book chapters. She is especially interested in the areas of prevention, emotional development, neuropsychoanalysis, and issues regarding the preservation of our Earth.

Mary Hansberry McCarthy directs service learning and character education in Hudson, Massachusetts. She taught English on the high school, junior high, and college levels and has served as a social worker, high school principal, college teacher, and supervisor. She has triple eagle status at Boston College with degrees in English and American Literature, Educational Administration, and School Leadership and coteaches a graduate course on service learning and a VHS course on service learning that she designed for high school students.

Ann Medlock founded the Giraffe Heroes Program after working as a curriculum developer at Science Research Associates and at Macmillan. A magna cum laude graduate of the University of Maryland, she expanded her education with a decade of living in Asia and Africa. She has been an award-winning commentator on public radio and a speaker at conferences around the world, she recently published a book of poetry, and she is in the final stages of writing a novel. Ongoing information about all aspects of the Giraffe Heroes Program can be found at www.giraffe.org.

Janet Patti has served as the Coordinator of the Educational Administration and Supervision Program at Hunter College (City University of New York) for the past 7 years. She is a member of the Leadership Team of CASEL, is the author of numerous articles on conflict resolution and intergroup relations, and is most recognized for her coauthored books, *Waging Peace in Our Schools* (Beacon, 1996) and *Smart School Leaders: Leading with Emotional Intelligence* (Kendall-Hunt, 2003).

Victoria Poedubicky is a School Counselor in Highland Park, New Jersey, and holds a degree in health and physical education and state certification in school counseling. She coauthored *Computer Facilitated Counseling for At-Risk Students in a Social Problem Solving Lab*, was a major contributor to the monograph *Promoting Social and Emotional Learning: Guidelines for Educators* (ASCD, 1997), and authored the article, "Students and Teachers Both Win When Social-Emotional Learning/EQ and IQ are Combined in Education" in the New Jersey Association for Supervision and Curriculum Development's annual journal (2002).

Rose Reissman has a PhD in Literature from New York University. She is an Associate Professor of Education at the Long Island University–Westchester campus. In addition, she is a consultant to the Department of Education in New York City for literacy, social studies, student leadership, test sophistications training, multicultural education, and new teacher/PATT training. She is President of the New York City Association of Teachers of English and a curriculum author/trainer for the New York Daily News' Newspaper in Education Program.

Pam Robbins consults internationally with school systems, universities, professional organizations, and corporate clients. Her professional background includes work as a teacher, basketball coach, and Director of Staff Development and Director of Training for the California School Leadership Academy. She has authored publications on emotional intelligence, coaching, leadership, and effective teaching, including *The Principal's Companion* (with Harvey Alvy, 2nd edition, Corwin, 2003) and *Thinking Inside the Block Schedule* (with Gayle Gregory and Lynne Herndon, Corwin, 2000).

Eliot Rosenbloom, MSW, MBA, is a returning doctoral student in human development and family studies at Penn State University. His interests include social and emotional development as well as cultural change to prevent bullying and foster concern for the community. Previously he worked in management and organization development mostly in the health sector, assisted (for the Department of Social Services) Virginia's counties in implementing programs to support families and children, and served as a regional director for the Giraffe Heroes Program.

Marcia A. Rubin, PhD, MPH, has been the Director of Research and Sponsored Programs for the American School Health Association (ASHA) since 1996. In that capacity, she has administered more than $4 million in extramural funding from both government and private sources. Prior to coming to ASHA, she taught for 5 years in the health education program at Kent State University.

Pamela Seigle is founder and Executive Director of the Open Circle Program, a social-emotional learning program based at the Stone Center at Wellesley College. She coauthored the Open Circle and Parent Program curricula, currently being implemented in more than 260 elementary schools in the Northeast. Through its curriculum and training, Open Circle works with all children and adults in the school community. She is a community activist and former classroom teacher, school psychologist, and staff developer.

Myrna B. Shure is Professor in the Department of Psychology at Drexel University in Philadelphia. Her I Can Problem Solve (ICPS) programs and her pioneering research with George Spivack have been recognized as best practice, model, or promising programs by the 1999 President's Report on School Safety, the Center for the Study of Prevention and Violence–Blueprints for Violence Prevention (1999); the Expert Panel, Safe, Disciplined, and Drug Free Schools, U.S. Department of Education (2001); and the Center for Substance Abuse Prevention (2001). In 2002, ICPS was chosen as a Select Program—the highest recognition—by CASEL.

Martin E. Sleeper is Director of Operations and Director of the New England Region of Facing History and Ourselves. He is former Principal of the Runkle School in Brookline, Massachusetts. His experience includes extensive teaching in secondary and higher education as well as curriculum design and teacher training in school and nonschool settings. He is the author of several articles on school administration and on the connection between history education and adolescent development.

Margot Stern Strom is Executive Director, President and Cofounder of the Facing History and Ourselves Foundation, an international, educational, nonprofit organization with headquarters in greater Boston and regional centers in the United States and Europe. Through partnerships with universities, civic leaders, and nongovernmental organizations across the globe, Facing History publishes educational materials, sponsors international symposia, and provides workshops, institutes, and online professional development services and resources to educators and students around the world.

Jennie C. Trotter, MEd, is co-developer of the Pre-School Stress Relief Project and the Founder and Executive Director of the Wholistic Stress Control Institute, Inc., a nonprofit, community-based organization that provides stress education services and materials for children and adults. She has developed several prevention models for users in educational settings. She obtained her master's degree from Bank Street College of Education in New York, where she majored in counseling and education.

Susan F. Wooley is Executive Director of the ASHA and oversees the day-to-day operations of the national office. Her responsibilities include representing the association, the school health community, and the health and well-being of children and youth at the national level as part of consortia and coalitions, in contacts with the media, and in advocacy work. She consults at the local, state, and national levels on curriculum development and program planning.

Introduction

About This Book

We organized this book into three parts, each introduced through interviews with one or more experienced, charismatic educators who have walked the walk and can also talk the talk. Their voices, like the voices of the authors who contributed to each chapter, are designed to help guide the way toward application of the ideas in the book. Their advice is theoretically grounded, but very strongly based in practice, and it builds on our companion book, *EQ + IQ = Best Leadership Practices for Caring and Successful Schools* (by M. J. Elias, H. Arnold, & C. Hussey, Eds., Thousand Oaks, CA: Corwin Press, 2003). There, educational administrators and other leaders provided firsthand accounts of how they brought social-emotional learning (SEL) and emotional intelligence (EI) into their schools in ways that built a positive climate, reduced violence and other problem behaviors, and promoted academic achievement. From Anchorage to New Haven, Minnesota to Louisiana, and California to Israel, in regular and special education settings for all age groups, administrators shared the paths they followed.

But much has happened in recent years, and many more teachers have added their voices as they have accumulated experience implementing SEL approaches in an era of strong academic accountability. Their stories are the main thrust of this book and comprise Part III. What they have to say confirms what visionary administrators knew all along: There is a fundamental connection between SEL/EI and academic performance. This connection is the focus of Part I of this book. Furthermore, SEL has become recognized as a connecting thread that provides synergy to other efforts that are of concern to every school district in which students attend and teachers teach. This is illustrated in Part II. We refer to the school's role in key areas:

- How we prepare students to become citizens and engage in service
- How we prepare students with both knowledge and character to enter the world of work
- How schools must attend to and take a comprehensive view of the health of students if they are to live up to their potentials
- How we prepare, orient and induct, nurture, and develop teachers and other educators

The most significant factors leading to school disaffection, failure, and dropout are social-emotional. When teachers leave teaching, it is much more for reasons related to student behavior, classroom and school climate, and matters of character than it is for anything having to do with technical aspects of teaching and pedagogy. Similarly, SEL is at the root of lack of civic participation, workplace difficulty, and poor decision making about health. Meeting the complex mission of schools for academics and character requires attention to SEL in tandem with intellectual factors. The best educators, like the best parents, have known this intuitively all along. Research and practice have now caught up with intuition.

AGE GROUPS ADDRESSED BY THE MATERIALS

As you will see, there is a great deal in this book that applies to every grade level. Part I addresses the connection of SEL and academics, brain learning, and multiple intelligences from preschool through high school. Although some of the contexts in Part II are age related (e.g., school-to-work), there are implications in each that are relevant to all developmental periods. Part III, bringing SEL to classrooms, contains examples from preschool through high school, as summarized in Figure 1.

That being said, many of the program developers are continuing their action research to allow their programs to have more developmental coverage and to connect to one another in more seamless ways when they are both found in the same schools or districts in contiguous grade levels. Examples of these include the newly developed Passages programs for elementary transitions, the new Social Decision Making/Social Problem Solving materials for middle school, and the strong connections between Responsive Classroom and Open Circle and PATHS. Also worth noting is the growing application of these approaches to special education populations, whether in general

Figure 1   Age Groups Addressed by Approaches to Social-Emotional Learning and Academics in Part III

	Early Childhood	Elementary	Middle	High
I Can Problem Solve (Chapter 10)	•	•		
Preschool Stress Relief (11)	•			
Morning Meeting/Responsive Classroom (12)		•	•	
Raising Healthy Children (13)		•	•	
Social Decision Making/Social Problem Solving (14)		•		
Open Circle (15)		•		
Promoting Alternative Thinking Strategies (16)		•		
Second Step (17)	•	•	•	
Quest (18)		•	•	•
Going for the Goal (19)			•	•
Service Learning and Literacy (20)		•	•	
Giraffe Heroes (21)		•	•	•
Best Practices in Prevention (22)		•	•	
Teenage Health Teaching Modules (23)			•	•
Facing History and Ourselves (24)			•	•
Senior Passage Course (25)				•

education/inclusion settings or in self-contained contexts. In the *EQ + IQ* book mentioned earlier, chapters by Cohen, Ettinger, and O'Donnell (2003) and by Frank Wallace (2003) describe how their schools for children with such problems as emotional disturbances, learning impairment, autism spectrum disorders, and hyperactivity are organized around SEL/EI approaches and the integration of specific curricula of the kind mentioned in Part III. Further information on these and ongoing developments is best obtained from the Web sites listed at the end of each chapter in Part III, the Web resources listed at the end of Chapter 1, or from periodic reviews and updates provided by the Collaborative for Academic, Social, and Emotional Learning (CASEL) at www.CASEL.org.

PART I

The first chapter shows the powerful connection between academic success and SEL/character education. It provides an overview of social and emotional skills and the essential role they play in everyday classroom organization, climate, and management, as well as student success. Much of this chapter is based on the work of CASEL. CASEL is the preeminent organization for gathering and disseminating research, theory, and practice information regarding SEL and its application to educational contexts of all kinds. At the conclusion of Chapter 1 is a listing of essential resources for SEL, especially Web-based information that will constantly be refreshed.

Perhaps the most important of these Web listings is the CASEL Web site, www .CASEL.org. There, readers will find an online version of CASEL's *Safe and Sound: An Educational Leader's Guide to Evidence-Based Social and Emotional Learning Programs.* In it, one can see a direct comparison and analysis of many SEL programs in a *Consumer Reports* format. This includes details about many of the programs in Part III of this book. CASEL's Web site will be an ongoing resource for updating information about SEL and triaging questions about resources and issues related to application, implementation, training, educator preparation, and educational policy related to SEL and academics.

Chapter 2 addresses the second fundamental connection, which is about brain research and how SEL is strongly implicated in what we are learning about learning. This chapter was specifically written for educators and illustrates in a very accessible way how we must make our pedagogy complement our physiology and the way in which SEL approaches foster this.

Chapter 3 helps us understand the grounding of SEL and EI in the broader context of Howard Gardner's theory of multiple intelligences (MI). In many ways, the emergence of SEL is a recognition that two aspects of MI, interpersonal and intrapersonal intelligence, have even more potential for general education success than perhaps was realized initially. This chapter helps readers realize that SEL is not something completely new and integrates well into Gardner's familiar and widely implemented approaches.

PART II

Chapters 4 through 9 in Part II consist of a series of brief essays that show the connection of SEL to service and citizenship, the school-to-work transition, comprehensive student health, and teacher preparation and continuing development. These are essential concerns of every school district, and as you will see from reading these chapters, using a common SEL approach across these areas can yield benefits of synergy. SEL skills are common to all these contexts.

As the last three chapters (7–9) in Part II show clearly, teachers who themselves have strong EI skills will be better able to deal with the challenges of their job, work well with colleagues and parents, and also impart SEL skills to their students. Early reviewers of this book suggested that Rose Reissman's chapter (Chapter 8) provides an excellent introduction to Dan Goleman's work on EI, and so we commend it to your attention if you want a refresher. Chapters 7 through 9 address teachers at various stages of their careers, starting with college-level training and teacher induction, two critical periods in education, given what we know about the staggering rates of teacher attrition due in large part to difficulties related to the behavior and social and emotional needs of students.

Part II closes with Pam Robbins's model (Chapter 9) for providing professional development to experienced teachers in SEL in a way that respects their professionalism and allows them to pace their own learning over time. Despite the brevity of the chapters in Part II, readers will find that the authors have made explicit suggestions about how SEL can be applied to strengthen children's learning in each context discussed and have shared their thoughts about the most effective ways to help educators make SEL a natural and integral part of their classrooms and schools.

PART III

Part III is the heart of the book, literally. It consists of stories told by master teachers who have worked with social and emotional programs for many years, in many classrooms. Each of the stories illustrates programs with the strongest empirical and pragmatic evidence of success. Each has been written in ways that allow readers to get a genuine feeling for the program. Vignettes and sample materials and activities will allow readers to try out aspects of what they are reading. Authors also address how educators can prepare to carry out the program, how the programs are related to a building-wide climate that promotes SEL, and how programs assess their effect. The purpose of these chapters is to inspire you to give SEL approaches a try. The intent of the articles is *not* to describe every nuance of each program or approach. The specific examples of activities and lessons are intended to foster an "I can do that" attitude, and then some specific guidance to actually do it!

Programs are presented roughly in developmental order, from preschool and early elementary through high school. Some extend across elementary, middle, and high school levels. Some are quite comprehensive (e.g., Quest, Open Circle, and Second Step), whereas others are more focused on critical SEL areas at key developmental periods (e.g., Going for the Goal, Giraffe Service Learning, Teenage Health Teaching Modules, Facing History and Ourselves). Some have found important applications in both regular and special education (e.g., PATHS, Best Practices in Prevention, Social Decision Making/Social Problem Solving). Some border on not being programs as much as ways to reorganize learning (Responsive Classroom, Raising Healthy Children, Senior Passage). In actuality, virtually all of these programs *do* transform the teaching and learning process in the classroom. They change relationships in the classroom and use emotions and problem solving constructively in the service of academic and social learning and application to everyday life.

READER'S APPLICATION/REFLECTION GUIDE

To help you bring the content of Part III into your educational practice, we have created a reproducible Reader's Application/Reflection Guide (see Figure 2). It serves as an organizer so that as you read, you will be able to consider the following to help you try out ideas from the chapter:

Figure 2   Reader's Application/Reflection Guide

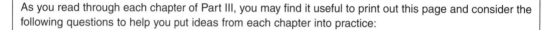

As you read through each chapter of Part III, you may find it useful to print out this page and consider the following questions to help you put ideas from each chapter into practice:

1. Visualize what this program would look like in your classroom.

2. Reflect on how this is similar to or different from your current practice.

3. Write down two or three specific ideas you can apply from this chapter most readily.

4. Ask a question for the developers/authors to clarify, extend your understanding, obtain more examples, and so forth, using the contact information at the end of the chapter and at www.CASEL.org.

We have found that this approach leads to less re-reading and also allows you to take ideas you are reading, bring them into practice quickly, and refine them through dialogue with others who have "walked the talk."

REFERENCES

Cohen, M., Ettinger, B., & O'Donnell, T. (2003). The Children's Institute Model for building the social-emotional skills of students in special education: A schoolwide approach. In M. J. Elias, H. Arnold, & C. S. Hussey (Eds.), *EQ + IQ = Best leadership practice for caring and successful schools* (pp. 124–141). Thousand Oaks, CA: Corwin.

Wallace, F. (2003). Social-emotional learning at North Country School: Resourcefulness, ruggedness, and resilience. In M. J. Elias, H. Arnold, & C. S. Hussey (Eds.), *EQ + IQ = Best leadership practice for caring and successful schools* (pp. 142–153). Thousand Oaks, CA: Corwin.

PART I

The Fundamental Connection of Social-Emotional Learning/Emotional Intelligence, Academic Performance, and the Process of Learning

Introduction to Part I

That social-emotional learning (SEL) and emotional intelligence are basic to education may seem intellectually obvious as one reads about it, but the pathways to a deep belief in this connection are forged through experience. Here is an indication of the journey, in the words of a district-level administrator, Larry Leverett, and a school-based educator, Denise Scala. Larry has been a self-described "mission warrior" on behalf of disadvantaged youth in a long and distinguished career in education and educational leadership. Denise has been on the front lines in that mission, dedicating her career to helping students who face the most roadblocks in life. They were asked to share some thoughts with educators who were beginning to learn about or make a deeper commitment to bringing SEL into the core of their practice.

Larry Leverett

I vividly remember my struggles as a young teacher filled with passion, eagerness, and a sense of mission focused on ensuring that every student succeeded in my classroom. Unfortunately, I hadn't been taught everything I needed to know to help my students to manage emotions, to be self-regulating, to communicate their feelings carefully and accurately, and to find ways to handle conflicts nonviolently with peers or adults in their learning environment.

Each day, our students arrive at the doors of classrooms across America with challenges that serve as barriers to their success as learners. These students are affluent and poor; they are English-language learners and English-language speakers; they are white, Hispanic, African American, and Asian; they are urban, suburban, and rural. Regardless of who they are, where they come from, or the extent of their poverty or wealth, the reality is that many lack the personal, social, and emotional competencies to receive the maximum benefit of a rigorous, standards-based instructional program.

I recall how frustrating it was for me to spend evenings planning lessons to engage students in the content of the curriculum. What I didn't do was to create a classroom environment that would help my students develop the skills, disposition, and discipline required for them to reap the benefits of my efforts to be a good teacher. The result was they didn't learn all they needed to, and I went home many nights feeling personal frustration and failure. I wanted my students to succeed and worked hard to make that happen, but I didn't know what I could do to actualize this goal.

The good news is that much has been learned that can help teachers and other educators to be more effective in creating classroom environments that can help learners to develop the knowledge, skills, and dispositions necessary for success. The field of SEL has grown, and there is solid evidence that links academic success to social-emotional competencies.

I have had the opportunity to work in a variety of school settings, and it is clear to me that children can benefit from the efforts of educators to integrate SEL into the curriculum of every child, across content areas. In my earlier work as an urban school superintendent in a low-performing urban district, my colleagues and I knew that our efforts to prepare students to meet rigorous academic standards would require us to integrate SEL competencies into our work. Our truth was that the goals of student achievement were inextricably linked to our efforts to help teachers and students develop the attitudes and behaviors that would enable them to sustain commitment and focus to improve.

We know that we are working in a tough accountability environment that places pressure on teachers and the students they serve. Many of us are working very hard to meet increasingly rigorous academic standards. The realities of No Child Left Behind require that we integrate SEL if we are to improve students' chances of experiencing the lasting life benefits that their time in school can provide and that teachers so much want to give.

Denise Scala

Why is emotional intelligence important? As a guidance counselor at an urban elementary school, I am constantly faced with the effects of a changing and sometimes struggling society. More specifically, our kids enter the school doors saddled with issues: shorter attention spans, being raised by single parents or grandparents, the need for instant gratification, anger problems, difficulty relating to structure, problems maintaining relationships with peers and adults, and pent-up negative emotions. As a school counselor, one of my primary responsibilities is to help remove the barricades that hinder their education. Easier said than done, I know.

SEL has been a key tool in helping me, and our teachers, remove educational hindrances at the school. Over the past 6 years, we have incrementally increased our test scores. Previous to educational reform and the introduction of a social-emotional program structure by Rutgers University, our school experienced test scores well below 20% proficient on state tests. Now, we consistently reach well above 60% and 70% of kids above proficient.

SEL by itself cannot move schools forward. However, balanced with an exciting and relevant curriculum, it can help to push students to the next level. All students have the potential to succeed . . . the emotionally healthy student will.

Larry Leverett is Superintendent of Schools in Greenwich, CT; held that position in Plainfield, NJ; and was Assistant Commissioner for Urban Education for New Jersey.

Denise Scala is currently a guidance counselor at the Stillman Elementary School in Plainfield, NJ.

1

The Connection Between Academic and Social-Emotional Learning

Maurice J. Elias

In every society, children will inherit social roles now occupied by adults. Our schools have the job of preparing children for this eventual responsibility. Therefore, around the world, people want to improve education. The pages of education newsletters, newspapers, magazines, books, and journals are filled with many different ideas about what should be emphasized. However, there are some areas of growing consensus. Numerous polls of parents and community leaders indicate clearly what we want our children to know and be able to do, and this defines what we want schools to teach. We want young people to

- be fully literate and able to benefit from and make use of the power of written and spoken language, in various forms and media;
- understand mathematics and science at levels that will prepare them for the world of the future and strengthen their ability to think critically, carefully, and creatively;

- be good problem solvers;
- take responsibility for their personal health and well-being;
- develop effective social relationships, such as learning how to work in a group and how to understand and relate to others from different cultures and backgrounds;
- be caring individuals with concern and respect for others;
- understand how their society works and be prepared to take on the roles that are necessary for future progress; and
- develop good character and make sound moral decisions.

All of these are aspects of what some refer to as the "education of the whole child." This is not a new idea; it is rooted in the writings and teachings of many ancient cultures. Yet achieving the kind of balance that encourages all children to learn, work, and contribute to their fullest potential has been a continuing challenge as our world has grown more complex and our communities more fragmented.

The final six points on the previous list refer to aspects of education that have been referred to as character education, service learning, citizenship education, and emotional intelligence. All of these can be expressed in the single term, *social-emotional learning* (SEL), and it is this form of education, when added to academic learning, that provides educators with the possibility of capturing the balance children need.

Since balance is necessary, efforts that elevate some factors at the expense of others are doomed to failure. A moment's reflection reveals how obvious this is. For children to become literate, responsible, nonviolent, drug-free, and caring adults, those of us who are educators, parents, business leaders, and policymakers must think cohesively and carefully about how to address this challenge and not divert attention to other goals.

Experience and research show that each element of this challenge can be enhanced by thoughtful, sustained, and systematic attention to the social-emotional skills of children (Greenberg et al., 2003). The Collaborative for Academic, Social, and Emotional Learning (CASEL; www.CASEL.org) has identified a set of social-emotional skills that underlie effective performance of a wide range of social roles and life tasks. CASEL has drawn from extensive research in a wide range of areas, including brain functioning and methods of learning and instruction to identify the skills that provide young people with broad guidance and direction for their actions in all aspects of their lives, in and out of school (Connell, Turner, Mason & Olsen, 1986; Elias, Tobias, & Friedlander, 2000; Elias et al., 1997; Goleman, 1995; Topping & Bremner, 1998; Zins, Weissberg, Walberg, & Wang, 2004). The skills are presented in Table 1.1.

Schools worldwide must give children intellectual and practical tools they can bring to their classrooms, families, and communities. SEL provides many of these tools. It is a way of teaching and organizing classrooms and schools that helps children learn a set of skills needed to successfully manage life tasks such as learning, forming relationships, communicating effectively, being sensitive to others' needs, and getting along with others. When schools implement high-quality SEL programs and approaches effectively, academic achievement of children increases, incidence of problem behaviors decreases, the relationships that surround each child are improved, and the climate of classrooms and schools changes for the better.

Table 1.1   The Collaborative for Academic, Social, and Emotional Learning's Essential Skills for Academic and Social-Emotional Learning

Know Yourself and Others

- Identify feelings—recognizing and labeling one's feelings
- Be responsible—understanding one's obligation to engage in ethical, safe, legal behaviors
- Recognize strengths—identifying and cultivating one's positive qualities

Make Responsible Decisions

- Manage emotions—regulating feelings so that they aid rather than impede the handling of situations
- Understand situations—accurately understanding the circumstances one is in
- Set goals and plans—establishing and working toward achievement of specific short- and long-term outcomes
- Solve problems creatively—engaging in a creative, disciplined process of exploring alternative possibilities that leads to responsible, goal-directed action, including overcoming obstacles to plans

Care for Others

- Show empathy—identifying and understanding the thoughts and feelings of others
- Respect others—believing that others deserve to be treated with kindness and compassion as part of our shared humanity
- Appreciate diversity—understanding that individual and group differences complement one another and add strength and adaptability to the world around us

Know How to Act

- Communicate effectively—using verbal and nonverbal skills to express oneself and promote effective exchanges with others
- Build relationships—establishing and maintaining healthy and rewarding connections with individuals and groups
- Negotiate fairly—achieving mutually satisfactory resolutions to conflict by addressing the needs of all concerned
- Refuse provocations—conveying and following through effectively with one's decision not to engage in unwanted, unsafe, unethical behavior
- Seek help—identifying the need for and accessing appropriate assistance and support in pursuit of needs and goals
- Act ethically—guiding decisions and actions by a set of principles or standards derived from recognized legal and professional codes or moral or faith-based systems of conduct

SEL is sometimes called "the missing piece," because it represents a part of education that links academic knowledge with a specific set of skills important to success in schools, families, communities, workplaces, and life in general. As national and world events continue to teach, there is a danger to each of us—locally and globally—when children grow up with knowledge but without social-emotional skills and a strong moral compass. Hence, a combination of academic learning and SEL is the true standard for effective education for the world as we now face it.

There are eight elements of SEL that create the strong connection with academic learning. These are supported collectively by the entire body of research cited in this chapter. But they are all based on one fundamental principle:

Effective, lasting academic learning and SEL are built on caring relationships and warm but challenging classroom and school environments.

There is abundant research in support of the idea that students are most responsive academically to classrooms and schools that are not threatening to students and challenge them to learn more but do so in ways that do not discourage them (e.g., Kriete & Bechtel, 2002; Lewis, Schaps, & Watson, 1996; O'Neil, 1997; Osterman, 2000; Zins et al., 2004). Also, these schools are places where students feel cared about, welcomed, valued, and seen as more than just learners—they are seen as resources.

In this kind of caring climate, educators can work on providing the eight elements necessary for the kind of academic-social-emotional balance that will lead students to success in school and life:

1. Link social-emotional instruction to other school services.

2. Use goal setting to focus instruction.

3. Use differentiated instructional procedures.

4. Promote community service to build empathy.

5. Involve parents.

6. Build social-emotional skills gradually and systematically.

7. Prepare and support staff well.

8. Evaluate what you do.

What follows is a brief explanation for each of these eight aspects to help underscore their importance and interrelationship. Although teachers cannot impact all of these elements in their daily roles, they can do so directly in many areas. In others, their awareness, advocacy, and leadership can be a source of positive change in their schools.

LINK SOCIAL-EMOTIONAL INSTRUCTION TO OTHER SCHOOL SERVICES

Social-emotional and life skills must be taught explicitly at the elementary and secondary levels. Like reading or math, if social-emotional skills are not taught systematically, they will not be internalized and become part of a child's lifelong repertoire of valued activities. Although this is necessary, CASEL research would suggest it is not sufficient (Elias et al., 1997). Children also benefit from coordinated, explicit, developmentally sensitive instruction in the prevention of specific problems, such as smoking, drug use, alcohol, pregnancy, violence, and bullying. Obviously, different communities and cultures will select and focus on preventing different problem behaviors. Perhaps of greatest importance and relevance to each teacher, children benefit from explicit guidance in finding a healthy lifestyle. Eating habits, sleeping patterns, and study and work environments are among the areas that are important to promoting academic learning and SEL.

Finally, schools should be attentive to difficult life events that befall students and try to provide them with support and coping strategies at those troubling moments. Typically, such assistance is not given until children show problems that are the result of those difficult life events; unfortunately, during this time, many students are distracted from learning. Even when they are not actively disrupting class, they are not taking in all that their teachers are working so hard to provide. Providing social-emotional assistance to children facing difficult events is a sound prevention strategy that also promotes better academic learning. Children with special education needs must also receive social-emotional skill-building instruction and be included in related activities (Adelman & Taylor, 2000; Comer, Ben-Avie, Haynes, & Joyner, 1999; Elias et al., 1997; Jessor, 1993; Perry & Jessor, 1985).

USE GOAL SETTING TO FOCUS INSTRUCTION

Children are required to learn many things, but without a sense of connection between and to those things, children are not likely to retain what they learn and use it in their lives. When their learning is presented in terms of understandable goals (goals that children can play a larger role in defining as they get older), children become more engaged and focused and less likely to exhibit behavior problems. Learning experiences that coordinate and integrate different aspects of learning across subject areas and over time, as well as those that link to their lives outside of school in the present and future, are especially valuable.

Children also benefit from learning problem-solving strategies that they can apply to new situations that face them. Instruction in reading that includes examining the problem-solving and decision-making processes used by various characters in stories, as well as history and current events instruction that allows students to focus on the different perspectives of individuals and groups involved and the problem-solving processes they used (or might have used), is particularly enriching. A similar process can be used to help students understand the process of scientific and mathematical problem solving. When this takes place, students find that as they encounter new books, new civic situations, and new group processes, they will have strategies to apply that enhance their learning and performance and enable them to make better progress (Cohen, 1999; Elias & Bruene, 2005; Elias et al., 1997; Pasi, 2001; Topping & Bremner, 1998).

USE DIFFERENTIATED INSTRUCTIONAL PROCEDURES

Academic learning and SEL take place best in different ways for different students. So educational experiences marked by instruction that uses different modalities are most likely to reach all children and allow them to build their skills and feel that the classroom environment is suited to their preferred way of learning. Modalities include modeling, role playing, making art, dancing, performing drama, working with materials and manipulatives, and using digital media, computer technology, and the Internet. Also important for sound instruction are regular and constructive feedback, discussions that include open-ended questioning, opportunities for student reflection, project-based learning, and frequent reminders to use social-emotional skills in all aspects of school life. Furthermore, differentiated instruction also recognizes the value of varying content, work processes, products, scoring systems, assessments, time, and grouping arrangements to meet student needs.

It is important to note that the pedagogy of sound SEL is not distinct from other sound pedagogy. Teachers should draw some reassurance from this, in that SEL does not demand dramatic changes in their roles or actions. However, the small changes that are required can produce quite dramatic and profound results, especially as children are exposed to SEL over a period of years (Gardner, 2000; Johnson & Johnson, 1994; Ladd & Mize, 1983; Lambert & McCombs, 1998; Noddings, 1992; Salovey & Sluyter, 1997; Topping, 2000).

PROMOTE COMMUNITY SERVICE TO BUILD EMPATHY

Community service plays an essential role in fostering generalization of SEL skills, particularly in building empathy. Properly conducted community service, which begins at the earliest level of schooling and continues throughout all subsequent years, provides an opportunity for children to learn life skills, integrate them, apply them, reflect on them, and then demonstrate them. This process solidifies their learning and also provides a climate in which others are more likely to engage in community service. Service experiences usually help students encounter other people, ideas, and circumstances in ways that broaden their sense of perspective and build empathic understanding and caring connections to the world around them. For many young people, community service provides an opportunity to nourish a universal need to be a generous and contributing member of important groups to which one belongs. This helps prepare children for their eventual roles in the larger society, as well as work and family groups of which they will be a part. Furthermore, it helps nurture the spirit of students to see themselves as part of a larger world, with sets of ideals and beliefs that are important to living a fulfilled life.

It is worth noting that service opportunities can be embedded in classrooms and schools so that even from the youngest age, students feel that they are making a contribution to the positive functioning of the classroom. Examples include putting chairs away, cleaning up, and helping the teacher and other students. As children get older, this can be augmented by opportunities for students to take on helpful roles in the community. Examples include improving the physical environment around the school, helping the elderly, and providing comfort and support to the injured or sick. Such opportunities begin with *preparation*, so that students understand the circumstances they will be involved with, such as the kinds of illnesses and difficulties that beset the elderly. Then, there is the *action* of carrying out the service, in which students should be as directly involved as is appropriate to their age and safety. Action is followed by *reflection*, as students have a chance to talk or write about what they experienced and their feelings about it. Finally, *demonstration* of learning should take place, as students creatively show their peers, younger students, parents, and other groups in the community what they did, why they did it, how they felt about it, and what they learned (Berman, 1997; Billig, 2000; National Commission on Service Learning, 2002).

INVOLVE PARENTS

Parents, schools, the community, and the larger society all agree that children's life success depends on building all forms of literacy, including social-emotional skills. When home and school collaborate closely to implement SEL programs, students gain more and program effects are more enduring and pervasive. As more and more children are being bombarded by messages of mass culture, Internet, television, music, videos, and other outlets unfiltered by adults, it becomes more and more important that key caregivers in children's lives send strong and coordinated messages. For this reason, school and community resources need to be mobilized to help parents provide home environments conducive to learning. This is the most fundamental form of parental involvement in the education of their children. Some examples include giving parents regular overviews of the academic and social-emotional skills students are learning at any given time, arranging opportunities for parents to meet to exchange ideas about how to support teaching in school and how to raise their children, helping parents learn how to organize the morning routine and homework routines to minimize conflict, and communicating with parents the importance of having positive times with their children, despite difficulties, to build children's sense of hope.

Such efforts will not occur adequately, especially in low-performing schools, without systematic and ongoing guidance and support from teachers and other school personnel (Christenson & Havsy, 2003; Elias et al., 2000; Epstein, 2001; Huang & Gibbs, 1992).

BUILD SOCIAL-EMOTIONAL SKILLS GRADUALLY AND SYSTEMATICALLY

Selecting and implementing an approach to SEL should follow consideration of local needs, goals, interests, and mandates; staff skills, workload, and receptiveness; preexisting instructional efforts and activities; the content and quality of program materials; its developmental appropriateness and sociocultural appropriateness to the range of recipient student populations; and its acceptability to parents and community members. SEL efforts are often implemented as pilot projects, and it typically takes 2 to 3 years for staff to have a confident and competent sense of ownership of the approaches being used.

Once implemented, SEL efforts are most likely to become a regular part of school schedules and routines to the extent to which they are aligned with local and national educational goals, comply with legal standards and mandates, and have the informed support of educational administration, organized groups of educators, and members of the community or government with responsibility to oversee high-quality education. Of particular importance is the connection between academic learning and SEL. SEL is not a separate subject area; rather, it must be linked to language literacy, instruction in math and science, history and current culture, health and physical education, and the performing arts. In all of these areas, the essential skills for academic learning and SEL mentioned earlier allow for deeper understanding of the content and improved pedagogy, with greater student engagement in learning and fewer behavior disruptions (CASEL, 2003; Elias et al., 1997; Novick, Kress, & Elias, 2002; Utne O'Brien, Weissberg, & Shriver, 2003).

PREPARE AND SUPPORT STAFF WELL

SEL is relatively new to many educators. Therefore, they need to be patient with themselves and allow themselves opportunity to learn this new area. Effective academic and social-emotional instruction benefits from well-planned professional development for school personnel; especially helpful is a system of support during the initial period of implementation. The kinds of professional development activities that are beneficial include training staff in children's social-emotional development, modeling and practice of constructivist and project-based teaching methods, multimodal instruction, coaching, and mutual feedback from colleagues. Staff also should become familiar with best practices in the field so that teachers can draw on what works most effectively. (Web sites that delineate best practices internationally can be found in Table 1.2.) CASEL is playing a significant role in identifying the best of what works. Its 2003 guide, *Safe and Sound*, is available on the Internet (www.CASEL.org) and provides guidelines and information to allow educators to

Table 1.2   Web Listings for Social-Emotional Learning Programs With International Presence

---

www.researchpress.com—I Can Problem Solve

www.quest.edu—Skills for Adolescence, Skills for Action, Violence Prevention

www.channing-bete.com—Promoting Alternative Thinking Strategies

www.esrnational.org—Resolving Conflict Creatively Program

www.responsiveclassroom.org—Responsive Classroom

www.cfchildren.org—Second Step

www.peaceeducation.com—Peace Works

www.open-circle.org—Open Circle/Reach Out to Schools Social Competency Program

www.umdnj.edu/spsweb; http://www.eqparenting.com—Social Decision Making/Social Problem Solving Program

www.tribes.com—Tribes TLC: A New Way of Learning and Being Together

Resources for Service Learning/Citizenship Education

International Partnership for Service-Learning
www.ipsl.org

National Center for Learning and Citizenship
www.ecs.org/clc

Center for Information and Research on Civic Learning and Engagement
www.civicyouth.org

National Service-Learning Exchange
www.nslexchange.org

National Service-Learning Clearinghouse
www.service-learning.org

find programs and procedures that work best for their particular situations. Finally, most schools that sustain SEL efforts for long periods of time have committees that are responsible for supporting implementation, especially during the initial years (CASEL, 2003; Kessler, 2000; Lantieri, 2001; Leiberman, 1995).

EVALUATE WHAT YOU DO

Although educators cannot guarantee the outcomes of all their efforts, they do have an ethical responsibility to monitor what they do and to attempt to continuously improve it. Therefore, educators need ways to keep track of student learning and performance in all areas, including the development of social-emotional abilities. SEL efforts should be monitored regularly, using multiple indicators to ensure programs are carried out as planned. Some of the best ways to gather the relevant information are to

- use checklists to keep track of whether SEL activities that are planned actually take place;
- provide teachers with the opportunity to rate or comment on the lessons they carry out, to note what went well and what might be improved in the future;
- use brief surveys of students to find out what they liked most and least about SEL activities, times they have put the skills to use, and ideas for improving instruction;
- ask people who work in the school (and parents, if possible) how they will know when students' academic and social-emotional skills are improving, and design indictors to measure the extent to which this takes place;
- place on the report card or other feedback system a listing of SEL skills or related indicators so that there can be accountability for this aspect of schooling and methods designed to improve instruction as needed (Elias et al., 1997; Fetterman, Kaftarian, & Wandersman, 1996; Harvard Graduate School of Education, 2003; Weissberg & Gullotta, 1997).

CONCLUSION

Education is changing. Academic learning and SEL are becoming the new standard for what are considered the basics that children should acquire during their schooling. Because this is so new to many educators, but not to all, this chapter outlines ideas to help get social-emotional efforts started as well as to sustain those that have already begun. It is designed to help all schools become places in which learning is valued, dreams are born, leaders are made, and the talents of students—the greatest resource shared by every community—are unleashed.

Our students are important not only to their schools and families, but also to their communities, to their future workplaces and families, and to the world around them. Each student has potential. Although that potential is not identical for all, every student deserves the opportunity to have his or her potential developed. The combination of academic learning and SEL is the most promising way to accomplish this goal. We need teachers to lead the way toward preparing students for the tests of life, for the responsibilities of citizenship, and for adopting a lifestyle that is literate, responsible, nonviolent, drug free, and caring.

REFERENCES

Adelman, H. S., & Taylor, L. (2000). Moving prevention from the fringes into the fabric of school improvement. *Journal of Education and Psychological Consultation, 11*(1), 7–36.

Berman, S. (1997). *Children's social consciousness and the development of social responsibility.* Albany, NY: State University of New York Press.

Billig, S. (2000). *The impact of service learning on youth, schools, and communities: Research on K–12 school-based service learning, 1990–1999.* Available from http://www.learningindeed.org/research/slreseaerch/slrschsy.html

Christenson, C. L., & Havsy, L. H. (2003). Family-school-peer relationships: Significance for social, emotional, and academic learning. In J. E. Zins, R. P. Weissberg, H. J. Walberg, & M. C. Wang (Eds.), *Building school success on social and emotional learning* (pp. 59–75). New York: Teachers College Press.

Cohen, J. (Ed.). (1999). *Educating minds and hearts: Social emotional learning and the passage into adolescence.* New York: Teachers College Press.

Collaborative for Academic, Social, and Emotional Learning (CASEL). (2003). *Safe and sound: An educational leader's guide to evidence-based social and emotional learning programs.* Chicago: Author.

Comer, J. P., Ben-Avie, M., Haynes, N., & Joyner, E. T. (Eds.). (1999). *Child by child: The Comer process for change in education.* New York: Teachers College Press.

Connell, D. B., Turner, R. R., Mason, E. F., & Olsen, L. K. (1986). School health education evaluation. *International Journal of Educational Research, 10,* 245–345.

Elias, M. J., & Bruene, L. (2005). *Social decision making/social problem solving for middle school students: Skills and activities for academic, social, and emotional success.* Champaign, IL: Research Press.

Elias, M. J., Tobias, S. E., & Friedlander, B. S. (2000). *Emotionally intelligent parenting: How to raise a self-disciplined, responsible, socially skilled child.* New York: Random House/Three Rivers Press.

Elias, M. J., Zins, J. E., Weissberg, R. P., Frey, K. S., Greenberg, M. T., Haynes, N. M., et al. (1997). *Promoting social and emotional learning: Guidelines for educators.* Alexandria, VA: Association for Supervision and Curriculum Development.

Epstein, J. L. (2001). *School, family, and community partnerships: Preparing educators and improving schools.* Boulder, CO: Westview Press.

Fetterman, D. M., Kaftarian, S. J., & Wandersman, A. (1996). *Empowerment evaluation: Knowledge and tools for self-assessment and accountability.* Thousand Oaks, CA: Sage.

Gardner, H. (2000). *Intelligence reframed: Multiple intelligences for the 21st century.* New York: Basic Books.

Goleman, D. (1995). *Emotional intelligence: Why it can matter more than IQ.* New York: Bantam Books.

Greenberg, M. T., Weissberg, R. P., O'Brien, M. U., Zins, J. E., Fredericks, L., Resnik, H., et al. (2003). School-based prevention: Promoting positive social development through social and emotional learning. *American Psychologist, 58,* 466–474.

Harvard Graduate School of Education. (2003). *The evaluation exchange.* Available from www.gse.harvard.edu/hfrp/eval/archives.html

Huang, L., & Gibbs, J. (1992). Partners or adversaries? Home-school collaboration across culture, race, and ethnicity. In S. Christenson & J. Close Conoley (Eds.), *Home-school collaboration: Enhancing children's academic and social competence* (pp. 81–110). Silver Spring, MD: National Association of School Psychologists.

Jessor, R. (1993). Successful adolescent development among youth in high-risk settings. *American Psychologist, 48,* 177–126.

Johnson, D. W., & Johnson, R. T. (1994). *Learning together and alone: Cooperative, competitive, and individualistic learning.* Needham Heights, MA: Allyn & Bacon.

Kessler, R. (2000). *The soul of education: Helping students find connection, compassion, and character at school.* Alexandria, VA: Association for Supervision and Curriculum Development.

Kriete, R., & Bechtel, L. (2002). *The Morning Meeting book.* Greenfield, MA: Northeast Foundation for Children.

Ladd, G. W., & Mize, J. (1983). A cognitive social-learning model of social-skill training. *Psychological Review, 90,* 127–157.

Lambert, N. M., & McCombs, B. L. (Eds.). (1998). *How students learn: Reforming schools through learner-centered education.* Washington, DC: American Psychological Association.

Lantieri, L. (Ed.). (2001). *Schools with spirit: Nurturing the inner lives of children and teachers.* Boston: Beacon Press.

Leiberman, A. (1995). Practices that support teacher development. *Phi Delta Kappan, 76,* 591–596.

Lewis, C. C., & Schaps, E., & Watson, M. S. (1996). The caring classroom's academic edge. *Educational Leadership, 54,* 16–21.

National Commission on Service Learning. (2002). *The power of service learning.* Newton, MA: Author.

Noddings, N. (1992). *The challenge to care in schools: An alternative approach to education.* New York: Teachers College Press.

Novick, B., Kress, J., & Elias, M. J. (2002). *Building learning communities with character: How to integrate academic, social, and emotional learning.* Alexandria, VA: Association for Supervision and Curriculum Development.

O'Neil, J. (1997). Building schools as communities: A conversation with James Comer. *Educational Leadership, 54,* 6–10.

Osterman, K. F. (2000). Students' need for belonging in the school community. *Review of Educational Research, 70,* 323–367.

Pasi, R. (2001). *Higher expectations: Promoting social emotional learning and academic achievement in your school.* New York: Teachers College Press.

Perry, C. L., & Jessor, R. (1985). The concept of health promotion and the prevention of adolescent drug abuse. *Health Education Quarterly, 12,* 169–184.

Salovey, P., & Sluyter, D. (Eds.). (1997). *Emotional development and emotional intelligence: Educational implications.* New York: Basic Books.

Topping, K. (2000). *Tutoring: Educational practices series, Booklet #5.* Available from http://www.ibe.unesco.org

Topping, K. J., & Bremner, W. G. (1998). *Promoting social competence: Practice and resources guide.* Edinburgh, Scotland: Scottish Office Education and Industry Department.

Utne O'Brien, M., Weissberg, R. P., & Shriver, T. P. (2003). Educational leadership for academic, social, and emotional learning. In M. J. Elias, H. Arnold, & C. Steiger (Eds.), *EQ + IQ = Best leadership practices for caring and successful schools* (pp. 23–35). Thousand Oaks, CA: Corwin.

Weissberg, R. P., Gullotta, T. P., Hampton, R. L., Ryan, B. A., & Adams, G. R. (Eds.). (1997). *Healthy children 2010: Establishing preventive services.* (Issues in children's and families' lives, Vol. 9). Thousand Oaks, CA: Sage.

Zins, J. E., Weissberg, R. P., Walberg, H. J., & Wang, M. C. (Eds.). (2004). *Building academic success on social and emotional learning.* New York: Teachers College Press.

2

Brain Development and Social-Emotional Learning

An Introduction for Educators

Carol A. Kusché and Mark T. Greenberg

Emotions play an integral role in daily functioning throughout life; we need and use our emotional system throughout every waking hour and even during sleep. Moreover, feelings are also crucial for success in education. Emotions are critical ingredients for optimal information processing, social communication, written communication, motivation, attention, concentration, memory, critical thinking skills, creativity, behavior, physical health, and even our very survival (Goleman, 1995; Jensen, 1998; Kusché & Greenberg, 1998; Sylwester, 1995). Although emotional growth takes place throughout life, childhood is a time of especially rapid maturation.

It follows that the manner in which behavior, emotions, and cognitions become integrated during the first decade of development has important implications for educators (Greenberg & Snell, 1997; Kusché, 1984). As Emde (1999) noted, "Affective processes are shown to provide integrative influences across systems in an individual's development, facilitating developmental change, as well as developmental continuity" (p. 317). Over the past 10 years, researchers have provided new information that adds to our understanding of how this occurs in the context of brain development and emotional maturation. In this chapter, we highlight some of these new findings and then discuss their implications for the effective implementation of social-emotional learning (SEL) in the classroom. Since brain development is a complex subject and we do not want readers to shun this chapter because of past experience with this topic, we have chosen to focus on a case study approach.

THE BRAIN IS BORN

Welcome the arrival of Baby May. It has long been held as conventional wisdom that Baby May was born with all of the brain cells she was ever going to have, but research has recently challenged this. New cell growth in the hippocampi of mature adults has been reported by neuroscientists (Gibbs, 1998). Nevertheless, Baby May was born with the vast majority of all of her lifetime's supply of brain cells. In fact, she was born with many more cells than she needs, and many of those that do not get used will die ("use it or lose it"). Somehow (no one yet knows how), her brain cells were produced and then migrated to their correct locations while she incubated in her (in this case healthy) uterine environment, and now they all "know" what their general function is supposed to be. Nevertheless, there is still room for considerable flexibility.

THE BRAIN DEVELOPS

As a newborn, Baby May's brain weighs only about 25% of what it will weigh when she is an adult, but it will rapidly increase its weight to 40% over the next 3 months (see Figure 2.1). By the time she is 2, May's brain weight will have tripled. Most of this dramatic increase in brain weight will be due to increases in the size of her neurons (nerve cells), in the density of the interconnections between them, and in the amount of fatty insulation around the nerve cell branches (i.e., myelination), which helps speed up the process of communication between neurons. Moreover, this rapid cortical development will correlate with May's functional progress in physical, emotional, and cognitive development. Although changes in her brain will slow down after the age of 2, they will nevertheless continue for the rest of May's life.

Compared with those of an adult, newborn Baby May's brain cells look rather like spindly little saplings, each having at most only a few branches and a meager root system. This will change rapidly, however, as the branches and roots of the surviving cells grow, proliferate, and become interconnected with one another to form intricate systems of communication known as *neural networks* ("neurons that fire together wire together"). At the same time, many of the synaptic connections that are not used will eventually be "pruned" away.

Thus, by the time Baby May is 2, her brain will have reached 75% of its adult weight, and what began as a crop of seedlings will have transformed into an interconnected forest of neuronal networks. These interconnections will continue to be made, and by the time May is an adult, each cell will be capable of communicating with thousands of other cells. Moreover, this forest will continue to grow and reorganize throughout May's lifetime.

Figure 2.1   The Development and Proliferation of Interconnections Between Nerve Cells in the Brain During the First 2 Years of Life

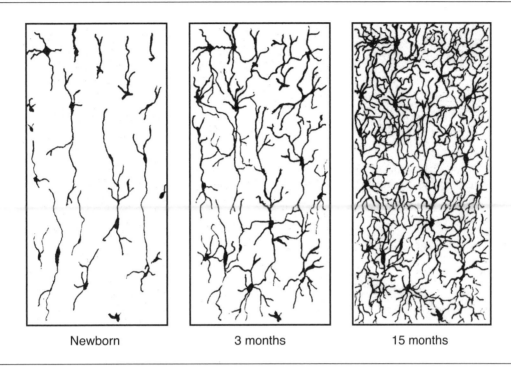

| Newborn | 3 months | 15 months |

We used to assume that this astonishing neural development unfolded rather automatically as a result of genetic codes. However, it now appears that much of the structuring and organization of the brain occurs as the result of interactive responses to environmental input. Using a computer as an analogy for the purpose of illustration, we could say that what each nerve cell communicates, and the other nerve cells in the networks with which it communicates, depend on what is fed into the "computer," and on the specific parameters of the computer itself. Unlike the computer in this analogy, however, we are living machines, in that the incoming information, interacting with our individual genetic codes, causes substantial changes in the structure and organization of our "hardware." As a result, May's brain will be unique, but at the same time, it will share certain characteristics in common with the majority of other human brains (i.e., just as each face has two eyes, a nose, and a mouth, but is nevertheless the only one of its kind). In addition, although the plasticity of brain development diminishes over time, some flexibility remains for change and reorganization throughout the lifespan.

There are at least two major aspects of brain development that are relevant to the relationship between May's brain growth and her emotional development. The first area involves the development of structures in the brain and their networks of association, whereas the second includes the neurochemical aspects of brain functioning. Although knowledge of neurochemical processes such as neurotransmitters (dopamine, norepinephrine, serotonin), amino acids (e.g., gamma-aminobutyric acid), neuropeptides, and hormones is critical to understanding the excitation and inhibition of neuronal pathways that regulate emotion and attention (Panskeep,

1998; Todd, Swarzenski, Rossi, & Visconti, 1995), this area of brain functioning is unfortunately beyond the scope of this chapter. Thus, we will focus on the development of brain structures.

THE TRIUNE BRAIN

To understand the developing brain, it helps to know that May's brain, being a product of evolutionary history, is an amalgamation of three different aggregates (brain stem, limbic system, and cortex) that originally evolved during disparate time periods (MacLean, 1978). Over the course of each individual's development, these three systems become increasingly interconnected. To appreciate the relevance of this for optimal emotional intelligence, it is important to first understand more about these structures.

The Brain Stem

As can be seen in Figure 2.2, the innermost and evolutionarily oldest part of the brain is the brain stem, which evolved more than 500 million years ago, long before the beginning of mammals (Ornstein & Thompson, 1984). Baby May shares the presence of a brain stem with other animals from reptiles to mammals (thus, its nickname of "reptilian brain").

Many important functions, including those at the basic level of life maintenance, are performed by the brain stem. For our present purposes, it is notable that information about the functioning of the internal world is transmitted from various parts of the body via the brain stem to be compared with data received from the external environment. Thus, our brains continuously monitor how we are functioning in relationship to the outside world. All of this takes place at an unconscious level.

Figure 2.2   The Triune Brain

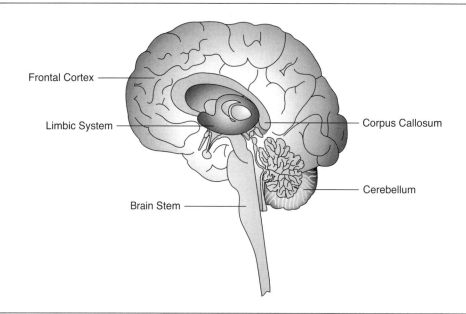

The Limbic System

The next layer of the brain is evolutionarily newer than the brain stem, dating from roughly 300 to 200 million years ago (Ornstein & Thompson, 1984). It is frequently called the limbic system, or "mammalian brain," because it is most highly developed in mammals. This area of the brain is not mature at birth, but it develops more quickly than the third, outermost part, and is also much more stereotypic and instinctual in its functioning. One of the important roles of the limbic system involves the initial processing of multiple aspects of emotion, including the recognition of emotional expressions on the face, action tendencies, and the storage of emotional memories (Aggleton, 1992).

Most definitions of the limbic system include the following set of subcortical structures surrounding the brainstem: the amygdala, hippocampus, thalamus, and hypothalamus (see Figure 2.3). All of these structures function at an unconscious level, although we can become conscious of the results.

The thalamus and hypothalamus can be considered akin to relay stations for incoming information. The thalamus receives all incoming sensory information from the external environment before it is relayed to other areas of the brain. In other words, information from the external world, transmitted in the form of energy or chemicals and received through receptors (nerve cells of various types), is carried first to the thalamus; from there, it is sent to other areas of the brain to be decoded, analyzed, stored, acted on, and so on. This occurs with data related to all sensory modalities (vision, hearing, touch, taste, and smell). The hypothalamus, on the other hand, receives signals from the body and is involved in the regulation of drives such as sleep, sexuality, and appetite (blame your hypothalamus the next time you overeat). Both of these structures relay information to the amygdala, the primary limbic structure involved in the neurobiology of emotion (LeDoux, 1991). Finally, the hippocampi store the contextual components of memories and also transmit this information to the cortex for additional analysis and storage. Sylwester (1995) referred to the hippocampus as the "card catalog for our library of memories" (p. 45), due to its role in assigning memories to networks in different brain areas.

Figure 2.3   The Limbic System

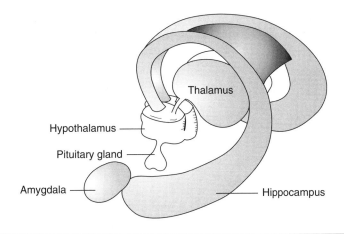

Each amygdala (there are two) is a relatively small, almond-shaped structure with multiple connections to other brain regions. The primary function of the amygdala appears to be the interpretation of incoming sensory information in the context of the individual's emotional and survival needs. Operationally, the amygdala can be likened to the body's "alarm system." That is, using incoming sensory information, an amygdala scans experience to examine even minute changes in the internal and external environments. It is constantly seeking emotionally related data: Is there something (important, interesting, attractive, fearful, distressing, irritating, etc.) here?

Another crucial function of the amygdala is the assigning of emotional meaning to memories. When a powerful emotion is experienced, especially under conditions of emotional stress (e.g., fear, anger), it appears that the amygdala imprints this memory with an added degree of strength (a highlighting of sorts). This may account for the fact that people tend to have strong memories for emotionally charged, personal experiences. It may also explain why children are more likely to learn in situations in which there is some type of emotional connection to the material (Jensen, 1998).

It has been speculated that emotional memories stored by the amygdala can be evoked and can impact current behavior without ever entering conscious awareness (LeDoux, 1993, 1995). In other words, we all have unconscious memories, especially for emotionally charged events (e.g., getting hurt, feeling abandoned), that affect our current functioning, without our being aware that we have them or that they are even memories.

Thus, it is believed that many early childhood experiences, particularly emotionally charged ones (e.g., important relationships, emotionally traumatic experiences), may exert a long-term impact on behavior through this mechanism. When an association in the present environment causes us to re-experience these emotional memories in the present, we automatically believe that the feelings are actually occurring in the present, when in fact they are associated with memories of the past. (This is much like we believe we are really experiencing our dreams when we are asleep.) This phenomenon has a profound effect on our relationships in the present, without our ever being aware of it.

Part of the reason this occurs is due to the separate storage of the nonlinguistic emotional component of memory (stored in the amygdala) from the contextual elements (stored in the hippocampus). In other words, the hippocampus, the limbic structure involved in the storage of contextual memory, and the amygdala (which adds the emotional imprint) appear to act as a team in the process of storing memories of meaningful life events. The hippocampi are believed to mature later in development than the amygdalae, which may be at least part of the reason why early memories are not available to consciousness. That is, early in life, the emotional component of certain experiences is stored in the amygdala, but the associated contextual information is not stored in (or possibly is stored but later cannot be retrieved from) the hippocampus. Verbal thinking is implicated, in that conscious retrieval of contextual memory in the hippocampus is enhanced after the development of the ability to think with internal language (on average by about age 5 or 6).

The Cortex

The outermost and evolutionarily newest part of the brain is called the cortex. Compared to the brain stem and limbic system, the cortex has much more flexibility in its development and is much more influenced by environmental input. It also develops more slowly than its two older counterparts. Moreover, the ratio of cortex to limbic system increases as one proceeds up the evolutionary scale (the adult human has approximately 90% cortex compared with 10% limbic system, whereas the reverse is true for the rabbit). The greater proportion of cortex in humans compared with other mammals plays an important role in our notable potential for variations in behavior and for adaptation to an impressive variety of environmental demands.

As will be described in greater detail, the cortex allows for secondary processing of emotions at a more refined level than is possible with the limbic system alone, and it also allows for greater (socialized) control over the more instinctual, automatic responses of the mammalian brain. In addition, the cortex allows us to accumulate and combine information over time (from various experiences first processed by the limbic system) to form schemas or templates about the external world. The cortex also contains "association areas" in which sensory data from different modalities can be integrated (tertiary processing), which in turn allows for complex verbal and non-verbal intelligence (the types of thinking that humans pride themselves in having).

AREAS OF THE CORTEX THAT SPECIALIZE IN SOCIAL, EMOTIONAL, AND ATTENTIONAL PROCESSING

The Neocerebellum

One of the evolutionarily newest parts of the cortex is the neocerebellum, the six outermost layers of neurons that cover the cerebellum (the two large "bumps" at the back of the brain just above the neck). It is only very recently that we have become aware of the apparent importance of this structure for facilitating semantic connections between words and for higher level processing of social intelligence (Ratey, 2001). Children who have a smaller than average neocerebellum (e.g., autistic children) show difficulty with social intelligence and interpersonal relationships, whereas children with a larger than average neocerebellum (e.g., children with William's Syndrome) are gifted in the area of social intelligence, even when they are retarded in other areas of cognitive development.

The Frontal Lobes

The left and right frontal lobes (the brain areas behind the forehead) are another evolutionarily newer part of the cortex that evolved at about the same time as the neocerebellum. The frontal lobes are responsible for the higher level processing of such functions as planning, anticipation, attention, concentration, insight, moral conscience, sense of identity, empathy, and altruism. Furthermore, the frontal lobes play an important role in processing complex information, sustaining attention to relevant versus irrelevant stimuli, and integrating incoming information with prior knowledge.

Attention and Concentration

Among other things, adequate frontal lobe organization and functioning are crucial for optimal ability to pay attention and to concentrate, which in turn, are essential for educational success. A well-functioning attentional system must fulfill several tasks, including identification of important elements in the environment, the ability to ignore irrelevant stimuli while sustaining attention to the primary focus, the ability to access inactive memories, and the capacity to shift attention rapidly as a result of new information (Sylwester, 1995). It is important to note, however, that attention, concentration, and memory are all powerfully influenced by a child's current emotional state, as well as by the child's overall development.

At least one of the reasons for this involves the fact that a crucial part of the prefrontal cortex that regulates emotions is located in the ventral area of the anterior cyngulate. It is very close to the module responsible for the regulation of cognitive processes (such as the maintenance of concentration and attention) in the dorsal area of the anterior cyngulate (Berger & Posner, 2000). Moreover, these two areas appear to be mutually inhibitory, so that when one of these areas is active, functioning of the other is compromised (Drevets & Raichle, 1998). In other words, physiologically, one can focus inward or outward, but not both ways at the same time.

Thus, a child who is emotionally upset, anxious, depressed, worried, angry, sad, frustrated, traumatized, or otherwise distressed (whose brain is preoccupied with attending to, processing, and managing these painful feelings in the internal world) will find it hard or even impossible to pay attention and concentrate on cognitive schoolwork in the external environment. It is extremely important for teachers to know and recognize that when a child is inattentive, this is generally due to the way the brain is designed and is not a function of the child's lack of effort.

Furthermore, it is very difficult to learn how to override or suppress strong emotional pain (and suppressing it is quite energy consuming and exhausting to maintain), so most children are not adept at doing this. These dynamics may at least partially explain why poor academic performance and achievement, as well as less than optimal frontal lobe functioning, are frequently found with both internalizing and externalizing types of emotional distress in young school-age children (Kusché, Cook, & Greenberg, 1993).

Of course, most children are not aware of how their brains are operating (nor are most teachers), so if a teacher reprimands a child for not paying attention and asks the child to try harder, this student is likely to feel shame, remorse, anger, and so on for not being able to comply. Because children think that they should be able to do things if adults expect them to, even when they cannot, this kind of situation is damaging to their self-esteem; if this happens frequently, it can result in a child giving up and learning to dislike school.

Emotion Regulation

The frontal lobes are also critically involved in emotion regulation. The frontal cortex has a unique relationship with the limbic system, in that it is believed to be the only cortical site in which information processed by the limbic system is represented (Damasio, 1994). The unique connections between the frontal lobes and limbic system make it possible for the prefrontal cortex to override or modify commands emanating from the limbic area. Dawson (1994), Schore (1994), and others have hypothesized that the frontal lobes play a regulatory role in emotional processes, in particular guiding our ability to contend with and control emotional expression. Similarly, Goleman (1995) referred to the frontal lobes as the "emotional manager," due to their apparent executive role in controlling emotion and overriding emotional impulses. He stated,

In the neocortex a cascading series of circuits registers and analyzes that information, comprehends it, and through the prefrontal lobes, orchestrates a reaction. If in the process an emotional response is called for, the prefrontal lobes dictate it, working hand-in-hand with the amygdala and other circuits in the emotional brain. (p. 25)

There have been numerous case studies that demonstrate how injuries and lesions specific to the frontal lobes are associated with dramatic changes in emotion regulation and social competence (Benton, 1991; Grattan & Eslinger, 1991). Although the patients in these reports often perform in the normal range on tests of cognitive functioning (intelligence testing, reading, mathematics), marked deficits in social functioning have been observed throughout the lifespan, primarily in the domains of emotion regulation, adapting to novel situations, and general social behavior. In the area of emotion regulation, limited frustration tolerance, increased impulsivity, poor peer relations, and frequent mood swings are often described. In the social domain, virtually all of these patients exhibit a failure to sustain meaningful relationships, extending across developmental levels.

Another crucial role played by the prefrontal lobes involves recovery from emotional trauma. When an individual has been traumatized, the emotional distress, as well as associations to the event, are all indelibly recorded at a subcortical level (i.e., in the limbic system). These memories cannot be erased, and any stimulus in the environment that matches an association stored in memory can trigger the emotional distress of the original trauma (with no conscious awareness of why this is happening). Historically, this probably had a high level of survival value, in that once a danger was experienced, anything that signaled a possibility of it happening again would automatically trigger a strong, automatic alarm. Unfortunately, this system of prevention does not readily protect us from the kinds of traumas encountered in today's complex world (e.g., car accidents, terrorism and terror threats, drive-by shootings). Rather, the triggering of associations and emotional distress frequently lead to trauma victims feeling overwhelmed with fear and avoidance, and this can become highly maladaptive (e.g., inability to drive, distrust of an entire ethnic group). However, it is possible for the prefrontal cortex to send an override message to turn off or modify the distress signals. Thus, although memories and associations of previous traumas cannot be deleted from the limbic system, they can be contained or modified through new programming in the prefrontal cortex.

Executive or "Vertical" Control

The limbic system promotes survival and is adept at responding especially quickly. For example, if you saw a car coming toward you and you startled and jumped to the side of the road, all of this rapid processing would have occurred primarily in the limbic system and brain stem, without any conscious awareness on your part. Afterward, however, you would take in and process more specific information at a cortical and conscious level (e.g., the thought, "That car almost hit me!"; the color of the car; the license plate number). In addition to the initial fear, you would probably start to feel angry, as well as relieved, and you might decide to report the incident to the police. Thus, rapid primary processing with the limbic system is sometimes crucial for survival, as in this case (you would have been dead before your cortex could have processed this); secondary and tertiary processing with the cortex, however, are also important, because these allow us to integrate cognitive and emotional data at a more complex level. This, in turn, allows us to better understand what has happened and to make appropriate plans for further action. Together, they can make an awesome team. However, this is not always the case.

In the previous example, it can be noted that the rapid speed of limbic system processing is undertaken at the expense of detailed accuracy. As a result, when the amygdala usurp control and initiate physical responses without cortical input or awareness, the outcomes are not always in our best interest. Goleman (1995) referred to these situations (i.e., maladaptive mishaps such as hitting a peer in response to getting hurt, shooting another driver during a fit of road rage) as "emotional hijacking" (p. 13).

Thus, having executive (prefrontal) control over our impulses (like having control knobs on a stove to turn down the heat) is often important for social adaptation and cultural survival. However, the neuronal interconnections between the prefrontal cortex and the limbic system develop relatively slowly over the course of childhood. Therefore, although the frontal cortex plays a role in emotional regulation as early as the first year of life, it takes many years before it gains executive control over the rapid and impulsive processing of the limbic system.

On the other hand, the connections between the limbic system and the brain stem, which allow for activation of motor responses without any cortical involvement, develop much earlier in life. The sensory and motor areas of the cortex also develop relatively quickly during the first 2 years. This is another reason why action often follows directly in response to strong feelings in young children (e.g., hitting one's sibling or throwing one's blocks when angry). These are examples of affective and sensorimotor intelligence at work, with no verbal or symbolic mediation needed. In other words, when children like Baby May are babies and experience emotions, they act or react.

Interestingly, the neural networks that transmit information from the limbic area to the frontal cortex develop faster than the networks that work in reverse. In addition, the development of pathways to dispatch messages from the frontal cortex to the limbic system appears to be much more dependent on environmental input. For example, when a mother comforts her overstimulated infant and helps her baby to calm down, she is teaching her child how to do this for himself or herself. At a neurological level, numerous successful experiences of this type will translate into the formation of optimal neural pathways from the frontal cortex to the limbic areas (ultimately resulting in well-developed self-control). If the child is frequently left in an emotionally overwhelmed state, on the other hand, the resulting networks will likely be deficient (the child will show deficits in self-control).

Perhaps even more surprising is the recent discovery of "mirror" neurons (Stamenov & Gallese, 2002). These nerve cells fire in response to observations of behaviors in others as if the individual were actually performing them. Thus, it is believed that neuronal networks can form through perception alone, which would explain, at least in part, why modeling has such powerful effects on learning. This of course implies that demonstrations of maintaining or regaining composure (or unfortunately, unhealthy alternatives) by significant others in the child's environment will also impact the manner in which neuronal pathways develop.

In summary, as a child matures in a "good enough" environment, interconnections between the frontal lobes and the limbic area increase and differentiate in an optimal way. These changes, along with developments in language and cognition (resulting from neuronal growth and maturation in other cortical areas), allow for dramatic changes in emotional maturation, self-control, and other aspects of development. Between the ages of 5 and 7, children normally show dramatic changes in functioning, sometimes termed the "5 to 7 shift" (Luria, 1976; White, 1970). As illustrated in Figure 2.4, pathways of vertical control from the frontal lobes lead to better regulation of impulses and action tendencies, greater independence, improved planning skills, and ability to assume greater responsibility. The capacity to automatically use inner speech also allows for verbal thought to serve as a mediator for behavioral self-control.

Following the successful transition of the 5 to 7 shift, a child is capable of using the following sequence: First the child experiences a feeling, then the child verbally processes this information, then the child makes a plan for responding, and finally, the child takes action. It can be noted that this critical change in development involving executive control occurs prior to societal expectations for the child to engage in formal schooling. In other words, we do not expect kindergartners to sit at desks for an extended period of time, but we do expect this by the second grade. (Since boys generally lag behind girls in neurological development at all ages, teachers usually expect that girls will have attained self-control by first grade, but are more tolerant with boys' "restlessness.")

Over the past 2 decades, however, the number of children showing difficulty with achieving the 5 to 7 transition (including the development of adequate self-control) seems to be growing. Children who do not form adequate orbital-frontal-limbic system neuronal networks by the age of 7 are at risk, because they will not be able to function in a manner that is expected for children of their chronological age. Furthermore, there seems to be a critical window of opportunity for the development

Figure 2.4   Pathways of Vertical Control From the Frontal Lobes to the Limbic System

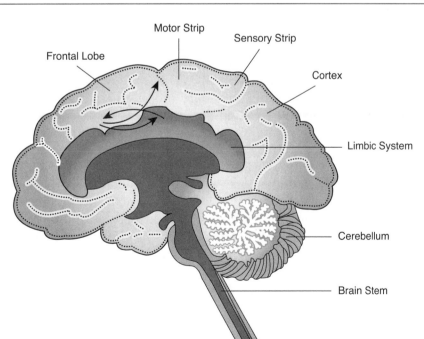

of these networks, and it appears to be very difficult to form them after adolescence. Risk for school failure, dropping out, drug use, violence, criminal behavior, and so on all increase as children grow older and continue to show deficits in this area.

Given the personal and societal problems inherent in less-than-optimal frontal lobe development, it is crucial for educators to promote the evolution of proficient neuronal networks (e.g., by actively teaching children, as well as modeling, how to calm down and achieve self-control over their behaviors). Children benefit greatly when specific models of bodily self-control, which are used during times of emotional arousal, are taught and mastered, followed by more advanced forms of verbally mediated self-control. In other words, the oft-used phrases, "You need to control yourself" and "You need to pay attention," need to be replaced with the understanding that many children lack the necessary neuronal structure and thus are unable to comply with the words alone. Teachers first need to instruct these children in how to control themselves and how to pay attention.

THE LEFT AND RIGHT HEMISPHERES

Interhemispheric or "Horizontal" Communication

As previously noted, the limbic system processes feelings at a primary level. The cortex, on the other hand, does so at a more refined, secondary level. Moreover, both sides of the cortex (left and right) are separate from one another and have specialized functions with regard to the processing of affect. In addition, coordination between the two hemispheres (in the mature brain) is made possible by the corpus callosum, a bundle of nerve cells that transverses the two sides and allows for communication between them. This also provides a means for integrating two different communication systems, that of emotion and that of language.

To better understand how this works, consider two symbiotic cities linked together by only one bridge. City L specializes in linguistic communication (e.g., expressive and receptive language), as well as in the secondary processing of the expression of pleasurable emotion (e.g., happiness, calm, excitement, love). City R, on the other hand, specializes in the secondary processing of the remaining aspects of emotional communication (i.e., the sending of unpleasurable emotional signals as well as the receiving of both pleasant and uncomfortable feelings).

Historically, things used to be much different: Approximately 1 million to 4 million years ago, City L and City R were probably symmetrical, mirror images of one another. Whatever could be done on one side, could also be done in the other (as with all other mammals). Apparently, with the advent of spoken language (which takes a considerable amount of processing space), there was simply not enough room to keep this duplication of functioning. Thus, the two sides began to specialize (Davidson, 1994; Fox, 1994), with City L processing language (plus expressive pleasurable feelings) and City R responsible for the secondary processing of receptive emotions and expressive uncomfortable feelings (Bryden & Ley, 1983). (For purposes of accuracy, it should be noted that infants and toddlers actually process verbal language in both hemispheres, but by about the age of 3, dominance for language-related operations shifts to the left hemisphere in the majority of preschoolers. However, it appears that a minority, primarily females, continue to process at least some language in both the left and right hemispheres, whereas an even smaller minority develop linguistic specialization in the right hemisphere.)

Linguistic processing has at least three advantages compared with nonverbal processing: (a) It permits metaconsciousness (i.e., the ability to observe and analyze one's own thoughts), which in turn, provides increased ability for self-control; (b) it allows for sequential thinking; and (c) it provides greater specificity and accuracy. Nonverbal intelligence, on the other hand, allows for global and holistic thinking (e.g., viewing a work of art or envisioning how to landscape a backyard), intuition, and faster processing of information. Emotions, for example, provide parsimonious packets of instantaneous data, and thus, afford an extremely efficient and highly adaptive method for conveying information quickly.

In addition, language requires a relatively long time to learn and is specific to the culture in which it is used, whereas the emotional communication system unfolds relatively quickly and is universal in nature. For example, by the end of the first year of life, an infant like young May is fluent in sending and receiving messages through emotional communication, and theoretically, could do so with any human from any culture. In comparison, a 1-year-old is only beginning to speak his or her first words in his or her specific mother tongue.

Thus, emotions and language are both important for different purposes, and to function in an integrated and optimal way, it is important to coordinate both systems of communication. In other words, City L and City R need to keep each other informed and work together for the good of the whole. To accomplish this, they need to use the corpus callosum as a bridge between them to allow a freely flowing conveyance of information back and forth between the two domains. Once the communication networks that cross the bridge have been created, nonverbal data emanating from City R can travel across the bridge to City L, where linguistic processing allows for metaconsciousness of internal responses to the external environment (e.g., emotional awareness). Information from City L, on the other hand, can travel across the bridge to City R to help clarify, influence, and control emotional processing (Fox & Davidson, 1984).

Moreover, this bridge is the only means by which the two cities can communicate with one another, and unfortunately, this situation has resulted in an interesting, and frequently dysfunctional, paradox. This occurs when unpleasant information processed in City R does not travel across the bridge (e.g., if access is blocked or if sufficient networks have never developed). When this happens, the individual, who is aware only of the comfortable affect in City L, is fooled into thinking that there are no uncomfortable feelings, when it fact, there are. In other words, this can trick individuals into thinking that they are free of emotional pain, a condition that most people prefer. In general, however, this lack of knowledge is not beneficial, because conscious awareness of external and internal conditions is usually necessary for optimal functioning and adaptation. Nevertheless, blocking the unpleasant communications from City R consciously feels better, so there is a strong tendency to want to do this and thereby mask discomfort. This defense is called emotional repression, and it is often dysfunctional.

To borrow from an old adage, if feelings processed in the right hemisphere are not "heard" or known by the left, they do still "make a sound." But due to the functional and structural arrangement previously described (which is also illustrated in Figure 2.5), the nonlinguistic information (such as an emotional signal) that is processed preconsciously by the right hemisphere will not reach conscious awareness until we verbally "think" about it with the left hemisphere. And to verbally label our emotional experiences, and thus become consciously aware of them, information from the right must be transmitted to the left via the corpus callosum. In other words, to be truly aware of our emotional experiences, we must use horizontal interhemispheric communication

Figure 2.5   Horizontal Communication Between the Left and Right Hemispheres

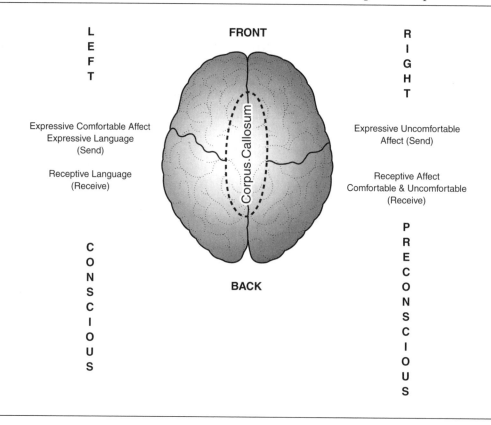

between the right and left hemispheres, a phenomenon originally described by Sigmund Freud in 1915 (1957/1915).

To summarize, if emotion information (e.g., the secondary processing of anger) does not reach the left hemisphere, an individual will experience the feeling but will not be aware of having the experience (as illustrated in Figure 2.6b). Moreover, other people can be aware of how this person feels (e.g., by observing facial cues or hearing the tone of voice), but the individual himself or herself will not be aware of his or her own feelings. (And if other people point out the feeling state to the person involved, this individual will frequently feel invaded, resentful, and frustrated. The logical but erroneous thinking goes something like, "They're my feelings; I would know better than you would if I were feeling that way!") A common illustration of this phenomenon occurs when a teacher clearly and correctly observes a child who is feeling angry, but the child truly has no conscious awareness of feeling that way ("I am not angry—I feel #@% # fine!").

Historically, children (at least in Western cultures) have frequently been inadvertently taught to use repression. It is very common, for example, to hear an exasperated adult tell a child, "Don't get mad!" In general, what the adult really means is, "Don't act out!" (e.g., throw a tantrum, scream, pout). However, the statement "Don't get mad!" results in the child thinking that it is bad to feel angry, and since it is impossible not to have a feeling when the feeling is there, often the best a child can do to comply is to repress it. Since the behavioral result is what the adult wanted in

Figure 2.6a   The Experience and Conscious Awareness of Anger

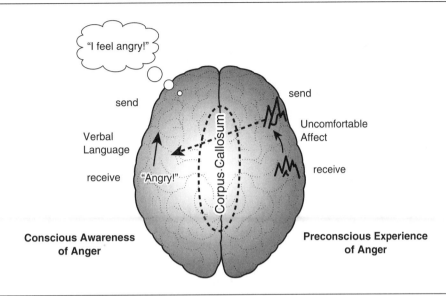

Figure 2.6b   The Experience of Anger, With No Conscious Awareness

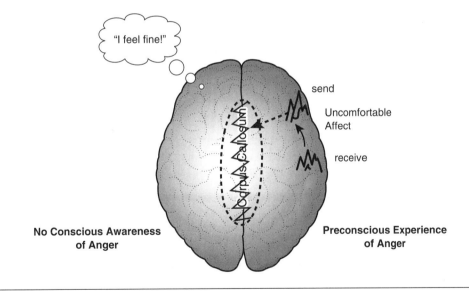

the first place, this response is usually reinforced as a good thing. Unfortunately, our ancestors were not aware of the substantial long-term costs that incur from the resulting lack of emotional awareness (paid at both an individual and a societal level).

In children, development of the corpus callosum is relatively slow. But the way in which interhemispheric structuralization occurs depends heavily on environmental input during development. Verbal identification and labeling of feelings should powerfully assist with managing these feelings, controlling behavior, and improving hemispheric integration. Thus, the use of emotion recognition cues such as pictures of facial expressions (mediated by the right hemisphere) in conjunction with verbal labels (mediated by the left) during the process of emotional experience should improve the development of interhemispheric communication. In addition, encouraging children to talk about emotional experiences (both at the time they are occurring and in recollection) should further strengthen cortical integration. Fortunately, these are all activities that teachers can promote in the classroom, both through SEL instruction and during daily interactions, especially when children are actually experiencing difficult emotions or social situations.

The Brain Gets Programmed

As if the story of brain development were not amazing enough, Schore (1994), Damasio (1994), and others have recently provided compelling evidence that all programming from the environment is not equal. Rather, neocortical brain development is especially responsive to the input of the "programmers" to whom we are emotionally attached, in interaction with our genetic potentials. For most higher mammals, including humans, the mother is generally the head programmer (pun intended), especially during the first few years, although other available caregivers and attachment figures (father, nannies, grandparents, etc.) are certainly important as well (Dawson, 1994).

Changes in affect associated with recovery from emotional pain (e.g., from despair to joy) in the context of the child-caregiver relationship result in increased secretion of dopamine and endogenous opiates which in turn promote synaptic growth in the prefrontolimbic regions of the brain (Schore, 1994, 1996).

Siegel (1998) summarized these ideas as follows:

> Our modern view of the brain and its response to experience has shed some new light on how experience directly affects gene function, neuronal connections and the organization of the mind. . . . emotion influences and is influenced by a wide range of mental processes. Another way of stating this is that emotion, thought, perception, memory and action are inextricably interwoven. (pp. 2, 7)

Moreover, these affective processes, with their powerful integrating influences, generally occur in the context of important relationships.

Thus, if Baby May's mother is generally successful in providing optimal, balanced stimulation (i.e., encouraging positive interest in the world while also supplying soothing comfort when her baby is distressed or overwhelmed), a very important positive foundation will be laid for the later achievement of such things as self-control, internal motivation, and paying attention. This will also result in a good foundation with regard to early brain development. Every time Baby May enjoys a learning experience with her mother, she will strengthen her love for learning along with her cortical interconnections.

May's cortex will slowly form schemas (templates processed by neural networks) about the world based on various experiences processed by her limbic system. If her caregivers continue to be reliable and responsive to her needs, she will eventually form schemas of basic trust and positive self-esteem. In contrast, the infant who frequently feels neglected or abandoned will come to see adults as untrustworthy and will likely form a basic sense of being unwanted, unloved, and unworthy (a recipe for depression, anxiety, aggression, or other disorders). However, this foundation is just the beginning, and the building blocks for motivation and control will continue to accrue along with the corresponding structural networks. Over the course of early childhood, the schemas and networks that develop will create expectancies or mind-sets that will affect May's perceptions of teachers and peers, as well as her classroom behaviors, when she finally begins school.

Her teachers will play powerful and crucial roles in May's brain growth and integration. The importance of attachment as catalyst for brain development will continue; the better May feels about her teachers (and perceives her teachers as feeling toward her), the more positive the effect on cortical development and learning. Strong negative feelings or the perception of negative feelings from her teachers, on the other hand, will likely cause significant interference with regard to motivation, attention, retention, and so on. In other words, the quality of emotional bonds (positive, negative, or indifferent) that develop between students and their teachers has a crucial impact on learning and brain development.

Gender Differences and Brain Development

Anyone who has worked with children knows that taken as a group, boys act differently than girls in many ways (although there are certainly individual differences). We now know that at least some of this diversity is due to differences in brain organization. Boys, for example, generally have more neurons in their motor cortex, whereas girls tend to have enhanced interconnections in the frontal lobes and verbal regions. As a result of this, boys tend to react more readily to anger with physical responses (e.g., fighting, hitting, etc.), whereas girls specialize in using verbal responses (e.g., "You can't come to my birthday party!"). Similarly, females usually have several million more neurons in their corpora callosa than do males (which theoretically augments interhemispheric communication and integration).

Until recently, it was believed that these variances were due primarily to differences in environmental input. Not surprisingly, we have recently learned that genetics also play a crucial role (Solms & Turnbull, 2002). For example, the "pilot light" in the male brain is programmed to maintain continuous awareness for the potential for attack (Who is the enemy? What weapons should be used? etc.), and males tend to have quick, aggressive reactions to the perception of danger (and, in today's world, to video games). With the female brain, on the other hand, the "pilot light" keeps vigil to maintain social order and harmony (e.g., Is everyone cooperating? Does anyone in the group need anything? etc.). Thus, compared with boys, it is usually easier to socialize girls (e.g., to teach them to cooperate, follow rules, etc.).

What makes this more complicated, however, is that the male or female brain does not always match the gender of the individual. When mothers are highly stressed during the second trimester of pregnancy, for example, a series of events occurs prematurely, which in turn precludes the boy from developing a male brain (the prototype being the female or social brain). As a result, the interaction of genetics with the environment (in this case, in utero) can result in individual differences in a gender.

IMPLICATIONS OF BRAIN DEVELOPMENT FOR SEL LEARNING

There are several important implications for educators that can be drawn from our current knowledge of brain organization and emotional processes:

1. The nature and quality of the teacher-child relationship impacts attention, learning, and brain development.

It is clear that brain development is highly malleable and is strongly impacted by experiences interacting with genetic potential to strengthen, prune, integrate, interconnect, organize, and reorganize neural networks. The creation of optimal neural networks between the left and right hemispheres and between the prefrontal lobes and subcortical areas are of special importance. We believe that the quality of the emotional attachment of a child to his or her teacher is of crucial importance with regard to the quality of attention, learning, and brain development.

2. Education can have a critical influence on the strengthening of neocortical control and self-awareness.

At a neurological level, teaching can be defined as the facilitation of neuronal growth, organization, and integration; that is, teachers have the potential to play important roles in strengthening pathways that lead to the integration of affect, language, and cognition. Although teaching content or subject matter is important, the process or manner in which it is taught is probably even more significant. Of particular importance is the manner in which teachers promote emotional literacy, interpersonal decision making, and problem solving in the classroom.

3. The strengthening of frontal lobe capacities is critical for optimal academic, social, and personal success.

The executive functions of the left and right frontal lobes (including such domains as attention, concentration, frustration tolerance, social problem-solving skills, self-control, and the management of affect) are crucial for both higher level learning and for mature behavior. Deficits in the functioning of any of these areas can affect the subsequent development of other domains. Moreover, it is important to note that these abilities do not automatically develop, but rather must be learned by each individual.

4. Helping children to develop awareness of affective processes (both in themselves and in others), using verbal labels to identify emotional experiences, and encouraging perspective taking and empathic identification with others improve the frontal lobe functions of interpersonal awareness and self-control.

In our own work, we have shown that children who display the most impulsive and aggressive behavior are the least able to verbalize and discuss their emotions. Furthermore, our work over the past 20 years with the Promoting Alternative Thinking Strategies curriculum (Kusché & Greenberg, 1994), a school-based program that focuses on emotional literacy, self-esteem, social problem solving, and so on, has demonstrated that SEL can lead to significant changes in such areas as emotional awareness, behavior, and academic success (please see Chapter 16 for further details).

5. Attending consistently and patiently to children's emotions and their consequences as a central part of classroom processes leads to improved personal and academic outcomes.

Teaching healthy strategies for coping with, communicating about, and managing emotions assists children in maintaining attention and focus during academic and interpersonal learning contexts. Most educators agree that, when possible, a balanced education is preferable for children to have. In neurophysiological terms, this means that many different areas of the brain are used in learning a diversity of skills. Education that does not include emotional literacy and SEL will be far from balanced. Furthermore, cognitive development alone, no matter how spectacular (e.g., high achievement test scores), is limited and is not likely to result in success in life without proficient emotional development. As Goleman (1995) has phrased this, "Emotional intelligence . . . can matter more than IQ."

6. When teachers listen to their students and show respect for their feelings, opinions, and ideas, they provide optimal conditions for attachment, learning, and brain development.

Children who feel listened to with respect by their teachers (and peers) feel valued, cared for, appreciated, supported, respected, and part of a social group. This, along with empathy from their teachers and peers, motivates children to value, care for, appreciate, and feel prosocial toward themselves, their environment, the social groups to which they belong, other people, and their world. In other words, emotional literacy and respect for the feelings of self and others are among the basic building blocks for healthy society and civilization.

REFERENCES

Aggleton, J. P. (1992). *The amygdala: Neurobiological aspects of emotion, memory, and mental dysfunction.* New York: Wiley.

Benton, A. (1991). Prefrontal injury and behavior in children. *Developmental Neuropsychology, 7,* 275–281.

Berger, A., & Posner, M. I. (2000). Pathologies of brain attentional networks. *Neuro-science & Biobehavioral Reviews, 24,* 3–5.

Bryden, M. P., & Ley, R. G. (1983). Right-hemispheric involvement in the perception and expression of emotion in normal humans. In K. M. Heilman & P. Satz (Eds.), *Neuropsychology of human emotion* (pp. 6–44). New York: Guilford Press.

Damasio, A. R. (1994). *Descartes' error: Emotion, reason, and the human brain.* New York: Grosset/Putnam.

Davidson, R. J. (1994). Asymmetric brain function, affective style, and psychopathology: The role of early experiences and plasticity. *Development and Psychopathology, 6,* 741–758.

Dawson, G. (1994). Frontal electroencephalographic correlates of individual differences in emotion expression in infants: A brain systems perspective on emotion. In N. Fox (Ed.), *Monographs of the Society for Research in Child Development: Vol. 59. The development of emotion regulation: Biological and behavioral considerations* (pp. 135–151). Chicago: Society for Research in Child Development.

Drevets, W. C., & Raichle, M. E. (1998). Reciprocal suppression of regional cerebral blood flow during emotional versus higher cognitive processes: Implications for interactions between emotion and cognition. *Cognition & Emotion, 12,* 353–385.

Emde, R. N. (1999). Moving ahead: Integrating influences of affective processes for development and for psychoanalysis. *International Journal of Psychoanalysis, 80,* 317–339.

Fox, N. A. (1994). Dynamic cerebral processes underlying emotion regulation. In N. Fox (Ed.), *Monographs of the Society for Research in Child Development: Vol. 59. The development of emotion regulation: Biological and behavioral considerations* (pp. 152–166). Chicago: Society for Research in Child Development.

Fox, N. A., & Davidson, R. J. (1984). Hemispheric substrates of affect: A developmental model. In N. A. Fox & R. J. Davidson (Eds.), *The psychobiology of affective development* (pp. 353–381). Hillsdale, NJ: Lawrence Erlbaum.

Freud, S. (1957). The unconscious. In J. Strachey (Ed.), *Standard edition* (Vol. 14, pp. 159–215). London: Hogarth Press. (Originally published in 1915)

Gibbs, W. W. (1998). New and analysis: In focus–dogma overturned. *Scientific American, 279*(5), 19–20.

Goleman, D. (1995). *Emotional intelligence: Why it can matter more than IQ.* New York: Bantam Books.

Grattan, L. M., & Eslinger, P. J. (1991). Frontal lobe damage in children and adults: A comparative review. *Developmental Neuropsychology, 7,* 283–326.

Greenberg, M. T., & Snell, J. (1997). The neurological basis of emotional development. In P. Salovey (Ed.), *Emotional development and emotional literacy* (pp. 92–119). New York: Basic Books.

Jensen, E. (1998). *Teaching with the brain in mind.* Alexandria, VA: Association for Supervision and Curriculum Development.

Kusché, C. A. (1984). *The understanding of emotion concepts by deaf children: An assessment of an affective curriculum.* Unpublished doctoral dissertation. (University Microfilms International, DAO 56952)

Kusché, C. A., Cook, E. T., & Greenberg, M. T. (1993). Neuropsychological and cognitive functioning in children with anxiety, externalizing, and comorbid psychopathology. *Journal of Clinical Child Psychology, 22,* 172–195.

Kusché, C. A., & Greenberg, M. T. (1994). *The PATHS (Promoting Alternative Thinking Strategies) curriculum.* South Deerfield, MA: Channing-Bete.

Kusché, C. A, & Greenberg, M. T. (1998). Integrating emotions and thinking in the classroom. *THINK, 9,* 32–34.

LeDoux, J. E. (1991). Emotion and the limbic system concept. *Concepts in Neuroscience, 2,* 169–199.

LeDoux, J. E. (1993). Emotional memory systems in the brain. *Behavioural Brain Research, 58,* 69–79.

LeDoux, J. E. (1995). Emotion: Clues from the brain. *Annual Review of Psychology, 46,* 209–235.

Luria, A. R. (1976). *Cognitive development: Its cultural and social foundations.* Cambridge, MA: Harvard University Press.

MacLean, P. D. (1978). A mind of three minds: Educating the triune brain. In J. Chall & A. Mirsky (Eds.), *Education and the brain, 77th national Society for the Study of Education yearbook* (pp. 308–342). Chicago: University of Chicago Press.

Ornstein, R., & Thompson, R. F. (1984). *The amazing brain.* Boston: Houghton Mifflin.

Panskeep, J. (1998). *Affective neuroscience.* New York: Oxford University Press.

Ratey, J. J. (2001). *A user's guide to the brain.* New York: Pantheon Books.

Schore, A. (1994). *Affect regulation and the origins of the self: Neurobiology of emotional development.* Hillsdale, NJ: Erlbaum.

Schore, A. (1996). The experience-dependent maturation of a regulatory system in the orbital prefrontal cortex and the origin of developmental psychopathology. *Developmental Psychopathology, 8,* 59–87.

Siegel, D. J. (1998). The developing mind: Toward a neurobiology of interpersonal experience. *Signal, 6,* 1–11.

Solms, M., & Turnbull, O. (2002). *The brain and the inner world: An introduction to the neuroscience of subjective experience.* New York: Other Press.

Stamenov, M. I., & Gallese, V. (Eds.). (2002). *Mirror neurons and the evolution of brain and language.* Amsterdam: John Benjamins.

Sylwester, R. (1995). *A celebration of neurons: An educator's guide to the human brain.* Alexandria, VA: Association for Supervision and Curriculum Development.

Todd, R. D., Swarzenski, B., Rossi, P. G., & Visconti, P. (1995). Structural and functional development of the human brain. In D. Cicchetti & D. Cohen (Eds.), *Developmental psychopathology: Vol. 1. Theory and methods* (pp. 161–194). New York: Wiley Interscience.

White, S. H. (1970). Some general outlines of the matrix of developmental changes between five and seven years. *Bulletin of the Orton Society, 20,* 41–57.

3

Multiple Intelligences and Emotional Intelligence

Finding Common Ground in the Classroom

Thomas Hatch and Mindy L. Kornhaber

In one corner of a kindergarten classroom, Kenny sits by himself, rapidly completing exercises in a first-grade language workbook. At the art table, Rosa, with a flourish, completes a whimsical painting of "frogs pulling a sleigh." In the dramatic play area, Maggie defuses a heated argument between Edith and Julia by suggesting they should "just play house" instead of playing Cinderella "because it won't be fair. Everyone will want to be a pretty lady, and there's no boys to be the prince."

All of these children are engaged in constructive activities, but which of these children displays intelligence?

Few would dispute that Kenny's ability to carry out an advanced language activity probably reflects his intelligence. But many people assume that Rosa's and Maggie's activities have relatively little to do with their intelligence. Why? As numerous researchers have pointed out, the term *intelligence* has been given a specific—and narrow—meaning by generations of psychologists and test makers who argue that intelligence can be measured by paper-and-pencil tests that focus on a handful of linguistic, logical, and mathematical abilities (Gardner, 1983; Gould, 1996; Sternberg, 1985).

Despite the pervasiveness of the traditional definition of intelligence, several people have proposed and pursued entirely different visions of intelligence that suggest that there are a broader range of capacities that are necessary to carry out many significant and meaningful activities. In recent years, Howard Gardner developed one of the most prominent alternatives. In *Frames of Mind* and several other publications, Gardner (1983, 1993) defined intelligence as the ability to solve problems and fashion products that are valued in one or more cultures. He has also argued that there are at least eight distinct capacities—linguistic, logical-mathematical, spatial, bodily-kinesthetic, musical, interpersonal, intrapersonal, and naturalist—that deserve to be called intelligences. According to Gardner, all of these capacities—not just the linguistic and mathematical abilities emphasized in traditional IQ tests and American schools—should "count" as intelligences because they meet eight criteria that demonstrate that these capacities develop relatively independently. These criteria include the existence of an identifiable set of core operations, a distinct developmental trajectory, and the potential of isolation by brain damage.

More recently, researchers like Peter Salovey and John Mayer and author Daniel Goleman have broadened the term *intelligence* in a different way. These authors argue that many of the capacities Gardner discussed as part of the personal intelligences constitute a distinct "emotional intelligence" (Goleman, 1995; Mayer & Salovey, 1997). In their views, emotional intelligence involves "the ability to perceive emotions, to access and generate emotions so as to assist thought, to understand emotions and emotional meanings, and to reflectively regulate emotions so as to promote better emotion and thought" (Mayer & Salovey, p. 22). This definition suggests that people have to have capacities to understand and deal with emotions to behave intelligently and that a failure to develop these capacities can interfere with thought and reasoning.

Over the past few years, interest in both multiple intelligences (MI) theory and emotional intelligence has grown considerably, inspiring many people and prompting considerable discussion and debate in educational circles, community groups, and the popular press. Understandably, these developments have created some confusion between these two views and their implications.

Although there are important differences between these views of intelligence that are worth exploring, recent efforts to document some of the most effective applications of MI show that, in the classroom, programs based on these two views may help to support the achievement of some of the same outcomes. Moreover, building on ideas and information drawn from both of these broader conceptions of intelligence can help create classrooms and schools that are characterized by a culture of care and respect. These are the kinds of environments in which students like Kenny, Rosa, and Maggie can develop many of the capacities they need to be content and successful in later life.

DIFFERENCES IN THEORY

It is possible to imagine classrooms and schools that draw on the ideas expressed in the MI and emotional intelligence theories because both areas are essential for understanding and dealing with our own and others' emotions. This in turn is central to the performance of a wide range of meaningful activities in our society. From making a marriage work to working as part of a team and from managing our own fears to motivating others, we have to learn to deal with our own and others' emotions. Furthermore, there is general agreement on the core capacities that involve the emotions. Although different researchers have produced slightly different lists, in general, people like Gardner, Salovey, Mayer, and Goleman suggest that the core capacities include perceiving and responding appropriately to the moods, motives, and desires of other people and understanding, dealing with, and expressing one's own emotions appropriately. Therefore, from the perspective of both the MI and emotional intelligence camps, there are good reasons to support explicitly the development of these capacities in schools and other educational institutions.

At the same time, from Gardner's (1983) point of view, it does not make sense to talk about a specific and independent emotional intelligence because there is not enough evidence that the abilities to process emotions meet the criteria established in *Frames of Mind*. From an MI perspective, the capacities to process emotions develop and are displayed in concert with the broader set of "core capacities" that characterize inter- and intrapersonal intelligence (Hatch, 1997b). These capacities include the ability to understand motivations and intentions, as well as moods and temperaments. From this perspective, the ability to process emotions is a critical part of what it takes to understand other people or oneself, to manage one's own behavior, or to influence the behavior of others, but not the only part. Thus, although inter- and intrapersonal intelligence are not the same as emotional intelligence, what has been learned about the processing of emotions helps to inform an understanding of how inter- and intrapersonal intelligence develop and operate.

Beyond the arguments over what capacities deserve to be called "intelligences," there are also some important implications of MI theory that are not necessarily shared by research and programs that focus on emotional development and emotional intelligence. First, MI is based on a theory of development that argues that intelligences are biopsychological potentials that cannot be seen, assessed, or developed directly. We can only see, assess, and foster competence in the domains of knowledge and expertise that have grown over time in different cultures. Thus, spatial intelligence can only be demonstrated and developed by using the tools, methods, and knowledge of domains like engineering and architecture to design machines or build buildings.

From this perspective, there are not just *more* intelligences than those proposed in traditional theories, the nature of intelligence is entirely different. In contrast to traditional views, MI suggests that intelligences are not fixed from birth and that how intelligence is defined, developed, and demonstrated will differ from culture to culture. As a result, although proponents of a traditional view of intelligence argue that a single test, like an IQ test, can predict the level of intelligence people will show in general across many different situations in their lives, MI suggests that their intelligences can only be assessed by seeing how people use their capacities in different contexts and over time. Kenny's, Rosa's, and Maggie's intelligences cannot be understood simply by observing them in a small set of activities on a given day. Furthermore, how they will use their intelligences cannot be predicted simply by observing or assessing them in kindergarten. How they develop and use their intelligences in later life will depend on the interests they express, the domains they encounter, and the communities in which they grow up (Hatch, 1997a).

Many theories of emotional intelligence, however, do not necessarily demand a rethinking of traditional conceptions of intelligence. Consequently, those who believe in emotional intelligence could simply argue that Kenny demonstrates traditional intelligence whereas Maggie demonstrates emotional intelligence. Correspondingly, programs that support emotional intelligence can simply be add-ons to the conventional curriculum or focus entirely on the development of emotional capacities. Those who believe in MI, on the other hand, would argue that Kenny, Rosa, and Maggie could all be displaying their intelligences in different ways and that the regular classroom activities should recognize and support the use of many of these capacities. Gardner (1999) has shied away from articulating a specific "MI approach" that explains how to do this; however, this viewpoint suggests that it is not sufficient simply to produce students who can do well on the academic tasks emphasized in traditional views of intelligence and who display emotional intelligence. Creating a curriculum that consists of three Rs (reading, writing and 'rithmetic) and an E (emotional processing) is not enough. From an MI perspective, the goals of schooling should include helping students to develop an appropriate and effective mix of capacities that builds on *many* of their intellectual strengths and takes into account the demands of the society. Thus, the development of particular intelligences— whether linguistic, spatial, or interpersonal—is not a meaningful end goal of education in and of itself. To have a high IQ, "EQ," or "MIQ" means little. What matters is helping students learn how to use their intelligences so that they can carry out the activities that will enable them to be productive members of society.

Second, although, as Goleman and others have noted, the role of the emotions was not highlighted in original discussions of MI (Goleman, 1995; Mayer & Salovey, 1997), the ability to understand, work with, and express emotions is involved in the use of many intelligences. For example, Rosa's picture of a frog pulling a sleigh is striking not simply because she produces recognizable representations, but because she can use her spatial skills to surprise and amuse the viewer. In this particular case, she depicts only the frogs, harnessed together, leaping through the picture, leaving the viewer to imagine the sleigh the frogs pull behind them. At the same time, she is not particularly adept at expressing her own emotions or influencing the emotions of others when writing stories or using other linguistic devices. Similarly, from an MI perspective, there is no general ability or intelligence that would suggest that a person like Maggie, who manages emotions expertly in interpersonal situations, would necessarily display the same emotional sensitivity when drawing or telling stories. Her spatial and linguistic capacities will influence her ability to process and express emotions in these different domains. The belief that the capacity to express and deal with emotions is used in concert with others reinforces the idea that efforts to develop emotional capacities should take place in the context of all of the meaningful tasks—painting, ballet, sports, and so forth—in which children use their intelligences.

All in all, one can imagine programs that support the development of emotional intelligence that neither confront views of traditional intelligence nor support the development of the other kinds of intelligences proposed in MI theory. However, it is hard to imagine programs consistent with the theory of MI that fails to take seriously the kinds of capacities that are emphasized in theories and programs focused on emotional intelligence and emotional development. Effective applications of MI include and encompass efforts to develop inter- and intrapersonal skills and enhance students' abilities to understand and express emotions appropriately in activities involving the other intelligences as well.

MIS IN THE CLASSROOM

Despite these differences in theory, the experiences of some of the most effective schools that use MI demonstrate that in practice, teachers work to develop children's abilities to process and manage emotions as part and parcel of addressing the many intelligences children bring into the classroom. These efforts have been noted during the work of Project SUMIT (Schools Using Multiple Intelligences Theory), an effort to identify effective applications of MI and create resources that will support educators' efforts to apply MI in sound ways (Kornhaber, Fierros, & Veenema, 2004). SUMIT researchers have identified 41 schools that have linked their application of the theory of MI to improvements in student achievement, student behavior, parent partici-pation, and the schooling of children with learning differences. By interviewing principals at these schools and visiting 10 schools to speak with and at which to observe teachers and students, SUMIT has established six "compass points" for using MI well. Rather than prescribing a single approach, these compass points provide a glimpse of some of the key practices of schools that appear to be using the theory effectively and the different routes these schools have taken in putting MI into practice. The compass points that have been identified are the following: a culture that is marked by care and respect for others, hard work, and joy in learning; collab-oration among adults; readiness built by understanding and exploring MI before implementing it; student choices in assessment and curriculum that are both mean-ingful to them and within the larger culture; the use of MI as a tool to develop high-quality work rather than as an end in and of itself; and a significant role for the arts in the life of the school (Kornhaber et al., 2004).

Although it is logical to assume that the distinguishing features of schools using MI are activities and assessments that focus on each intelligence, visitors to the most successful MI schools are likely to be struck first by something else: a school culture that reflects an abiding concern and respect for each individual. The principals and staff demonstrate this concern and respect in their efforts to recognize and build on the strengths of every child, but the students demonstrate this concern and respect as well in their behavior and interactions with one another. In fact, more than 60% of the schools that have been identified credit improvements in discipline to their applications of MI. For example, at the Dover School outside Tampa, Florida, dis-ciplinary referrals dropped from more than 400 in 1990—when the school began to apply MI—to 13.

Beyond the numbers, in these schools, it is common to see students regularly displaying a knowledge of and concern for their peers unusual in most settings. For example, in a third-grade room in a highly heterogeneous school in Albuquerque, a boy with Tourette's syndrome who was new to the school did not want to show his work to the researchers. As the researchers moved on, they overheard the student's classmate ask the boy why he did not want to share his work. The boy said, "It isn't any good." His classmate reassured him that it was good and would get even better as he spent more time in the school.

This culture of concern and respect grows alongside activities that foster the development of students' inter- and intrapersonal abilities and projects that often focus on the real issues that affect children's lives and support the development of a sense of collective responsibility. For example, at McCleary Elementary, a high-poverty school in Pittsburgh, lunch initially took place in a dingy basement area and was punctuated by behavior problems. The principal decided to make this problem into a project. The lunchroom was transformed into a restaurant, with students taking on some of the front jobs, like greeter and menu board writer. Teachers and students decorated the space to make it into a warm and more inviting environment, and students (many of whose restaurant experiences had been limited to fast food outlets) learned about volume levels, etiquette, and social exchanges that contribute to enjoyable dining.

In MI schools, the shared belief that every child has worthwhile intellectual strengths provides a foundation for collaboration that does not exist in other places: Teachers often need to collaborate to address the range of children's strengths. The theory enables educators to recognize that just as students have strengths in some but not all areas, teachers and administrators also have specific areas of strength. Thus, teachers with spatial skills often find themselves using pictures and diagrams to explain concepts and incorporating drawing and designing activities into their curriculum; at the same time, they may struggle to incorporate activities that focus on other intelligences in a meaningful way. This problem gives many teachers an important reason to recognize their colleagues' strengths and work together. As a result, administrators and teachers of successful MI schools provide a model of the kinds of attitudes and behaviors that many programs focusing on emotional intelligence seek to foster in students.

At the same time, explicit efforts to recognize and support the development of interpersonal and intrapersonal intelligences among the students help provide them with the skills and understandings they need to get along with one another. For example, at the New City School, a private K through 5 school in St. Louis, one teacher builds her students' intra- and interpersonal understanding by having them draw a map of the school. She asks them to put down "trouble spots" where they are likely to have difficulty with others. In the process, she gets students to reflect on their behavior in ways that help them both to better understand their own activities and to manage their interactions with their peers. As Tom Hoerr, principal of the New City School, put it, these kinds of activities help students to "learn more about themselves as people" (personal communication).

In turn, the knowledge and feelings of competence the students gain as they learn more about themselves helps them to become accepted and effective members of the school community. As one teacher described it, a child who had experienced some behavior problems and likely would have been classified as learning disabled in another setting, was able to become a "player" in his peer group by coming to understand his own strengths and by developing his skills as an artist. This kind of personal knowledge is also a key part of establishing a culture of concern and respect. As Sheryl Hamer, principal of Glenridge Elementary, put it, "Kids really have a respect for each other and an empathy for each other because they realize that they have strengths and weaknesses" (personal communication).

As these examples demonstrate, many effective MI schools do not establish a separate series of activities that focus on the development of the personal intelligences. Instead, teachers in these schools strive to give students opportunities to develop interpersonal and intrapersonal skills in concert with a variety of other abilities and in the contexts of the kinds of real activities and problems they are likely to encounter outside school. In addition to integrating the development of inter- and intrapersonal skills into the curriculum, these projects help support the development of a culture of concern and respect by providing students with an opportunity to make a contribution to their community and to develop a sense of collective responsibility.

At the Searsport Elementary School in Searsport, Maine, for example, fifth graders carried out an archeological dig. The culmination of the project was to create an exhibition of their findings to be placed in a nearby museum. To achieve this goal, the students had to work together in groups to organize, label, and present what they had found. In the process, they had to use their logical-mathematical, spatial, and linguistic intelligences to create coherent displays and write descriptions. But they also had to use their inter- and intrapersonal intelligences to determine what kinds of displays might engage museumgoers and to figure out how to communicate an appropriate amount of information in a succinct way. But rather than simply completing the exhibitions and sending them on to the museum, the work was first displayed in the school lobby where everyone in the school was invited to review it and point out any problems or flaws. The fifth graders displayed their exhibition at the museum only after it had passed the review of their classmates and the entire school, thus reinforcing the idea that they were all responsible for the work and reputation of their school.

Many of the projects carried out in effective MI schools also focus explicitly on social-emotional issues that students have to deal with in their own lives. At the McCleary School in Pittsburgh, for example, fourth and fifth graders engaged in projects focused on the life cycle. Among other issues, the projects helped the students explore the concept of loss and deal with the departures and deaths of parents, family members, teachers, peers, and other significant individuals. As a result, one student was able to write a story that described how her cousin cried every day after her mother's murder. In the process, she had an opportunity to try to understand her cousin's feelings of loss and to explore her own feelings about her own teacher's departure.

BUILDING ON BOTH PERSPECTIVES

Although there are significant differences in the theory of MI and views of emotional intelligence, these examples from some of the most effective MI schools demonstrate that efforts to support intelligences and to foster social-emotional development can go hand in hand. As a result, the compass points developed by SUMIT may prove useful for those interested in creating programs that build on both perspectives. Correspondingly, many of those interested in applying MI theory may benefit by carefully examining and drawing on some of the most effective programs that aim to support social-emotional development. In fact, many of the programs discussed in this book and other Collaborative for Academic, Social, and Emotional Learning publications provide guidelines and discussions of classroom applications that are quite consistent with the educational approaches that SUMIT has documented in MI schools.

Whatever their differences, building on both approaches demands a commitment to examine regularly any applications that develop and to reflect on whether those applications are working. It requires assessing practices while recognizing that the formal scientific instruments available to measure effectiveness may be based on views of intelligence and education that are not necessarily compatible. It requires creating a community of educators, students, and parents, who—even if they disagree about the nature of intelligence or the kinds of activities that matter in schooling and society—can work together. Ultimately, these efforts will have to be carried out in ways that enable people to find common ground and to understand—not ignore or erase—important differences in perspective, theory, and practice.

Authors' Notes: The authors would like to thank the Geraldine R. Dodge Foundation and the Charles and Helen Schwab Foundation for their support of some of the work described in this chapter. In addition, we would like to thank Howard Gardner and the editors of this volume for helpful comments on an earlier draft and Edward Fierros for valuable assistance in the preparation of materials used in the chapter. The authors are solely responsible for the content presented here.

For more information on the theory of MI and Project SUMIT, see http://pzweb.harvard .edu/sumit/default.htm.

REFERENCES

Gardner, H. (1983). *Frames of mind.* New York: Basic Books.

Gardner, H. (1993). *Multiple intelligences.* New York: Basic Books.

Gardner, H. (1999). *Intelligence reframed.* New York: Basic Books.

Goleman, D. (1995). *Emotional intelligence.* New York: Bantam Books.

Gould, S. J. (1996). *The mismeasure of man* (Rev. ed.). New York: Norton.

Hatch, T. (1997a). Friends, diplomats and leaders: Interpersonal intelligence in play. In P. Salovey & D. Sluyter (Eds.), *Emotional intelligence and emotional literacy* (pp. 70–89). New York: Basic Books.

Hatch, T. (1997b). Getting specific about multiple intelligences. *Educational Leadership, 54*(6), 26–29.

Kornhaber, M. L., Fierros, E. G., & Veenema, S. (2004). *Multiple intelligences: Best ideas from research and practice.* Needham Heights, MA: Allyn & Bacon.

Mayer, J. D., & Salovey, P. (1997). What is emotional intelligence? In P. Salovey & D. Sluyter (Eds.), *Emotional intelligence and emotional literacy* (pp. 3–31). New York: Basic Books.

Sternberg, R. (1985). *Beyond IQ.* New York: Cambridge University Press.

PART II

How Social-Emotional Learning/Emotional Intelligence Creates Synergy in Key Contexts in Education

Service and Citizenship, School-to-Work, Health, Teacher Preparation, and Professional Development

As noted in the introductory material, schools have a great deal to address besides academics, and they cannot address academics effectively without doing so. Schools are essential in preparing students to be active and thoughtful citizens, productive and ethical workers, and healthy and caring family members. Educators are the ones who must carry out the work of schools, and their preparation is essential if schools are to reach their goals. Victoria Poedubicky has been a teacher and counselor dedicated to preparing students for the tests of life, and not a life of tests. She was asked to speak about her experiences in using social-emotional learning (SEL) for these purposes. Raymond Pasi has a gift for leading schools to adopt SEL with depth and enthusiasm. He reflects on the preparation and nurturing of teachers and how SEL is at the core of teacher success.

Victoria Poedubicky

Many can say what they would like about the importance of high-stakes testing and the federal mandate of No Child Left Behind, but what is more important than arming our children (of all ages) with the proper skills and tools so *no* child will be left behind as they go through life's most difficult tests: the tests of life? Children come to school with many things on their minds, and many of these things are not from the academic world.

Twelve years ago, as a health educator, I began teaching my students concrete skills that would enable them to regulate their emotions so they could make sound, rational decisions in stressful situations while also being more available to learn. I wanted them to be able to make the kinds of healthy decisions that would help them live long enough to be able to use the academic skills that they were learning.

There was nothing better than watching my students learn a common language, concrete skills, and a decision-making framework and then see the applications spill out into the school itself. Teachers like you would then integrate the same language, skills, and decision-making framework into all aspects of standards-based curriculum. With every teacher in the school teaching and reinforcing the same skills, no matter where students would go or who they would encounter (administrators, counselors, etc.), they would hear and use the same language, skills, and framework. It actually was pretty amusing! The students could not get away from it. However, this is what provided multiple opportunities for students to practice and become more skilled.

As a result, over the years, students have been able to put their newly learned skills to practice in the real world. I have seen students able to call up the appropriate skill to regulate their emotions. I have seen students use a decision-making framework to reflect on poor choices so that they could make a better choice the next time. I noticed my classroom issues were cut down because students were solving their own problems, leaving me more time to teach. Yes, I actually saw students decide on their own that they needed to go to the "keep calm" area and solve a problem on their own. I have had teachers from various disciplines show me their students' work, applying SEL concepts in an academic context. They were becoming more critical in their thinking. They were not just talking about goals but were developing the plans to make them happen. And I have also seen many students take responsibility for their actions, all because they were given the words and proper skills.

When you think that there is not enough time to do it all, or that the middle or high school is no place for SEL, remember that we as educators have a responsibility to guide *all* of our students to become responsible, caring people in this world. In turn, they are more likely to become productive citizens. As educators, we need to teach the whole child, allowing the social and emotional aspects of our students' learning to sit side by side with academics.

Raymond Pasi

More than professional training, although this can be a part of it, I believe strongly that schools that effectively promote SEL have teachers who are competent *and* caring. The competence is easier to measure: What did the candidate study, what type of grades did he or she get, did he or she like their academic program, what else do they do to advance their knowledge in the field? The caring piece is more difficult to get a handle on, but as important.

It is hard to train someone to care. At the same time, some educators simply need exposure to professionals who truly do care, to benefit from their example. Someone who indicates, by word or manner, that he or she is only interested in teaching the "best and brightest" would likely not be hired where I work. We make no secret about it: We want individuals on our staff who are interested in all students of all levels of ability and motivation. I believe that new teachers who join our faculty quickly learn that we do not just give lip service to this ideal. They learn almost by osmosis that attitudes and actions that are harsh, punitive, demeaning, or unfair stick out in our school. It is simply not how faculty deal with students—or if they do deal with students that way, they know it will almost always be addressed.

I say this not to brag about the faculty, but to explain a key piece in the training of new educators. It involves exposure to caring, compassionate, dedicated teachers. A strong mentor program in the school is essential. An orientation program that runs throughout the year covering topics dealing with student-teacher interactions can also be extremely instructive. Finally, working hard each day at having an institution of learning that does not ignore behaviors and attitudes that do not fit in with a caring and competent philosophy is also important training. And at the core of all this, one finds SEL.

Victoria Poedubicky is a School Counselor at Bartle School in Highland Park, NJ. She is a Social Decision Making/Social Problem Solving trainer and consultant, and coauthor of several articles and book chapters in the area of SEL.

Raymond Pasi is the principal of Yorktown High School in Arlington, VA, and a faculty member in Education and Human Development at George Washington University. He is the author of Higher Expectations: Promoting Social Emotional Learning and Academic Achievement *(Teachers College Press, 2002).*

4

The Connection Between Character, Service, and Social-Emotional Learning

Sheldon Berman and Mary Hansberry McCarthy

HOW ENVIRONMENTAL SCIENCE, SERVICE, AND SOCIAL-EMOTIONAL LEARNING (SEL) ARE LINKED: A SNAPSHOT

Once a month, fourth-grade students in Dawn Sather's classroom venture into the woods that adjoin the Forest Avenue School playground and field areas. Students are wearing rubber boots and are equipped with data sheets, pens, measuring sticks, and guidebooks. Accompanying the students are eight parent volunteers, wearing boots or waders and already engaged in discussion with their small group of students. Students chat with their parent or grandparent volunteers who serve as leaders for the project and as caring adults for the students. There is a sense of purpose as well as excitement as the students and parents traipse off to the special area that opens through a gate whose sign reads "The Johnson-Sather Wetlands," and onto a boardwalk stretching into the wetlands. The sturdy boardwalk was funded through a National Science Foundation's President's Award for Elementary Science that Mrs. Sather received and designed, and it was built by volunteers from Intel, one of Hudson School District's community partners.

As everyone enters the gate, the group stops. There is complete silence. Everyone is listening intently to the sounds of the wetlands. On Mrs. Sather's request, students volunteer specific bird or other sounds they have heard. After documenting their listening, each group heads off to its special plot. Each group has a designated plot that they attend to each time they visit the wetlands to document the changes they observe and study the ecosystem of the area. Students engaged in decision making back in September to determine which area they would adopt and monitor for the year.

The wetlands are named for veteran teacher Dawn Johnson-Sather because her students, along with the students from three other fourth-grade classes, collected sufficient data to certify the area as an environmentally protected vernal pool. They submitted the documentation and were successful in having the vernal pool certified by the National Heritage Program of the Massachusetts Division of Fisheries and Wildlife. Succeeding classes of fourth graders have assumed the role of conservationists as they systematically log the data and take care of the area. The classes have agreed on six wetland rules, including walking, stay with your group leader, stay focused, talk quietly in your group, respect nature, and keep your hands to yourself. Their data logs chart the date, air temperature, water temperature, muck temperature, water level of the vernal pool, water level near the wood bridge, water level near the drain pipe, sunrise and sunset times, and weather conditions.

The study of water in the Massachusetts Curriculum Frameworks is designated for fourth grade, and the study of water through the wetlands is the hands-on, experiential learning that is structured with student inquiry so essential to the scientific process of learning. Reflective activities include journals that students write when they return to their classrooms from the wetlands. The students use rubrics to guide their writing that also connect to the Massachusetts Frameworks composition strand. The class reads the book *She's Wearing a Dead Bird on Her Head!*, which explains the founding of the Audubon Society. Students create posters to promote Hat Day at their school. The students collect money and donate half to the Organization for the Assabet River, a strong community partner of the wetlands, and the other half to the Audubon Society. They also create a species biodiversity poster of various species native to Massachusetts and especially to their wetlands. These biodiversity posters have been given to the Department of Education, representatives of the Massachusetts House and Senate, the local board of selectmen, public works, and the superintendent of schools.

BACKGROUND OF SEL AND SERVICE LEARNING IN THE HUDSON SCHOOLS

We will hear a bit more about the wetlands project later in the chapter. For now, it stands as an exciting, inductive example of how students can be engaged in learning multiple areas at multiple levels.

Over the past decade, several movements have emerged that focus on the social-emotional and civic components of learning. These include character education,

SEL, and service learning (Berman, 1997; Edutopia Online, 2003; McCarthy & Corbin, 2003). Each provides a powerful lens through which to assess if we are helping children become active, caring, and thoughtful members of the larger human community. Each has its own organizations and advocacy networks. And yet from an educator's perspective, they are inextricably linked. Each enhances the impact of the other and enriches the learning experience for children. In fact, these movements have their most powerful impact when they are brought together in an integrated approach in the classroom and a comprehensive approach in a school or school district.

For the past 10 years, the Hudson Public School District in Hudson, Massachusetts, has consciously worked to create a comprehensive approach to SEL that draws from the best in each of these movements. Hudson is a socioeconomically and culturally diverse community 30 miles west of Boston. About one third of the population is of Portuguese descent, with immigrants coming each year from Brazil, the Azores, and other countries. With 2,800 students and 240 teachers, the school district is able to work closely with teachers and administrators to develop consistent approaches to curriculum.

Building on the core values of empathy, ethics, and service, we have layered programs that foster children's social skill development, ethical understanding, and confidence that they can make a difference in the world. We believe that providing an education that integrates challenging academics with a commitment to nurturing a caring and civil community will ensure a safer, more secure, and more productive environment for students and adults. In fact, the time we take for this makes it far easier for us to accomplish our academic goals.

The base of our program is social skill development. School is the most significant social experience for children. Each child interacts with diverse groups of children in a variety of social and task settings. The social skills necessary for effective functioning in these groups are complex and take years to develop. They include skills in listening, perspective taking, conflict resolution, impulse management, and empathic response. We have found that it is best to teach these skills directly, rather than by only trying to infuse them through the curriculum. We begin this work in our preschools with a program developed by Educators for Social Responsibility entitled Adventures in Peacemaking. Through games, music, art, dramatic play, and storytelling, young children are taught basic ways to resolve conflict. As we move into the elementary grades, we use a program developed by the Committee for Children in Seattle, Washington, entitled Second Step. The program provides 30 lessons a year of direct skill instruction in anger management and empathy development. Through pictures of social and emotional situations, children engage in reading social cues, role playing these situations, and generating positive alternatives. The theme of each lesson is then revisited throughout the week in the classroom. Second Step is taught in each elementary classroom and continues into the middle school as part of our health program.

However, direct instruction is insufficient to teach social skills. They must be modeled in the daily life of the classroom and the school. To create a classroom environment that models these skills on a daily basis, almost all our elementary- and middle-school teachers have chosen to be trained in the Responsive Classroom program developed by the Northeast Foundation for Children. It is based on two core principles: (a) the social curriculum is as important as the academic curriculum, and (b) a specific set of social skills fosters children's academic and social success. The program enables teachers to effectively use class meetings, rules and their logical consequences, classroom organization, academic choice, and family communication to create a caring classroom environment. The program blends well with the direct social skill instruction provided by the Second Step program.

Although Hudson selected these programs to create the right blend of skill instruction and modeling for our circumstances, a number of excellent programs available to schools are equally effective. Such programs as the Educators for Social Responsibility's Resolving Conflicts Creatively Program, the Stone Center at Wellesley College's Open Circle, Rutgers University's Social Decision Making/Social Problem Solving Program, or the Developmental Studies Center's Caring School Communities are all effective avenues for teaching these skills (cf. the Collaborative for Academic, Social, and Emotional Learning's *Safe and Sound* publication at www .CASEL.org for more information on these and similar evidence-based programs). Through the school's curriculum and culture, students gain experience in behaving in ways that are sensitive to and considerate of the feelings and needs of others, while at the same time learning that there are ways to deal with differences other than avoidance or fighting.

Layered on the direct teaching of social skills and the modeling in a caring classroom environment is a focus on ethical development. In the area of ethics, there is little evidence to show that moralizing to children or giving them direct instruction in moral principles has much impact. Those of us who are parents can also attest to that through direct experience. What seems to work best is considered dialogue about moral dilemmas, practice in situations of moral conflict, and role modeling by adults. It is for this reason that we have avoided the "value of the week" or "value of the month" approach to character education with its emphasis on posters and moralistic stories. Instead, we have focused on several strategies. The first is identifying ethical dilemmas in literature and examining how the characters in the story try to handle these dilemmas. The Developmental Studies Center in Oakland, California, has developed rich sets of literature for each grade level that provide examples of ethical dilemmas. However, the plots of most high-quality literature embody ethical dilemmas that are equally useful.

For many years, we purchased literature with prosocial themes, and recently we selected a reading series that, at the upper grades, deals with broader social issues. We left it up to the teachers to draw out the ethical understandings from this literature. Currently, we are focusing in our professional development program on a deeper analysis of this literature. To help young people grapple with ethical dilemmas embedded in what they read, we encourage teachers to begin by helping students identify the dilemma implicit in a problem. Usually, the ethical dilemma is not simply one of good versus evil but rather of choosing between two conflicting goods or the lesser of two evils. Next, we encourage teachers to examine the dilemma from multiple perspectives with a focus on the moral reasoning used to justify each perspective. After this, we suggest setting the dilemma in a larger social or political context so that children can see its broader implications. Finally, teachers help students analyze solutions based on moral principles. This helps children better understand the literature they are reading and gives them a deeper sense of the ethical choices people face on a daily basis.

At each grade level, this becomes more complex, culminating at the high school with a ninth-grade core combined social studies and English civics course focused on the essential question of "What is the individual's responsibility for creating a just society?" As part of this course, we use the Facing History and Ourselves curriculum, which explores the question of how genocide became state policy in Germany and Armenia. We add to this an analysis of other genocides from that of Native Americans in the United States to the civil war in Rwanda. From this material, students confront issues of intolerance, individual complicity with state policy, and the potential for human destructiveness. The course raises significant ethical questions and sensitizes students to injustice, inhumanity, suffering, and the abuse of power. It is a powerful curriculum that helps students develop a sense of moral responsibility and a commitment to make a difference. There are other courses at the high school as well that draw out ethical themes, including numerous English literature courses, social studies courses, and an elective ethics class.

A second strategy for teaching ethics is direct engagement in classroom and school decision making. One aspect of Responsive Classroom is the co-creating of classroom rules and the holding of class meetings that deal with conflicts and other classroom issues. These are excellent vehicles for discussing and living the ethics we are teaching. At the high-school level, we have begun an experiment in democratic decision making involving the entire high school. We have broken down a 1,000-student high school into teams at the 8th and 9th grades and cross-grade clusters at the 10th through 12th grades. These clusters meet weekly for one hour to discuss school and cluster issues that are then taken to a community council of students and teachers to be voted on. Although we have just begun this experiment, it has the potential of engaging young people in deliberation on the ethical dilemmas we face as a community.

A third strategy is to analyze the ethical dilemmas embedded in the service-learning projects our students engage in from kindergarten to graduation. By surfacing the ethical issues implicit in many community problems, students can begin to understand the social and political implications of these ethical dilemmas, look for root causes of the problems, and explore the difference between short-term assistance and long-term change.

Service learning is an excellent instructional method for building character, developing effective social skills, understanding the perspectives of others, and developing students' self-confidence that they can make a difference in the world. In fact, service learning enables students to apply their social-emotional skills in the real world. At the same time, it is also an excellent vehicle for bringing the academic curriculum to life and improving overall student performance. In Hudson, it is a comprehensive pre-K to 12 service-learning program that brings all the elements together.

We have attempted to integrate service learning into all classes and grade levels in a way that enhances the effectiveness of our instructional program. As seen in the following vignettes, when service learning is a natural extension of the curriculum and is built on curricula teaching social-emotional skills and ethical sensitivities, students understand the significance of the content they are learning. At the same time, experiencing service learning each year helps young people develop an ethic of care and service and experience being a contributing member of their community. From these experiences, they learn to empathize with others, respond in positive ways to individual and community needs, and learn social decision-making models that enable them to function effectively in a broad range of group and social situations.

VIGNETTES OF SERVICE LEARNING AND SEL IN ACTION

Kindergarten Brings Smiles to Homeless Children

Each year as spring begins, it is time for teaching the letter Q and launching the Quilt Project at the Hubert Kindergarten Center. One by one, the kindergartners are entrusted with taking home a large bag containing a colorful cloth quilt that has been created by each student in the class and a student-written book that accompanies the quilt. The students bring the quilt home for an overnight visit so that each family can admire the quilt and write a special message in the quilt book. These quilts are destined for babies who are born to mothers in homeless shelters. On the quilt squares and in their quilt book, the kindergartners include messages of love and happiness for the babies who will receive their quilts. This special project, the fourth service-learning project these kindergartners will experience this year, provides the 5- and 6-year-old students with the opportunity to think about people who are in need and to realize that even young children can provide help and make a difference. It also provides them with a rich academic instruction about the letter Q, the geometric shapes sewn onto the quilt, the writing of a book for a specific audience, and the history and cultural meaning of quilts.

This service-learning project builds on the skills they have learned using Second Step and participating in Responsive Classroom throughout the year. The quilt project becomes a living example of the skills in empathy taught through Second Step as the students try to understand the situation of someone less fortunate then themselves and to write something that appropriately helps the mother and child. Their Responsive Classroom experiences have helped them practice the listening and decision making that are necessary for the project to succeed. Students learn to listen to each other through Morning Meetings as well as to listen in a school assembly through the thematic presentations that are led by Principal Linda Corbin and their teachers. Each service-learning project is introduced to the whole school community through an assembly in which students are asked to consider situations and needs related to the focus of service (in this example, babies born into a homeless situation) and to generate helpful ideas. For the quilt project, teachers in each classroom read *The Quiltmaker's Gift*, a story about a woman who makes quilts for homeless people in a nearby village. In the book, a greedy king has a rule that everyone in the village must give him gifts at the two birthdays he declares for himself each year. The quiltmaker has a rule too. She will only make quilts for needy or homeless people. The king wants a quilt, but she refuses to make a quilt for him until he has experienced the joy of giving. The students are asked to consider what rules they would write for the town after reading the story. One student offered, "If I were the queen, I would celebrate my birthday once a year and give away some of my things to the poor and to people with some money, but not lots." The classes also read *Home Is Where We Live*, about a child who lives in a shelter. Children hear the historical and cultural background of quilts, and they also talk about the physical and emotional comfort that quilts provide.

Practicing the group decision-making skills they are learning in their Morning Meetings and class meetings, the children make many decisions regarding the quilts, from voting on the material that will be used to the design of the quilt. Geometric patterns are used to create the quilt squares, and the students also contribute their own creative drawings and messages to personalize the quilts. Parent volunteers stitch the quilts together and then bring the quilts to school for each student to spend some quality time with the parent in tying off each student's square.

At the conclusion of the quilt service-learning project, one of the expectant mothers or the director of the homeless shelter comes to Hubert Kindergarten Center to receive the quilts. Each quilt is unique, and each book that accompanies the quilt is full of hope and love for the new baby. The kindergartners' families become intimately involved in the project, which enables parents to become strong partners with the school and to contribute to a project that captures everyone's heart. This becomes a rich academic and SEL experience that is shared by children and their parents.

Note: The Quilt-Makers Project at the Cora Hubert Kindergarten Center is featured in the National Youth Leadership Council (2004) publication, Growing to Greatness, *which chronicles progress in service learning in 18 states.*

Second Graders Learn Community Through Service

Reflecting on Service

Sitting cross-legged on their class rug, the second graders in Laura Mullen's class begin the daily ritual of Morning Meeting with a special greeting. "Konnichiwa," they wish each other, as well as the visiting educators from Japan who join them that day. The classroom community is visibly etched in the circle of students whose attention is tuned to their teacher. Mrs. Mullen asks the students to describe their service and service-learning activities for the year. Eager hands reach for the opportunity to begin the recounting. Taking turns, students render reflective accounts. Their teacher reminds them to include why as well as what they did. Students shared their concerns for others and the ways that together they had decided to help. There was the Freedom Car Wash when they washed the cars and trucks of the fire and police departments to say thank you and to make the anniversary of September 11, 2001, a positive day. October brought Read to Feed, in which the students collected enough money from the books that they read to buy livestock for people in an underprivileged area. The students loved deciding on chickens, pigs, a cow, and seeds for planting. In November, the children read the book *A Coat of Many Colors* and participated in a coat drive that was organized by the school nurse. January brought the news that the local food pantry was very low on toiletries, so the students decided to join with the other second-grade class in a drive after they read *Uncle Willie and the Soup Kitchen.* Involving the whole second grade and second-grade teacher, Patricia Lima, the Barkery Project involved studying about different kinds of helping dogs and the high costs of pet medical bills. The students and teachers made edible "dog biscuits" and sold them to students and teachers at lunch. In each project, students identified the community they were serving. Their stories provided a testimonial to the community of learners and servers that they have become.

Senior Literacy Coaches

Throughout the year, a husband and wife, both senior citizens, trained as senior literacy tutors through a Learn and Serve America grant, worked with individual students, small groups, or the whole class at least once a week. These surrogate class grandparents extended the class's circle of community and service. One senior literacy tutor had retired from Verizon, and he organized service to the school community. The company sent volunteers to work with the students, teacher, and parents in painting a map of the United States on the Mulready School playground in conjunction with Youth Service Day.

Participatory Rule Setting and Creating "Peace Places"

Through Responsive Classroom, students began each day with Morning Meeting, and they also developed their own community rules and consequences. Confirming their agreement on these rules, each student signed a ball, making a commitment to use the Peace Place, where they could go to resolve conflicts. As Mrs. Mullen explained, by allowing students the autonomy and responsibility to decide when they need to visit the Peace Place, problems and disputes do not have the time to brew into more serious conflicts. The sessions that the school psychologist led in Second Step also contributed to students' practice with empathy development and the role playing that developed situations of peaceful conflict resolution.

Afterschool, Cross-Grade Tolerance Building

In addition to the academic learning connected to serving real community needs and the social skill building during the school day, there is also an afterschool program that Laura Mullen instituted in November 2001. Modeling the program on "Don't Laugh at Me," the Peter Yarrow program that was written by Educators for Social Responsibility, the program is named "U Matter at Mulready." Students in Grades 1 through 5 meet once a week with the purpose of learning about tolerance and keeping the Mulready School as a ridicule-free place. The first year of U Matter brought 23 students, in the second year there were 75, and in the current year, there are 60 students enrolled. Fortunately, Laura Mullen has the assistance of her second-grade colleague Patricia Lima and a teacher of special-needs children, Shel Tscherne. The group has strong parent support, as well as parent volunteers, and has engaged in many activities from making comfort quilts for the fire department to a service auction that raised $800 to buy toys for hospital pediatric units. Through U Matter, the entire school community of the Mulready School is served and strengthened.

Note: The second-grade classes of Laura Mullen and Patricia Lima are featured in the video Hudson Public Schools: Educating for Social Responsibility *by Antioch University's Heritage Institute (Michael Seymour, 800/445-1305).*

Curricular Connections in the Wetlands Project

Dawn Sather's wetlands service-learning project, mentioned at the beginning of the chapter, has extended to all of the fourth-grade classes, and the curricular connections continue to develop. In science, students study ecosystems, environmental issues, changes over time, the life cycles of species in the wetlands, and the process of predicting, reasoning, and observing. There are numerous language arts and writing experiences integrated into the wetlands study. There is also a great deal of mathematics integrated into the project through measurement activities and the collecting, graphing, and analyzing of data.

The wetlands project is a year-long service-learning project that is deeply integrated with academics and the social skills the students have developed through Second Step and Responsive Classroom. However, it is not the only service-learning activity these students experience. The four fourth-grade classrooms also participate in other service-learning projects including Trick or Treat for UNICEF; a Math-A-Thon for St. Jude Children's Research Hospital; Towers of Kindness, which promotes awareness of community and respectful behavior; Letters to Service People; and Helping Hands to Little Ones during their lunch recess, where on a rotating basis, fourth graders read to Head Start preschool students every day and engage them in simple science experiments and in physical education activities. All of these service experiences provide fourth graders with multiple opportunities to develop the interpersonal and intergenerational skills they are learning in their SEL programs.

Note: "Dawn Sathers' Wetlands as Classroom and Service Opportunities" is featured in Kids Taking Action: Community Service Learning Projects, K-8, *by Pamela Roberts (2002).*

Drama as an Exhibition of SEL

Sixth-grade drama students in Gail DiPace's classes at the John F. Kennedy Middle School (JFK) are engaged for the 3rd year as actors in a living museum program called Stare and Share. At the middle school, Responsive Classroom's Morning Meeting evolves into the Circle of Power and Respect (CPR). Students use CPR time to think about situations that occur in their lives that have to do with prejudice, fear, and apprehension. In drama class, which all sixth graders take, groups of students discuss and then create living tableaus that use pantomime to generate alternative solutions to prejudice, stereotyping, and conflict and to build a positive classroom environment in which students can examine their own feelings, ideas, ethical principles, and misconceptions about those who seem different. Students perform the pieces for fellow students, for parents and the community, and for students at the elementary schools. After each scene, the docent asks the actors to rewind the scene, and the audience is invited to interpret the situation and to offer solutions.

One of the most successful tableaus involved a scene with a bully played by a student who admitted he actually had been a bully at times. The open discussions provided a forum for breaking down some of the barriers among students, who gained the confidence to address bullying. The positive reinforcement the boy received from his participation, in fact, mitigated his bullying tendencies. Parents had opportunities to ask questions of the actors (their children), who come out of their Stare and Share roles and answer candidly at the end of the performance.

The Stare and Share project began through a Massachusetts Department of Education and Learn and Serve America Community, Higher Education, School Partnership that brought together Fitchburg State College, Hudson Public Schools, and groups concerned with disabilities. It has evolved as a well-integrated curricular program that ties together writing, speaking, and performing with discussions in students' CPR. The service-learning component not only enables them to demonstrate their SEL in a public setting and feel that they are contributing to others, but it brings them into contact with important mentors such as university theater students and faculty and adults with disabilities who help foster further social-emotional growth.

Middle Schoolers Model Conflict Resolution Through Peer Mediation

Four JFK students sit facing each other in the cafeteria, and the conversation is serious but not strained. Each student speaks in turn, and the students listen carefully to each other. Two of the students paraphrase what has been said and wait for confirmation that they got it right. They keep trying until the other two students say that the rephrasing is correct. Visitors are allowed to stand by and listen because the two peer mediators and the two JFK students who are involved in a conflict situation are all actors. But the situations that they are enacting came from real-life situations that the peer mediators had successfully mediated.

Middle school is an age of developing hormones, sudden mood swings, and huge developmental differences among students who are the same age. Hurt feelings and misunderstandings are an inevitable occurrence that can undercut learning in any classroom. The opportunity to employ trained peer mediators has proved a successful approach that is used at the middle school as well as at Hudson's elementary schools.

Students and teachers were trained for peer mediation by Educators for Social Responsibility in Cambridge, Massachusetts, over the past 3 years. Now, as students move up through the grades, they carry their mediating skills with them. Even if they do not have the opportunity to serve as active peer mediators, the knowledge and skills of mediating are positive qualities that contribute to a sense of community and harmony in classrooms and schools. Their efforts at peer mediation are both an exhibition of the conflict resolution and SEL skills they have gained over their school years as well as a service project that helps create a more positive and responsive school environment.

Civic Ethics as a Foundation for High School

In the spring of each year, the community of Hudson feels the impact of 200 ninth-grade students who contribute in numerous ways to serving their community as part of their civics class at Hudson High School. The creator of this course, social studies teacher Todd Wallingford, collaborates with other ninth-grade social studies and English teachers in a course that integrates civics and English and centers on the essential question, "What are the rights and responsibilities of a citizen in a just society?" This core ninth-grade course combines freshman social studies and English in a year-long, 90-minute-a-day course team taught by a social studies and English teacher.

In the fall semester, the students study the development and structure of our democratic form of government while reading literature that raises important governance issues, such as *Lord of the Flies* and *Animal Farm.* During the second semester, the students read such novels as *Night* and *Hiroshima* and use the curriculum Facing History and Ourselves, developed by the Facing History and Ourselves Foundation, as they explore the conditions that gave rise to the Holocaust and the Armenian genocide. The curriculum confronts young people with the human potential for passivity, complicity, and destructiveness by asking how genocide can become state policy. It raises significant ethical questions and sensitizes them to injustice, inhumanity, suffering, and the abuse of power. At the same time, it is academically challenging and helps complicate students' thinking so that they do not accept simple answers to complex problems. In the process of studying both a historic period and the personal and social forces that produce genocide, students confront their own potential for passivity and complicity, their own prejudices and intolerance, and their own moral commitments. The curriculum develops students' perspective-taking and social-reasoning abilities, and students emerge with a greater sense of moral responsibility and a greater commitment to participate in making a difference.

Building on their study of the genocide, students are asked to design a service-learning project and exercise their role as a responsible citizen by making a difference in their school, town, or world. As part of this service-learning experience, students grapple with the questions of whether their project would have been allowed in Nazi Germany and how their service-learning project connects to deeper societal issues today in the United States and in our global society.

Five of the Hudson High School students who participated in the ninth-grade civics course enrolled in the Virtual High School (VHS) course in service learning designed and taught by Mary McCarthy, Hudson's director of service learning and character education. VHS is a collaborative of high schools from around the country that have banded together to offer more than 150 virtual courses to their students. Students from across the United States and from as far away as Venezuela took the VHS service-learning course either in the fall 2003 or spring 2004 semesters. These students are self-selected young people who are interested in contributing through service and service learning. In comparison with most of the other 36 students, the Hudson students demonstrated a stronger knowledge base and more readiness for designing their own service-learning projects than the students from other areas.

The civics course is foundational for the high school's instructional program and for the experiment in democratization that is under way at Hudson High School. It enables students to think through serious ethical dilemmas and the meaning of justice and individual responsibility and then put them into practice in the world around them. It sets the base for students to become engaged, thoughtful citizens capable of making decisions for the common good.

Note: The Hudson High School civics course is delineated in "Responsibilities of Citizenship" in Community Lessons: Promising Curriculum Practices *(Bartsch, 2001).*

CONCLUSION

The examples presented are intended to show teachers how a combination of service learning and SEL can create a layered, consistent instructional approach that is marked by continuity, depth, and meaningfulness. Achieving success across grade levels and buildings requires years of effort and continuous professional development. Effective teaching of social-emotional skills is best built on a structured, evidence-based, multiyear curriculum. Although Second Step provides a very structured curriculum and Responsive Classroom has a high-quality professional development program to support teachers, both require that teachers develop skills in facilitating social skill development in the classroom. Using dilemmas in literature and daily classroom life to teach ethical understanding requires an ability to clearly identify the dilemma and help students consider multiple perspectives and principled reasoning. Even the work in service learning requires that teachers think carefully about whether service extends the curriculum and helps meet a real need. Helping young people reflect on their service experience, look beyond short-term assistance to long-term change, and develop both critical understanding and a vision of a better world are important, yet challenging, elements of using service learning as an instructional method.

When teachers effectively combine SEL, character education, and service learning, young people bring their academic learning to life and develop the personal and interpersonal skills to help them function effectively as a contributing member of the community.

Authors' Note: Ongoing information about all aspects of character education, social-emotional learning, service learning, and related programs in the Hudson Public Schools can be found at www.hudson.k12.ma.us.

REFERENCES

Bartsch, J. (2001). Responsibilities of citizenship. In *Community lessons: Promising curriculum practices.* Available from http://www.doe.mass.edu/csl

Berman, S. (1997). *Children's social consciousness and the development of social responsibility.* Albany: State University of New York Press.

Edutopia Online. (2003, May). *A+ for empathy.* Available from http://www.glef.org

McCarthy, M., & Corbin, L. (2003, January). The power of service-learning. *Principal, 82*(3), 52–55.

National Youth Leadership Council. (2004). *Growing to greatness.* Available from http://www.esc.org

Roberts, P. (2002). *Kids taking action: Community service learning projects, k-8.* Greenfield, MA: Northeast Foundation for Children.

5

From School to Work

Social-Emotional Learning as the Vital Connection

Cary Cherniss and Daniel Goleman

During the last decade there has been increasing concern about the weak link between schooling and the realities of the workplace. Employers report that too many young people lack the social-emotional competencies that are most critical for success on the job.

For instance, the U.S. Department of Labor sponsored a national survey of what employers are looking for in entry-level workers (Carnevale, Gainer, & Meltzer, 1988; Secretary's Commission on Achieving Necessary Skills, 1991). The skills most often cited included motivation to work toward goals, adaptability in the face of setbacks and obstacles, personal self-management, confidence, group and interpersonal effectiveness, cooperation, and skills in negotiating disagreements. Employers also value social-emotional competence in higher level employees. Another study asked corporations what they are looking for in people with master's degrees in business administration who they hire. The three most desired capabilities were communications skills, interpersonal skills, and initiative (Dowd & Liedtka, 1994).

Research on the competencies that actually lead to superior performance in jobs tends to support the conventional wisdom among employers. Goleman (1998) reviewed competency studies that have been conducted in more than 200 companies, focusing on dozens of different types of jobs. He found that competencies such as initiative, self-confidence, and collaboration matter more than twice as much as IQ plus technical skill in what sets apart outstanding performers from average ones. And the importance of these competencies increases as one moves up the workplace hierarchy: For top leaders, they account for more than 85% of the difference. IQ, often thought to be one of the most powerful predictors of success, accounts for only about 4% to 25% of the factors that determine success at work (Hunter & Schmidt, 1984; Sternberg, 1996).

We are not suggesting that IQ and technical skills are unimportant or that schools should stop teaching basic academic subjects. Cognitive abilities and general knowledge are essential. However, in the world of work, these tend to be "threshold" competencies. For instance, to secure a job as a computer programmer, one needs a fairly high level of cognitive ability and technical skill. However, once one has landed the job, these capabilities no longer make much difference because everyone has them. Social and emotional abilities make the difference between superior computer programmers and average performers, or those who are likely to lose their jobs.

Unfortunately, many computer programmers, as well as other kinds of workers, seem to lack these critical social-emotional competencies when they emerge from school. One survey found that more than half the people who go to work in this country lack the motivation to keep learning and improving in their job (Harris Educational Research Council, 1991). Furthermore, 4 in 10 are not able to work cooperatively with fellow employees, and only 19% of those applying for entry-level jobs have enough self-discipline in their work habits.

Even more alarming is the fact that the situation seems to be getting worse rather than better. Achenbach and Howell (1993) initially asked parents and teachers to evaluate the social-emotional competence of a random sample of children, aged 7 to 16, in the mid-1970s. Then they repeated the study in the late 1980s. On almost every measure, the children in the more recent study did worse. They were more lonely and depressed, more angry and unruly, more nervous and prone to worry, as well as more impulsive and aggressive. And these are the individuals who now are entering the workforce.

It is not surprising, therefore, that companies increasingly are spending money to help their employees overcome deficiencies in the "soft skills." A recent survey conducted by the American Society for Training and Development (1997) found that four of five companies are trying to promote emotional intelligence in their employees. Although American employers clearly are willing to help their workers become more socially and emotionally competent, they would prefer to have the schools do it before those employees grow up and go to work. And for good reason: It is easier to learn these skills when one is young (Goleman, 1998).

But what are the competencies that are most important for success and fulfillment in the world of work? Research suggests that there are 25 social and emotional competencies that are most often linked to success (Goleman, 1998). These are presented in Table 5.1. Some of these competencies, such as self-awareness, self-control, and achievement drive, relate to how one handles oneself. Others, such as empathy, influence, and cooperation, concern one's ability to manage relationships with others. Also, there is some evidence that the competencies build on one another. The first set, which relates to self-awareness, is the foundation for the others. For instance, one's ability to control disruptive emotions (self-regulation) is enhanced by the ability to

Table 5.1 The Social and Emotional Competencies Linked With Success at Work

Self-Awareness

Emotional awareness: Recognizing one's emotions and their effects.

Accurate self-assessment: Knowing one's strengths and limits.

Self-confidence: Sureness about one's self-worth and capabilities.

Self-Regulation

Self-control: Managing disruptive emotions and impulses.

Trustworthiness: Maintaining standards of honesty and integrity.

Conscientiousness: Taking responsibility for personal performance.

Adaptability: Flexibility in handling change.

Innovation: Being comfortable with and open to novel ideas and new information.

Motivation

Achievement drive: Striving to improve or meet a standard of excellence.

Commitment: Aligning with the goals of the group or organization.

Initiative: Being ready to act on opportunities.

Optimism: Persisting in pursuing goals despite obstacles and setbacks.

Social Awareness

Empathy: Sensing others' feelings and perspectives and taking an active interest in their concerns.

Service orientation: Anticipating, recognizing, and meeting customers' needs.

Developing others: Sensing what others need to develop and bolstering their abilities.

Leveraging diversity: Cultivating opportunities through diverse people.

Political awareness: Reading a group's emotional currents and power relationships.

Social Skills

Influence: Wielding effective tactics for persuasion.

Communication: Sending clear and convincing messages.

Leadership: Inspiring and guiding groups and people.

Change catalyst: Initiating or managing change.

Conflict management: Negotiating and resolving disagreements.

Building bonds: Nurturing instrumental relationships.

Collaboration and cooperation: Working with others toward shared goals.

Team capabilities: Creating group synergy in pursuing collective goals.

sense when one is becoming upset (self-awareness). Similarly, one's ability to sense others' feelings (empathy) is enhanced by the ability to sense one's own feelings and by the ability to control one's disruptive emotions.

Not all of these competencies are equally important for all jobs. Developing others is particularly important for supervisory and managerial work, whereas optimism is particularly important for sales positions. However, research suggests that to be successful in most jobs, one needs at least one or two competencies in each of the five categories found in Table 5.1 (Goleman, Boyatzis, & McKee, 2002). Thus, this list of competencies provides a useful guide for teachers and principals who want to be sure that their students are prepared for the world of work. (More information about these competencies is available on the Web at www.EIConsortium.org.)

These emotional and social skills always have been important for success in work and in life, as our parents and grandparents well knew. They realized that it is character, not just how smart we are, that makes the difference between a fulfilled life and a wasted one. But in the new world of work, these abilities are more important than ever. With constant change and downsizing, people in every field need these competencies to survive. They must be able to work in a team, but they also must be highly self-reliant. They must be resilient and adaptable, but they also must be able to take initiative. They must be realistic about their own abilities, but they also must be optimistic. Educators can prepare children for this new world of work by helping them to learn those social-emotional competencies that are most critical for success. We owe our children nothing less.

Authors' Note: Ongoing information about all aspects of the Consortium for Research on Emotional Intelligence in Organizations can be found at www.EIConsortium.org.

REFERENCES

Achenbach, T., & Howell, C. (1993). Are America's children's problems getting worse? A 13-year comparison. *Journal of the American Academy of Child and Adolescent Psychiatry, 32*, 1145–1154.

American Society for Training and Development. (1997, October). *Benchmarking forum: Member-to-member survey results.* Unpublished study. Alexandria, VA: Author.

Carnevale, A. P., Gainer, L. J., & Meltzer, A. S. (1988). Workplace basics: The skills employers want. *Training & Development Journal, 42*, 22–26.

Dowd, K. O., & Liedtka, J. (1994, Winter). What corporations seek in MBA hires: A survey. *Selections, 10*(2), 34–39.

Goleman, D. (1998). *Working with emotional intelligence.* New York: Bantam.

Goleman, D., Boyatzis, R. E., & McKee, A. (2002). *Primal leadership: Realizing the power of emotional intelligence.* Boston: Harvard Business School Press.

Harris Educational Research Council. (1991). *An assessment of American education.* Unpublished study. New York: Harris.

Hunter, J. B., & Schmidt, F. L. (1984). Validity and utility of alternative predictors of job performance. *Psychological Bulletin, 96*, 72–98.

Secretary's Commission on Achieving Necessary Skills. (1991). *What work requires of schools.* Washington, DC: U.S. Department of Labor.

Sternberg, R. (1996). *Successful intelligence.* New York: Simon & Schuster.

6

Physical Health, Social-Emotional Skills, and Academic Success Are Inseparable

Susan F. Wooley and Marcia A. Rubin

As knowledge has increased exponentially in the 21st century, our approaches to educating children have narrowed and specialized. The results of this trend have raised alarms about the condition of American education and the academic performance of American students. Although laudable in its insistence on eliminating disparities while raising the achievement bar, the focus on accountability for math and reading scores under the No Child Left Behind Act has led many schools to narrow their focus even more and has dramatically increased stress on both students and staff. By compromising the health of our students, this narrowing actually threatens genuine and lasting academic progress.

These reform initiatives are unlikely to succeed unless schools address all interacting dimensions of students' lives: the physical, emotional, intellectual, social, and spiritual. Recent research on the brain (Wolfe & Brandt, 1998) reveals the intimate connections between the brain's physical structures, emotions, and learning. Research in medicine confirms the importance of emotions and spirituality on healing and longevity (Seeman, Dubin, & Seeman, 2003). Schools have traditionally emphasized the intellectual dimension and given far less attention to the others. For all students to succeed, we, as a society, can no longer afford such narrow approaches.

A successful, competent person achieves high-level functioning in all dimensions. An optimally healthy student is more likely than a less healthy student to succeed in school. In the physical domain, an optimally healthy student will have body systems that function efficiently with capacity to spare. School health programs promote this dimension by teaching students information and skills for selecting a diet that provides good nutrition, engaging them in activities that foster physical fitness, and encouraging them to get sufficient sleep. In the emotional domain, optimally healthy students can express a wide range of feelings in culturally acceptable and effective ways and thus can function well in the classroom and in life. Offering opportunities in dance, music, poetry, and painting is one way schools can help youth develop this dimension. Intellectually healthy individuals exhibit a reflective curiosity about life and learning; they are open to new ideas and new experiences and exercise critical thinking. Teaching strategies that employ inquiry-based, interactive methods can contribute to this dimension. In the social domain, optimally healthy students interact effectively with a variety of people, not just those like themselves. Teaching multicultural perspectives, using cooperative learning techniques, and allowing students to practice effective communication skills in multiple settings are some of the techniques used to develop this area. Spiritually healthy people can articulate the principles and values by which they live and that govern their behavior. School norms and policies that encourage students with axioms such as "don't hit," "share," "pick up after yourself," "tell the truth," "keep your promises," and "respect others" reinforce and nurture the spiritual dimension.

Educational approaches that fail to recognize the interactive nature of these dimensions and limit programming to the intellectual dimension cannot meet the educational needs of the whole child. Schools need a continuum of programming that integrates these dimensions. A more universal approach begins with teaching basic learning skills while promoting social and emotional health and effective peer relations. Programs for adolescents include targeted programs that aim at preventing particular high-risk behaviors such as drug and alcohol abuse, provide early intervention for students exhibiting one or more at-risk behaviors, and offer treatment services for students in crises such as attempted suicide.

To provide the full scope of this continuum, some schools have established school health advisory councils as mechanisms for coordinating classroom instruction, mental health services, nutrition services, medical services, administrative policies, faculty and staff development, and family and community involvement. Coordinated programs encourage positive practices across all five dimensions. For example, in the elementary grades, such councils design ways to introduce students to the tools of learning along with practices to ensure safety, positive oral health habits, personal hygiene, and healthy food choices. This learning is further reinforced by teaching students skills for interacting effectively with others, the importance of telling the truth, and using "I" messages to communicate feelings. In addition to education in the classroom, coordinated health programming includes nutritious meals served in the school cafeteria, opportunities for students to be physically active, a physically

Table 6.1   National Health Education Standards

The National Health Education Standards state that students will

- comprehend concepts related to health promotion and disease prevention;
- demonstrate the ability to access valid health information and health-promoting products and services;
- demonstrate the ability to practice health-enhancing behaviors and reduce health risks;
- analyze the influence of culture, media, technology, and other factors on health;
- demonstrate the ability to use interpersonal communication skills to enhance health;
- demonstrate the ability to advocate for personal, family, and community health.

and emotionally safe environment that sets high expectations for students, and strong bonds among the school, students, their families, and communities.

SOCIAL-EMOTIONAL LEARNING AND HEALTH EDUCATION: PARTNERS IN HEALTH PROMOTION

Social-emotional learning (SEL) programs and health education are complementary approaches. SEL enhances students' ability to express their feelings effectively and appropriately, to solve everyday problems and resolve conflicts, and to interact successfully with many kinds of people. These elements are an integral part of the national standards for health education (Fetro, 1998; Joint Committee on National Health Education Standards, 1995; see Table 6.1). Although quality health education includes social skills training, there is rarely enough class time to develop mastery of these skills. The more students practice social-emotional skills in different situations, the more likely they are to transfer that learning to new situations and incorporate those skills into lifelong habits. Together, health education and SEL can provide students with the knowledge and skills they need to be emotionally and socially competent in a variety of situations that might promote or endanger their health, safety, or well-being and contribute to their academic success.

TARGETED PREVENTION EDUCATION PROGRAMS

Targeted prevention education focuses on one or more specific practices that compromise students' health and well-being, as well as academic achievement. For example, an estimated one in four children in the United States aged 10 to 17, or 7 million youth, are at extreme risk for using drugs, engaging in early unprotected intercourse, participating in violent or delinquent acts, experiencing depression or post-traumatic stress, or dropping out of school. An additional 25% are moderately at risk for these outcomes. The remainder, who are at relatively low risk, nonetheless require ongoing support to remain at low risk (Dryfoos, 1990).

Self-contained health classrooms often focus considerable time on primary prevention or targeted instruction in priority areas identified by the Centers for Disease Control and Prevention (n.d.):

- injury and violence,
- nutrition,
- physical activity,
- tobacco use,
- alcohol and other drug use, and
- sexual behaviors.

Many of these problems are often symptoms of dysfunctional social practices and emotional distress. SEL programs with a targeted focus reinforce and complement health educators' efforts to teach students how to avoid high-risk situations or minimize harm.

EARLY INTERVENTION AND TREATMENT PROGRAMS

When educational programming fails to address the multidimensional nature of students' needs, the result often is students who do not succeed in schools and who have multiple, complex problems requiring intervention and treatment services. Once identified and referred by the classroom teacher, these students' needs are usually addressed by other professionals in the school and community such as a speech pathologist, reading specialist, school nurse, counselor, social worker, or psychologist. An example of this type of program is the Primary Mental Health Project (PMHP; Cowen, Hightower, Pedro-Carroll, Work, & Wyman, 1996), which identifies children in kindergarten through Grade 3 who are experiencing minor school adjustment difficulties. Children are taught various strategies for coping with stress in weekly, 30-minute sessions for several months. Older children through Grade 5 who need assistance with aggression, shyness, inattentiveness, or restlessness also receive assistance. Evaluations have consistently demonstrated that PMHP effectively strengthens young children's behavioral adjustment skills and academic achievement across diverse populations. Many other similar, evidence-based programs have been identified that can also be closely coordinated with health education (Collaborative for Academic, Social, and Emotional Learning, 2003). By coordinating early intervention and treatment services with educational programs in a systematic fashion, schools can help all students succeed.

PREPARING FOR COMPREHENSIVENESS

The complex needs of children and youth cannot be met by any single class or one individual. Teachers trained in SEL, and those who provide health education, as well as school counselors and mental health providers, help students develop emotionally and socially. Art and music instruction provide additional opportunities for students to express their feelings. Science teachers reinforce and apply inquiry skills, social studies teachers expose students to other cultures and peoples, and principals establish the environmental climate that sets the spiritual tone of the building. Health teachers, nurses, and physical educators teach students how to maintain the body's health. Promoting healthy functioning in all dimensions of a student's life is the responsibility of everyone working for students' success in schools. School programs that recognize and foster the social-emotional dimensions as well the physical, intellectual, and spiritual dimensions of individuals' lives provide structured, interactive opportunities for developing self-management skills, effective communication strategies, cooperation, social decision making, and problem-solving skills. These characteristics, in turn, contribute to well-functioning schools that foster learning, safety, and positive interpersonal relations and that graduate healthy, competent young people well prepared for the 21st century.

REFERENCES

Centers for Disease Control and Prevention. (n.d.). *Coordinated School Health Program.* Available from www.cdc.gov/HealthyYouth/CSHP

Collaborative for Academic, Social, and Emotional Learning. (2003). *Safe and sound: An educational leader's guide to evidence-based social and emotional learning programs.* Chicago: Author.

Cowen, E. L., Hightower, A. D., Pedro-Carroll, J. L., Work, W. C., & Wyman, P. (1996). *School-based prevention for children at risk: The primary mental health project.* Washington, DC: American Psychological Association.

Dryfoos, J. G. (1990). *Adolescents at risk: Prevalence and prevention.* New York: Oxford University Press.

Fetro, J. V. (1998). Implementing coordinated school health programs in local schools. In E. Marx & S. F. Wooley (Eds.), *Health is academic: A guide to coordinated school health programs* (pp. 15–42). New York: Teachers College Press.

Joint Committee on National Health Education Standards. (1995). *Achieving health literacy: An investment in the future.* Atlanta, GA: American Cancer Society.

Seeman, T. E., Dubin, L. F., & Seeman, M. (2003). Religiosity/spirituality and health: A critical review of the evidence for biological pathways. *American Psychologist, 58*(1), 53–63.

Wolfe, P., & Brandt, R. (1998). What do we know from brain research? *Educational Leadership, 56*(3), 8–13.

7

Addressing Social-Emotional Education in Teacher Education

Janet Patti

I n today's marketplace, whether we are buying a household item, providing customer service, or leading a Fortune 500 company, our social skills, the skills that we use to interact with others, make a difference. Plain and simple: People respond better to those who are optimistic, empathic, trustworthy, and inspirational. Moody, highly explosive, uncaring, or pessimistic people are often avoided or feared. The way we express our emotions and respond to others' emotions matters. In the classroom, the social-emotional competencies of adults and young people have great impact on the teaching and learning processes.

The good news is that advances in our knowledge about how the brain learns and the role that emotions play in that process have made it possible to include the teaching of emotional and social competencies in schools. As a result, programs in character education, service learning, social-emotional learning (SEL), and the development of emotional intelligence (EI) have become desired ways to create safe and caring learning communities in America's schools. The bad news is that few teachers and school leaders have the social and emotional skill preparation to do this right.

In this chapter, we address the knowledge, skills, and belief systems that teachers need to ensure their students have the full range of intelligence—both intellectual and emotional. We look inside classrooms and provide snapshots of SEL teaching and learning. We talk about the role of teacher as model and teacher as learner. We present some instructional strategies that make this kind of teaching and learning possible. Finally, we address the role that preservice education needs to play in the preparation and development of today's educators.

REFLECTION

If you are a teacher who is reading this chapter, take a moment of reflection to ask yourself the following questions:

- Where in my day do I model reflective teaching and learning?
- Do I provide opportunities for students to be in touch with their own feelings?
- Do I give them time to reflect on their feelings about their learning, the lessons I am teaching, and the strategies I use?
- Beyond my focus on academic learning, do I model good interpersonal behavior?
- Do I see my students engaging in caring behavior with their peers?
- Finally, who makes the decisions in the classroom and school? Are young people involved in this process? Do they know how to make wise, responsible decisions? Do I help them set goals about their learning?

If you are a school leader, a parent, or other school support staff, take an hour or so to visit a classroom. Use the following questions as a guide to determine if good SEL teaching habits are visible:

- What do I see that informs me that SEL is alive in this classroom?
- What kind of feeling tone exists in this classroom?
- What kind of teaching strategies does the teacher use as the lesson unfolds? Are the students engaged? Is the content meaningful? Does there appear to be a sense of ownership on the part of the learners?

The answers to these questions are telling. They reveal what the adults in the building know about SEL, the extent to which they value it, the skills they have to impart it, and the level to which young people apply SEL in their learning as they travel through their school day.

The following two scenarios provide brief examples of what you might see as you visit classrooms:

In School Less, third-grader Ronald busily draws a picture during his social studies class. Teacher Janice strolls over to his desk, snatches the picture, and tells Ronald that he should pay attention. Ronald says nothing but soon retaliates by creating a series of disturbances. He sharpens his pencil three times, drops his books, talks to his neighbor, and reads a comic book. Exasperated, Teacher Janice sends Ronald down to the office with a referral. She attaches the picture that Ronald was drawing along with the list of misbehaviors. She asks that Ronald not return to her class and that his mother be called. The class laughs as Ronald is admonished, which further angers Teacher Janice and Ronald. Ronald storms out of the room toward the office. Meanwhile . . .

At School SEL down the road, third-grader Annie stares out the window while Teacher Joan and her class make puppets. Teacher Joan notices Annie's behavior. She asks Annie to join her group but gets no response. She then asks third-grader Sara to show Annie her puppet and see if she can cheer her up. Sara walks over to Annie and says, "Look at my puppet, Annie. She wants to play with your puppet." When Annie does not respond, Sara gently asks her, "Why are you so sad? Do you want to tell my puppet?" Annie manages to force a smile at Sara and begins to pick up her materials and work on her puppet. Sara helps her. Teacher Joan walks over to the two girls a little later and says, "I'm glad that you are not so sad now, Annie. Thank you, Sara, for helping Annie." Turning to Annie, she asks, "Maybe we can talk a little later about your sad feelings?" Wide-eyed, Annie nods her head. She would like this. Teacher Joan makes a note to check in with her during lunch. She plans to stop by the counselor's office after school to chat with her about Annie.

What is similar about each of these scenarios is that the children involved did not comply with the teacher's requests. What is different is the way each teacher responded to the children. In the first scenario, Teacher Janice, angry over Ronald's drawing in class, incited Ronald further by using punitive classroom management strategies. How she responded was influenced by her feelings in the moment. Perhaps she was feeling angry, frustrated, or disregarded? Rather than personally acknowledging these feelings or expressing her feelings to Ronald, she allowed these negative feelings to get the best of her. This response escalated the situation. Consider these questions and the importance of teachers being prepared to deal with them as situations transpire in the classroom:

- How might she have better managed her emotions and diffused the situation?
- What skills or strategies might have better prepared her to deal with Ronald and her feelings about his behaviors?
- What about Teacher Joan's feelings? What might she have been feeling at the time? (Perhaps she was concerned, annoyed, or angry with Annie.)
- What skills or strategies did she use to handle the problem with Annie?
- How did she address her feelings?
- What about her actions helped to get Annie involved in the class again?
- What kind of preparation might Teacher Joan have received along her path of professional development that guided her in this situation?

An analysis of both situations tells us that Teacher Janice lacks the social-emotional competencies needed to regulate her anger and manage her emotions. Furthermore, the children in Teacher Janice's room also lack a sense of community and caring for one another. In Annie's class, Teacher Joan has clearly worked on developing her own emotional competencies and those of her children. Children in this room are accustomed to caring for and helping each other, especially when in distress.

Teachers who recognize that social and emotional health and growth are critical to learning carefully work with children's outbursts or unacceptable behavior. They know that their modeling is critical to how children will react toward others. They know that children can learn social-emotional skills that will enhance the quality of learning. Finally, they believe that children can resolve conflict and become responsible decision makers and problem solvers.

TEACHER AS MODEL

Think for a moment about a teacher you had during your early school days. What role did your teacher play in shaping your social-emotional competencies? Too often, when we reflect on our early models, negative images come up. I remember Teacher Jones, who repeatedly pinched my arm when she was mad at me. And then there was Teacher Hyatt, who kept us after school for hours when we got three checks after our name. But fortunately, most of us have had at least one positive role model whom we fondly remember. When asked to describe the qualities of this teacher, words such as *caring*, *warm*, *kind*, *smart*, and even *funny* are common.

Positive relationships between teachers and students are essential for today's youth. They can even make a difference in a young person's willingness to stay in school, especially at high school. The lack of a significant relationship with another adult has been cited as a major cause of student drop out (Black, 2002). Many teachers find a variety of ways to model this caring relationship with and for students. They fight against constraints that limit their time for social interactions with their students. In some cases, however, teachers contribute to the problem. They use punitive, degrading measures to deal with students' misbehavior instead of positive discipline. A teacher's ability to create a caring classroom can be learned. But this kind of preparation is sorely lacking, and the profession is further challenged by the difficulty in attracting the right people to this vocation and then keeping them committed to this career path.

More than 50,000 people who lack the preparation required for their jobs enter the teaching profession annually on emergency or substandard licenses (National Council of Accreditation of Teacher Educators [NCATE], 2003). Twenty-seven percent of newly hired teachers are not fully licensed. Twelve and a half percent have no license, and almost 15% possess temporary, provisional, or emergency licenses. Furthermore, the least well-prepared teachers typically work with the most needy students. The percentage of unlicensed teachers hired in schools in which more than half of the students are minority or poor is at least four times that of other schools. In schools with the highest minority enrollments, students have less than a 50% chance of getting a science or mathematics teacher who holds a license and a degree in the field he or she teaches.

The accountability measures placed on teachers and the steady increase in teacher salaries have helped improve teaching as a viable, competitive profession. But there are still obstacles to consistently attracting high-quality teachers. Work conditions are a significant challenge, especially in high-need areas. Teachers in high-poverty, high-minority schools, in particular, express a lot of frustration with issues such as student misbehavior, including tardiness and disrespect for teachers (Ingersoll, 2003).

Teachers and students alike need to learn the social and emotional norms of behavior that allow for success in life. Some everyday examples include being able to handle a hostile person without attacking back, being flexible and able to adapt to sudden changes, telling someone your true feelings without putting them on the defensive or offensive, not letting daily moods bring us down or those around us, and remaining optimistic even in the case of setbacks. These are all factors that have a dramatic impact on learning. Those involved in educational policy making and professional preparation need to rethink the teacher's role, help teachers become reflective practitioners, and provide them with the social and emotional skill development they need to create the relationships that both they and the young people they teach need to be successful.

TEACHER AS LEARNER

Being a teacher at any grade level is no easy task. Now, add to that the charge to develop one's own personal and emotional competencies as well as teach SEL to students. Many overburdened teachers might say, "Forget it. I don't need that stuff. Let someone else teach it to the kids." But we know that the more competent the adult in the classroom is, the more caring the learning community will be. Corporate middle managers and top-line supervisors learned this lesson some time ago. In the last decade, they have brought EI development into the workplace through workshops, seminars, and executive coaching models. These models are designed to improve individual competencies in the four quadrant areas: self-awareness, social awareness, self-regulation, and relationships management. Competence in these areas, Daniel Goleman (1998) told us, is a capability that one can learn, which in turn will lead to outstanding performance in the workplace. He identified self-awareness as the threshold skill, the one that when increased, ensures that the other competencies will also grow. Developmental psychologist Carolyn Saarni described the characteristics of a self- aware person. Such a person exhibits

> (a) a rich vocabulary of feeling words; (b) the ability to recognize and differentiate among emotions; (c) the ability to identify physical cues; (d) ability to discern what external event or internal cognition triggered the emotion and: the knowledge that at times, we may not be aware of an emotion because of unconscious dynamics or selective inattention. (as cited in Patti & Tobin, 2003, p. 15)

The more self-aware teachers are, the more willing they will be to take risks to try new instructional strategies, receive feedback, improve their craft, and build learning teams with colleagues. Goleman, Boyatzis, and McKee (2002) told us that for adults to change long-time habits, they need to:

a. bring bad habits into awareness,

b. consciously practice a better way, and

c. rehearse the new behavior until it becomes automatic.

To accomplish this, teachers need role models. Although modeling by observation is fruitful, the teacher as learner needs guided practice to try new strategies. The teacher also requires immediate supportive feedback. These opportunities should be consistent and long term for success to occur. Even the reluctant, jaded, seasoned teacher can find a place of willingness to learn with the proper support. This might require opportunities to work with a trusted colleague or attend a conference or training program. Direct support, however, is the key element in lasting change.

When teachers strive to be the best that they can be, they will model this for students and help them to grow in their personal and social competencies too. The

American Psychological Association (1997) provided a set of guiding principles for all learners, including adults. As we think about providing our teachers with the support to improve their professional skills and personal competencies, four of these principles, in particular, need to be remembered:

- The successful learner, over time and with support and instructional guidance, can create meaningful coherent representations of knowledge.
- What and how much is learned is influenced by the learner's motivation. Motivation to learn, in turn, is influenced by the individual's emotional states, beliefs, interests, and goals, and habits of thinking.
- As individuals develop, there are different opportunities and constraints for learning. Learning is most effective when differential development in and across physical, intellectual, emotional, and social domains is taken into account.
- Learning is influenced by social interactions, interpersonal relations, and communication with others.

FITTING SEL TEACHING INTO THE CROWDED SCHOOL DAY

A challenge for many teachers is when and how to teach SEL in their classrooms, given their already overcrowded school day. Skills such as communication, conflict management, decision making, perspective taking, and goal setting can easily be incorporated into many academic content lessons. One point to remember, however, is that SEL instruction requires sequential, skill-building opportunities. To ensure that young people unlearn negative, patterned behaviors such as aggressive responses to conflict, teachers need to teach SEL skills in an ongoing and consistent way. Young people, in time, acquire positive new behaviors that replace their former patterned responses.

Critical learning tools for the teacher of the SEL classroom instruction are the use of sound, discovery-oriented instructional strategies. These teaching strategies lay the groundwork for creating a climate of trust and safety for learning. SEL strategies may include but are not limited to the use of reflection, inquiry-based learning, problem solving, good communication, cooperative learning, and team-building exercises. The following lesson plan guide can assist teachers with infusing SEL strategies into their regular teaching instruction.

- *Setting the Stage for Learning:* Teachers begin their lesson with a "gathering" or a "go-around" that gets students ready for the new learning that is going to be presented to them. For example, if teaching a lesson on the types of writing, you might begin with a go-around such as, "Tell me a person to whom you recently wrote a letter." Young people might answer, "a friend," "my teacher," "my mother," or "a politician." This is a good way to get them relaxed and ready to talk about the different purposes of writing.

- *Body of the Lesson:* This is the part of the lesson in which the teacher presents new knowledge and concepts. Whether this lesson helps children identify the many purposes of writing or the reasons why an airplane flies, the body of the lesson should contain opportunities for active engagement of young people. Ways to accomplish active engagement include the use of pair shares, interviews, microlabs, fishbowls, cooperative learning groups, concentric circles, and other interactive learning tools.

- *Learning Styles and Special Needs:* Teachers plan lessons geared toward multiple learning styles. They involve the primary learning modes of their students and foster the development of other modalities. Training in multiple intelligence theory and differentiated instruction can be helpful to the SEL teacher. Constructivist approaches encourage teachers to help each student progress from the knowledge they already have to the acquisition of new knowledge.

- *Time for Reflection:* Reflection is a critical part of any teaching lesson. Teachers ask young people to reflect in pairs, in small groups, or in their private journal. Students can reflect on their learning experiences at the end of the lesson or even at the end of the school day. Reflection increases students' self-awareness and expands learning.

- *Practice of the New Learning:* As in all good teaching, young people need multiple opportunities in which to practice the new learning. School leaders should help teachers learn ways to build in multiple opportunities to practice effective strategies.

- *Whole Class Debrief:* Teachers who promote dialogue about the learning process increase the potential for learning in the classroom community. When a lesson ends, teachers encourage young people to share what they have learned. The teacher also asks students to comment on the instructional strategies and knowledge that most enhanced their learning. This process enhances students' meta-cognitive processes. It also helps them recognize that the way they learn may be different from that of another class member. Whole class debriefing helps to bring the class together as a team. It also gives the teacher a sense of the learning that has occurred.

Additional details concerning these procedures can be found in Patti and Tobin (2003).

THE CALL FOR TEACHER PREPARATION PROGRAMS

Given that we know the technology and pedagogy for building SEL skills in teachers and in students, how do we create preparation programs that allow this knowledge to be incorporated into the practice of teacher educators? The NCATE, the official accrediting body recognized by the U.S. Secretary of Education for schools, colleges, and departments of education that prepare teachers, administrators, and other professional school personnel, accredits college programs based on six standards. NCATE's mission and scope explicitly calls for reform of teacher preparation toward ensuring that every child is taught by caring, competent, and qualified educators who are committed to imparting not only basic skills but the skills necessary for responsible citizenship and economic contribution (see www.ncate.org).

Of the six standards that NCATE requires of teacher candidates, three are essential to our discussion:

Standard 1: Candidate knowledge, skills, and dispositions

Standard 4: Diversity

Standard 5: Faculty qualifications, performance, and development

The first standard requires that teachers need to develop the dispositions necessary to help all students learn in addition to the content and pedagogical knowledge.

Dispositions, or belief systems, are not easy to develop or change. To do so, we have to create a vehicle for reflection and support in our teacher training. Teacher education programs have been sorely lacking in their abilities to help prospective teachers learn how to communicate effectively, resolve conflict, deal with differences, and manage strong emotions. As universities across the country prepare for NCATE accreditation, they are seeking ways to teach and measure dispositions in the personal and social competencies we have been discussing in this chapter. What is critical is that professors of education realize that talking about teaching dispositions will not suffice; we have to develop these skills through active engagement in appropriate learning experiences.

Diversity, the fourth NCATE standard, requires a focus on the knowledge, skills, and dispositions needed to prepare future teachers to work with diverse student populations. My belief is that we cannot really prepare teachers to help all students learn unless they have explored their own feelings and attitudes about the biases and prejudices they have and bring to their own classrooms. We talk a lot about diversity in college classrooms. What we do not do is allow the time for adult learners to dialogue, express divergent views, and practice verbal techniques to interrupt bias and promote social justice.

The fifth standard, faculty qualifications, performance, and development, asks faculty to model best professional practices. To do this, they need to assess their own performance effectiveness. College professors need to model the reflective process, as well as teach teachers how to do this.

What would it look like if we were to put these standards into action? Imagine if every teacher who enters a teacher preparation program begins their program with an assessment that calculates their EI in areas such as self-awareness, social awareness, self-management, and relationship management. Imagine if, after receiving this feedback, they develop a professional growth plan that helps them to consciously develop skills such as positive expression of emotion, accurate self-assessment, self-regulation, conflict management, the ability to collaborate, empathy, and more. Consider this: Throughout their teacher education program, they are assigned a personal advisor who checks in with them regularly to see how they are progressing in their EI. Imagine if a major assignment includes the ongoing written reflection of this conscious development, with feedback from college advisors and recommendations for further growth. Finally, on completion of the program, teacher candidates take a posttest to evaluate their EI competencies and determine growth. And last but not least, they demonstrate in a portfolio assessment process how they have used these competencies to improve their performance with students in the classroom.

There are small pockets of programs around the country that are looking at a variety of ways of doing this. The Lesley College master's degree in curriculum and peaceable schools is one such degree that prepares teachers to take leadership in SEL. The Ohio Commission on Dispute Resolution and Conflict Management is working with more than 30 universities across the country to integrate conflict resolution into their programs. In New York City, at Hunter College, EI has been taught and assessed since 2002 in the preparation of education administrators and a leadership center was established as of the time of this writing. In the summer of 2004, the Graduate Center of the City University of New York began its first course in a four-course sequence certificate program in SEL for teachers and other educators.

CONCLUSION

In this chapter, we have explored issues surrounding the inclusion of the development of social-emotional competencies of teachers in teacher preparation programs. We have examined the benefits of preparing teachers with these skills, who in turn model them for children and infuse them into the teaching and learning process. We recognize that the teaching profession involves continual learning; the more teachers continue their professional growth in ways that incorporate SEL, the more intelligent our children will be in every aspect of their lives.

REFERENCES

American Psychological Association. (1997). *Learner-centered psychological principles: A framework for school redesign and reform.* Available from http://www.apa.org/ed/lcp.html

Black, S. (2002). *NCATE summary data on teacher effectiveness, teacher quality, and teacher qualifications.* Available from http://www.ncate.org

Goleman, D. (1998). *Working with emotional intelligence.* New York: Bantam Doubleday Dell.

Goleman, D., Boyatzis, R., & McKee, A. (2002). *Primal leadership: Realizing the power of emotional intelligence.* Cambridge, MA: Harvard Business School Press.

Ingersoll, R. M. (Ed.). (2003). *Quality Counts 2003: If I can't learn from you.* Arlington, VA: Editorial Projects in Education.

National Council of Accreditation of Teacher Educators. (2003). *NCATE standards.* Available from http://www.ncate.org/public/standards.asp

Patti, J., & Tobin, J. (2003). *Smart school leaders: Leading with emotional intelligence.* Dubuque, IA: Kendall Hunt.

8

Raising Your New Teacher's Emotional Intelligence

How Using Social-Emotional Competencies Can Make Your First Year of Teaching Less Stressful and More Successful

Rose Reissman

As a brand new teacher, whether straight out of graduate school or a second- or third-career mature newcomer to the teaching field, you already know about the minefield that awaits you: accountability stress, political pressures, supervisor overloads, classroom management issues, the necessity of implementing new theoretical models you do not fully comprehend, parent pressures, weeping and screaming students, and other overwhelming tensions (both real and imagined). Take a deep breath. Just recording these few of the myriad pressures heaped, if not dumped on the new teacher, is a formidable task. Imagine living and struggling under this heap each day.

In 1995, Daniel Goleman articulated five competencies of emotional intelligence (EI) that markedly enhance life and learning for a broad spectrum of multisector adult, student, senior, special-needs, and culturally diverse individuals. Almost immediately, business leaders and educators recognized the broad applicability and tremendous potential in developing these competencies for both the global marketplace and the school community. Within a decade, a vast body of research was compiled documenting the positive academic, economic, and corporate benefits of EI and competency enhancement. Ironically, one group of individuals in the school community that is tremendously in need of EI to deal with day-to-day stress has been left behind as the theory and data advance. Which educational stakeholders have been left behind? Those most stressed out and at risk of dropping out: new teachers. If you are a new teacher, serve as a mentor for a new teacher, or are an administrator charged with retaining and nurturing new teachers, I urge you to read on.

You can keep the pressures of being a new teacher from burying you (or your charges) in a hole of despair. Take heart and raise your EI and emotional competence powers. Consider Daniel Goleman's (1995) first competency of EI.

GOLEMAN'S (1995) SOCIAL-EMOTIONAL COMPETENCY 1: SELF-AWARENESS—KNOW YOUR STRENGTHS AND WEAKNESSES

Teach to and from your personal and past professional, intellectual, artistic, and entertainment (yes, entertainment) strengths. No matter what the topic (I myself have had stressed-out veteran and new teachers dancing the "hokey pokey" as they learned how to implement the Balanced Literacy Workshop model), infuse it with singing, dancing, writing, collecting art, moving, cooking, sculpting, movie viewing, or exercising, wherever your expertise lies.

Remember that although you may be new to the teaching profession, your lifelong gifts, talents, and entertainment capacities are not new to you. Use them, don't lose them. By using them, you will begin to relax and enjoy your teaching. In turn, your students will benefit from your pleasure in teaching them while also sharing a talent you enjoy. When you, as a new teacher, provide a personal flair to teaching and learning, you will enhance your self-esteem and reduce your personal stress.

On the other hand, use this competency to also admit and to recognize aspects of content knowledge, skills, or capacities that are not your strengths. Take these into account as you work through your first year of teaching and learning. If you are a childhood or elementary educator and are weak in science content or teaching skills (and have no personal monies or time to take a professional development workshop or training course), try to team up with a colleague who possesses experience in that subject or license area. Barter your own subject content expertise or talents for your colleague's curriculum writing, advising, and mentoring. If team teaching is not possible, contact the district subject content coordinator or a colleague who excels in that subject or license area. Try your local subject-specific nonprofit teacher's organization. For example, during my tenure as president of the New York City Affiliate of the National Council of Teachers of English, our organization sent out retired people to serve as mentors and provided phone and curricula support. Beyond reaching out to local human and collegial resources, you can also sit down online and do a search for the topic you are required to teach. Within 90 seconds, you will have a list of no fewer than 20, but perhaps hundreds of downloadable lesson plans. Many of these come complete with worksheets and activities. If you try some author sites, you can even get actual authors to respond to your students' work or at the very least hear from the site's Web staff. Check out the Scholastic Web site (www.scholastic.com) or the PBS teacher resource site (www.pbs.org) for a treasure trove of resources!

Another wonderful way to enhance your own area of content or license expertise is to model adult cultural investigations for your students. Translation: Take them on a real school bus or train or subway field experience. Learn with them and bond together on a shared adventure, outside the physical classroom. Debrief your up-to-date constructivist learning when you return to the classroom!

Above all, as you empower yourself through the self-awareness competency, stop beating up on yourself for not excelling in a specific content or license area. Do not blame yourself for the economic, political, or staffing vicissitudes that landed you in this placement. Use colleagues, the Internet, field trips, and teachers' organizations, and model lifelong learning for your students!

GOLEMAN'S (1995) SOCIAL-EMOTIONAL COMPETENCY 2: HANDLING YOUR STRONG EMOTIONS

The first year of teaching is fraught with intense emotion. There are moments of sheer joy and power, as you finally get that single child to understand a concept, demonstrate skill mastery, and complete a project. But there are also many moments of frustration, powerful hurt, and disappointment. There are times of tremendous physical exhaustion, coupled with self-doubts and anguish. And yes, tears, plenty of them.

During this tremulous period, you tend to think that everything that happens in your classroom or to your students is a direct consequence of your teaching. This is particularly true of negative student behaviors toward you or peers. However, in reality, students' behaviors, responses, outbursts, and reactions often are not about you at all. These outpourings generally grow out of the students' lives, experiences, and needs in their own family and caregiver circles. Count to 10 and remember that a specific student screaming session, even if it includes shrieking your name out loud, could be a cry for your attention due to lack of attention at home. Your fault? No. Done on your watch? Yes.

Student outbursts and insults on the kindergarten through 12 levels go with the territory of teaching, much as they go with the territory of parenting. They accompany strong relationships and caring. Ironically, your very genuine and justly motivated display of reciprocal anger, tears, and facial expressions of pain accompanied by your screaming, slamming the door, or hitting the desk—will not help the situation. Indeed, if done in full view of the entire class, you will justly be diminished in the eyes of all your students. You are the adult teacher. They are watching you very carefully.

Yes, you are also a real person with feelings that can be easily hurt by an unthinking, out-of-control 5-, 9-, 10-, or 16-year-old. Screaming back and acting out in response to this unmerited attack on you may be your natural, real-life response in a family or relationship setting. But control yourself and consider the source of this painful upset: an immature student.

If you are an "emotions to the surface" individual, you may need to practice holding back the tears that spring to your eyes, controlling your facial responses, and toning down your body language. If necessary, clench your fist or clasp your hands behind your back to release tension. Softly modulate and lower your voice. Respond with deliberate, slow calm to an outburst. Use a delay by always counting, perhaps to 5, maybe even only to 2 or 3. Students may come from home environments where they fire up caregivers' yelling by their outbursts. Your flying off the handle will not negate the students' doing so. Rather, your emotional response models undesirable behavior for them! You send a message: "Yes, this will be just like home. There is nothing special here, no special safety." You are the ultimate classroom role model for the students. Do not allow them to become your negative role models.

As an emotionally competent teacher, you must manage your own strong emotions. In doing so, you then can be better at helping offending students find their way to a calm space, in which they can reflect on what they were actually upset by (probably not you or your classroom). Gradually, you can then teach through your own example the skills necessary for better expressing their strong emotions (perhaps through art, writing, or exercise) rather than through berating you or others. This will result in diminished outbursts.

GOLEMAN'S (1995) SOCIAL-EMOTIONAL COMPETENCY 3: EMPATHY

Two wonderful vehicles for building your sensitivity to the feelings and perspectives of the students in your class are the use of role play and of an empathic lens for viewing the students.

Role play works best with another person or when you physically get up and stand in different positions as you replay a situation or event from your classroom experience. For example, reenact (painful as it may be for you) the student outburst scenario that so hurt you. Role-play the offending student or students. What are they actually reacting to? What situations in their lives outside of class are contributing to their in-class remarks? Where do you and your ongoing teaching fit into these outside-of-class situations? Sometimes, your innocent, classroom-appropriate remarks may add fuel to students' burning internal emotional fires. For example, I have seen students react intensely to a story being read that describes a happy family, which they resent not having. And this will happen at some times, but not others. Try to see what is happening from the children's point of view. You are not making excuses for their behavior—you still need to teach them how to react appropriately when they are upset in school. But if you first confront the challenge of tempering your own reaction to the situation, you can better appreciate why your students, who are younger and less mature than you are, will have even more need to learn emotional competency skills. Practice some empathy and find some ways to comfort yourself when your feelings start to get the better of you.

When you begin to examine upsetting classroom confrontations from students' perspectives, you better position yourself to develop teacher responses that will defuse or at least lessen the disruption to learning. The use of empathy in reflections about students' actual concerns also offers you, as a new teacher, a degree of enlightenment and meta-cognition in dealing with what initially appears to be a deliberately defiant "student versus teacher" standoff. When you are able to shift from perceiving students as your classroom antagonists to perceiving the classroom as your students experience it, your own stress level is very likely to diminish. This means you will need to find time and ways to get to know students' families and about how they live their lives in their communities. You cannot teach them from a bubble.

Much job stress for you as a new teacher is generated by the demands, likes, and dislikes of administrators and supervisors whose mandates sometimes appear to be in direct opposition to yours. You may need to accede to their demands because you need and want to remain on the job. You also have a sense of responsibility to your students. Rather than concentrating on employing negative combative energy to protest, defy, or elude these authorities, view them through an empathic lens.

Perceive them as themselves subject to even higher placed administrators. Ask yourself what outside pressures, mandates, and personal factors might cause them to be so inflexible and difficult. Surely they are not this way by choice, nor is it likely that they have a personal vendetta against you or your students. Rather than waste needed positive energy on destructive protests, acting out, or revenge, try to demonstrate your support by showing empathy for the stresses these administrators confront.

As you use this perspective, you will feel your level of stress diminishing. Use the same role play and empathic lens approach for dealing with angry parent (or guardian) letters, calls, and demanding visits. Too often, you, as a vulnerable new teacher, cast the parent who phones, writes, or comes in to see your supervisor as a villain of the highest order. This stereotyping often reflects your self-consciousness as a new teacher, rather than awareness of the actual cause for parent concern. It drains you of positive energy and creativity. It can lead you to do less, in the kind of tit-for-tat mentality you see students engage in (and with so little positive outcome, as I am sure you have noticed).

It is crucial that you take a step back and switch roles with the parent or guardian. What feedback or information from class (accurate or not) led to this response? Why might he or she have gone over your head to complain? In what ways might you quickly defuse the concern or correct the misinformation? What positive thing is the parent or guardian trying to accomplish for the child he or she cares about? How can you put this parent's fears to rest or, better still, how can you engage this parent's hopes and trust?

What steps, actions, and words would you want to hear from the teacher, if you were the anxious parent or guardian? While you are switching roles and reviewing the situation from the perspective of the parent, you may notice your own anxiety and stress levels going down. In the act of focusing on an empathic analysis of the distress of parents and guardians, you relieve your own.

GOLEMAN'S (1995) SOCIAL-EMOTIONAL COMPETENCY 4: MOTIVATION—SETTING GOALS, DEMONSTRATING HOPE AND OPTIMISM

The process of goal setting is a simultaneous act of hope, optimism, and motivation. You set a direction for yourself and for your students. As you continue to incorporate the use of the emotional competencies into your array of professional tools and strategies, you will begin to see how raising your EI can relieve stress and improve classroom management. Use a journal to begin the school year by setting attainable (the focus is on doable and viable) academic and behavioral goals for your class. Set goals for individual students, as well. Actually, you can start doing this at the beginning of any marking period, not just at the start of the school year.

As you continue to maintain your journal and any other internal or posted goals (charts or graphs), list the steps, strategies, tools, and measures you are using to monitor progress toward your whole class or individual student goals. Try to find a way to involve your students in also monitoring and charting their own progress toward individual and class academic and behavioral goals. You can do this with students at any age, from preschool through high school. Is it a lot of work? Yes. But you are a professional teacher and should no more resist a time-consuming but effective technique than a doctor should resist a time-consuming but life-saving new medical procedure. More students than you would imagine, at every socioeconomic level, are adrift and in need of goals. They even feel more out of control and clueless than you do, although they will not admit it.

Precisely because the first year of teaching is often marked by a feeling that you are not in control of your professional life and of your classroom, the use of the goal-setting emotional competency helps you regain the sense of being in charge of your day-to-day destiny. As you set your own goals and, if possible, involve your students in the process of setting goals for themselves and the classroom, you immediately breathe optimism into your professional life. Rather than being subject to the vicissitudes of day-to-day classroom successes and failures, you have a powerful plan to steer your own destiny. If you get pulled off course, you can and will get back on track! You will have the charts, graphs, and journal notes to help you remain on course for your destination and let the students know that they are not just coming to school to pass the time. They are getting somewhere!

GOLEMAN'S (1995) SOCIAL-EMOTIONAL COMPETENCY 5: SOCIAL SKILLS AND MANAGING RELATIONSHIPS

Question: Should a serious, dedicated first-year teacher socialize on the job? Answer: Who has time?

Wrong answer. A new teacher not only needs time to socialize, he or she must take the time!

Sometimes with pressures imposed by you and your school setting, you can overlook a key component of stress relief, classroom management, and personal contentment—socializing! Here are things that many new teachers stop doing in the name of efficiency and productivity, at their peril:

- Be certain to take a few moments each day to have a personal, friendly, and collegial exchange with both new teacher colleagues and veteran teachers.
- Take time to chat about family, feelings, books, movies, music, fashion, and household concerns.
- Purposefully inquire about and support colleagues in their ongoing out-of-school pursuits.
- Compliment colleagues throughout the building who are doing wonderful work.

- Be there for teacher colleagues who are facing classroom challenges and need a sounding board.
- Contact someone outside the school if you need to talk to a colleague who can give you an impartial but expert opinion on a classroom issue.

One of the unique joys of teaching is that to some extent, you can create a community with your students. By all means, do that. But for most teachers, especially new ones, that is not enough. There is no need to be an island unto yourself. You will gain much through sharing your concerns and triumphs with those in your building.

Socializing reduces the stress of addressing immediate classroom problems in a vacuum. Become a part of your school's professional family who shares common positive goals and experiences (as opposed to banding together only to combat the "alien administrators"). Interestingly, supporting you serves to reinvigorate your colleagues by validating their own professionalism.

Socializing can also extend in a more guarded fashion to your relationship with your students. Although you will always be distanced from them as their teacher, spend some time seeing them as social beings, getting to know the whole student. Eat with them once in a while. Listen to their conversations about home, movie stars, special events, worries, and tensions. In your classroom, provide opportunities for them to talk with one another and not at one another. Once in a while, go to recess with your students and stay with them during a performance or experience (even if you are scheduled for a break).

Experience them as individuals and give them a chance to experience you as a person. Since social-emotional skills are a key part of personal development and job success, you will want opportunities to nurture these student skills in addition to students' academic skills. You can use your new perspectives on your students to customize learning experiences for them. This will help you be more empathic, set better goals, and put yourself in a relationship with students that is likely to promote better awareness of feelings and more self-control. It all comes full circle.

CONCLUSION

Despite the many stresses that exist, it is vital that you, the newest, crucial recruit to the profession, feel empowered to lend your talents, expertise, passion, and strength to meeting students' academic and social-emotional goals. The five emotional competencies popularized by Goleman (1995) have been used by many new educators just like you to immediately transform stress, worry, fears, anxiety, and isolation into proactive, self-directed, confident, optimistic, joyful, and collegial designs for successful, pleasurable teaching and learning. Start now!

Author's Note: The Peak Learning Systems Web site, http://www.new-teacher.com, has a collection of articles on emotional intelligence specifically for new teachers.

REFERENCE

Goleman, D. (1995). *Emotional intelligence: Why it can matter more than IQ.* New York: Bantam Books.

The Professional Inquiry Kit

One Avenue for Exploring, Enhancing, and Applying Emotional Intelligence in Schools

Pam Robbins

Lucky Moore, a Department of Defense teacher at Bad Aibling American High School in Bad Aibling, Germany, and his 10th-grade class are discussing insights derived from an interpersonal style inventory they just took. They ponder the implications for interpersonal relationships at school and at home. They talk about how differences in style might be a source of conflict if they are not understood. They reflect on literary characters they have studied, the interpersonal styles they depict, and what role style played in their interactions. At the end of the period, many students express an interest in administering the inventory to their parents, with a goal of fostering an enhanced understanding of self, relationships with others, and interactions with family members. There is an air of excitement and marvel among students as they grab their book bags and walk to the door.

Lucky watches them leave with a smile on his face, reflecting on their session together and noting how students who rarely spoke had become energized by the topic. He walks to his computer and e-mails a colleague about this experience.

He wanted his colleague to know about it, since they had collaboratively discussed the lesson plan earlier.

At an elementary school in Highland Park, Illinois, teachers meet around the table in the faculty room and plan curricular integrated units using children's literature. Their interest is in weaving lessons of emotional intelligence (EI) into lessons designed to prepare students to meet or exceed content standards in language arts and reading. They talk about how they might also address thinking skills and multiple intelligences in the process.

These two examples portray possible outcomes of study groups composed of professional colleagues who meet together to design experiences for students to develop, enhance, and extend skills in EI. Their work together is based on Daniel Goleman's (1995) book, *Emotional Intelligence: Why It Can Matter More Than IQ* and facilitated by activities in the *Professional Inquiry Kit on Emotional Intelligence* (Robbins & Scott, 1997). As they collaborate, these same professional colleagues are increasing their own awareness of how they are modeling aspects of EI in interactions with one another. Students, in turn, will be more likely to demonstrate those behaviors that they see enacted by the adults in the school.

PROFESSIONAL DEVELOPMENT THROUGH STUDY GROUPS

The *Professional Inquiry Kit on Emotional Intelligence* (Robbins & Scott, 1997) is designed to foster professional dialogue about and exploration of the topic of EI. The forum for this endeavor is a study group. A study group is a collection of individuals who gather together to examine a particular topic. They are often formed in response to a recognized need or interest. Study groups provide participants with an opportunity to learn together and, in the process, build both enhanced individual and organizational capacity to serve students. Activities in the study group may include doing professional reading; doing constructivist tasks; sharing expertise and experiences; problem solving; creating new knowledge; and designing, delivering, and evaluating student work. Also possible are collecting and analyzing data, doing site visits, viewing, or attending conferences. Collectively, these interactions leave their mark on perspectives, attitudes, policies, and practices.

Perhaps one of the greatest challenges of study groups is finding quality professional time. Schools have approached the time issue in a variety of ways:

- Using faculty meeting time for study groups
- Using staff development hours spread over several months to create chunks of time to meet
- Beginning school late 1 day a week
- Adding 15 instructional minutes to 4 school days a week and dismissing students 2 hours early on the remaining day
- Sending students from one class to another to form a double class, freeing teachers for study group activities. In one elementary school, for example, primary teachers were freed for study groups by sending students to elementary classrooms where they were assigned study buddies. Later in the month, elementary teachers were freed up by sending students to tutor (and reinforce skills) in primary classrooms

Study groups in some schools are held after the end of formal professional duties on a given day, particularly when teachers opt not to use time during the traditional day because of existing commitments. But in most cases, this approach tends to be least appealing.

A MENU OF OPTIONS

Since the content, processes, and sequence of study group activities may vary considerably given members' needs, time available, and the topic, the *Professional Inquiry Kit on Emotional Intelligence* (Robbins & Scott, 1997) offers a menu of options. These options are introduced in a series of folders.

Folder 1 addresses how to convene, organize, operate, and evaluate study groups. Folder 2 focuses on "What Is Emotional Intelligence?" Materials included in this folder present a variety of perspectives on the nature of EI and its consequences. Participants are invited to make sense of this concept through a constructivist task and identify connections to their own lives and schools. They also are invited to explore how EI affects day-to-day interactions among adults and students and how this ultimately plays a critical role in school climate. This folder provides several foundational activities to help study group members develop an understanding of EI, its value, and implications for staff, students, and parents. These include the following options:

- A KWL chart (i.e., what I *Know*, what I *Want* to know, what I *Learned*) to generate questions that study group members want to pursue regarding EI
- A cooperative activity using excerpts from Daniel Goleman's (1995) book *Emotional Intelligence: Why It Can Matter More Than IQ.* This reading introduces five domains of EI: self-awareness, managing one's emotions, motivating one-self and delaying gratification, empathy, and handling relationships
- An article summarizing Daniel Goleman's ground-breaking and field-inspiring talk at the Association for Supervision and Curriculum Development's 1997 annual conference
- An opportunity to view a video about EI in schools, especially about issues of dealing with angry and impulsive behavior
- An invitation to construct a personal definition of EI as a result of readings and video viewing
- A chance to examine the historical roots of EI and the cost of emotional illiteracy
- A task in which study group members analyze the fit between the concepts of EI and multiple intelligences

Many study groups choose to complete all the activities in this foundational folder; some elect to select from among the options. Study group members often comment that Folder 2 activities have made them more conscious of what they are already doing in the classroom or at a school level that relates to EI and that the activities have piqued an interest in what more they might do. Several individuals have observed that if school faculties spent more time focusing, modeling, and teaching EI, the incidents of school violence would be reduced.

Activities in Folder 2 build an interest in delving deeper into the five domains of EI. Folder 3 addresses the first of these domains: self-awareness. In addition to supplemental readings on this topic, Folder 3 offers study group members several adult and student activities designed to develop, extend, and enhance one's own sense of self-awareness. Study group members are invited to complete multiple intelligence and EI inventories to learn more about themselves. In the process of exploring, expressing, assessing, and developing self-awareness, group members gain insights, ideas, and strategies that will help them in working with students. Many take the same study group experiences they have had and modify them so they are suitable for students. After providing these as classroom experiences for students, study group members share and compare the results they derived from putting their ideas into practice. They also explore how the topic of self-awareness can be integrated into a variety of curricular areas. Some study groups have spent time developing lessons to accomplish this goal and see them as an engaging way to address state standards in a variety of curricular areas. In addition, many of the suggested adult (and corresponding student) activities offer a way to study self-awareness using a variety of multiple intelligences to accomplish this goal.

Folder 4 focuses on the topic of managing emotions. In this folder, participants find readings that offer an opportunity to study managing emotions in greater depth. The readings include an excerpt entitled "Passion's Slaves" from Daniel Goleman's (1995) book *Emotional Intelligence: Why It Can Matter More Than IQ*, a reading on the brain's emotional architecture, quotations regarding windows of opportunity for the development of skills in the area of managing emotions, and several journal articles by leading authors in the field of social-emotional learning. The menu of activities in this folder invite participants to explore an eight-step problem-solving model for social decision making, examine conflict resolution techniques, and complete a classroom analysis task related to how students manage emotions. Participants can also explore cultural influences on managing emotions. This folder often initiates continuing dialogue and study of the implications of its information for the playground, passing periods, and policies and procedures for preventative measures associated with behavior management.

Folder 5 addresses self-motivation, self-control, and the ability to delay gratification. In this folder, participants have the opportunity to explore how emotions affect our capacity to use our mental resources to the extent that they get in the way of or enhance our ability to think, plan, and act. As a consequence, they influence how well we do in life. Goleman (1995), in *Emotional Intelligence*, stated that

> to the degree to which we are motivated by feelings of enthusiasm and pleasure in what we do—or even by an optimal degree of anxiety—they propel us to accomplishment. It is in this sense that emotional intelligence is a master aptitude, a capacity that profoundly affects all other abilities. (p. 80)

This folder focuses on those behaviors that help individuals develop this "master aptitude." Materials in this folder include excerpts from Goleman's (1995) *Emotional Intelligence*; activities addressing self-control, motivation, and delayed gratification; a reading about learning and the concept of "flow"; a reading and reflection about building resilience in students; and five steps to inner leadership. Many teachers have followed study group activities from this folder with collaboratively planned lessons to help students be more self-motivated, exercise better self-control, and delay gratification. This also has inspired dialogue about special-needs students, such as the child with attention deficit disorder, and what implications information from this folder has for classroom practice. Action steps that follow have taken the form of problem solving, communicating with parents, sharing, and lesson planning.

Folder 6 addresses the domain of empathy. Empathy refers to the ability to recognize, read, and respond to others' feelings. Empathy allows one to create and maintain rapport with others. It plays a critical role in a wide range of settings: teaching, administration, management, public relations, sales, parenting, and romance. Students who are able to read others' feelings and respond appropriately are often both popular and emotionally stable.

Newspaper headlines remind us daily of what a lack of empathy can produce: murderers, rapists, psychopaths, and child molesters. Among young people, delinquents often lack the ability to sense their victim's pain, thus making their deviant behavior possible. Activities in Folder 6 invite study group members to explore empathy from both a verbal and nonverbal perspective. These activities include readings, an opportunity to view a video clip, a chance to explore the link between caring and empathy, a simulation to practice reading nonverbal expressions, and an exploration of how caring and empathy are communicated in works of art.

Many study group members have had students create picture dictionaries of emotions as a result of participating in adult activities in this folder. Others have developed lessons using children's stories, wherein students experience empathy by taking the role of a character in a story. Several study groups have begun collecting musical selections that address empathy. Others have begun discussing how lessons in empathy, including empathy-building activities such as well-planned community service, may have the capacity to reduce incidents of school violence.

Folder 7 addresses handling relationships. Goleman (1995), in *Emotional Intelligence,* suggested that "much evidence testifies that people who are emotionally adept—who know and manage their own feelings well, and who read and deal effectively with other people's feelings—are at an advantage in any domain of life" (p. 36). This ability is also inextricably linked to physical and mental health.

Folder 7 also explores behaviors that help individuals develop and maintain relationships. It includes readings as well as activities to support students in learning how to handle relationships. Study group members are invited to learn about the "social arts," display rules, how to turn conflicts into learning experiences, ways to gain parental support, and strategies to lift a school's spirit. They also can explore the critical link between the home and the school, and why nurturing and maintaining relationships is so essential.

After completing activities in this folder, many study group members have explored how this folder's content relates to school improvement efforts at their sites in the area of home-school partnerships.

Folder 8 is entitled "Extending Your Learning." Its intent is to offer suggestions for ways to keep the focus on EI an integral part of life at the school and in home-school and community-school relationships. There is growing evidence that, of the individual and organizational variables most closely linked to the implementation of an innovation in a school, teacher beliefs play the most salient role in determining implementation success. The activities in the EI kit were designed to provide experiences that will help organizational members value and believe in the capability of EI for transforming relationships and improving the quality of interactions in schools and classrooms and with parents and community members. One intended consequence of this endeavor would be enhanced levels of student achievement.

Schools are busy places, and it is difficult to stay focused on any one innovation. But one way to do so is to build the innovation into the culture of the school. When developing and supporting EI become a common thread in a school, relationships blossom. A focus on EI will add strength to school change and school reform efforts as teachers and others see the positive results of such a focus. As a result, activities in Folder 8 are designed to build EI into the school culture and to provide a way for analyzing the effects of EI on students. The menu of activity options include suggestions for developing an EI activity box for students, opportunities to contact others involved in programs to develop social-emotional learning, ideas for faculty meetings, topics for action research, activities for peer coaching, and plans for a schoolwide exhibition on emotions as an integrated curriculum project. Together, these activities have engaged study group members in integrating EI into all aspects of life in the school and have served as a springboard for further study and action.

CONCLUSION

As a result of embedding the professional inquiry kit activities into the daily life of administrators, teachers, paraprofessionals, and students at the school, new policies are being created, insights are developing, and practices to nurture EI are emerging at many sites. Some sites have also included parents in study groups. Collectively, the individual endeavors of staff are fueling the capacity of the school as an organization to serve students. As one study group member reflected,

> Our faculty is more collaborative and our resources have been enhanced as a result of our study of emotional intelligence. As an individual, I am more aware of how important it is to model those practices I am committed to teaching our students. For it is our students who will create the world of tomorrow. They need to be both bright and emotionally intelligent.

Author's Note: Updated information about Pam Robbins's work can be found at http://user .shentel.net/probbins.

REFERENCES

Goleman, D. (1995). *Emotional intelligence: Why it can matter more than IQ*. New York: Bantam Books.

Robbins, P., & Scott, J. (1997). *Professional inquiry kit on emotional intelligence*. Alexandria, VA: Association for Supervision and Curriculum Development.

PART III

Educators
Tell Their Stories

How to Bring Social-Emotional Learning/ Emotional Intelligence Into Classrooms

In Part III, educators share their stories about bringing social-emotional learning (SEL)/emotional intelligence into their classrooms. They do this for several reasons. First, they have come to believe in its importance and would like others to appreciate it as well. Second, they realize that it was not a core part of their preparation as educators; they would like to help make the path that they followed a bit more clear and accessible than it appears in typical academic book writing. Third, and perhaps most important, is their view that if they can do it, so can you. SEL does not require complex pedagogy or some extraordinary techniques or knowledge. As noted in the introductory discussion about Part III, these educators felt that with a few stories and some examples of activities and approaches, you would have something to try "on Monday morning." And that is the best way to use the materials in Part III— read some and try them out.

You will find activities that focus on all age levels, from preschool to high school, and there is a chart in the introductory materials that can guide you as to which chapters might be the best starting points for you. In addition, we encourage you to make copies of the readers' reflection/application guide we provided in our introductory section "About This Book" (see p. xviii) to help you cull specific activities and techniques from what you are reading, try them out, and then follow up to get clarification, greater depth, or support in implementation.

To bring you into these chapters, three educators were asked to share their experiences working with the kinds of approaches to be presented. Jacqueline Norris has served in every role, from teacher to district administrator to education professor, and has trained many educators in the use of SEL programs. Christopher Lommerin has spent the last few years guiding an urban school and urban educators in bringing an SEL program to their students. And Suzanne Evans, with whom we begin, has been a teacher and teacher leader using these approaches. Each has found the experience transformative in ways that they can best describe.

Suzanne Evans

I have been on staff at Yorktown High School for the past 5 years. My previous teaching experience was as a high school math teacher (teaching everything from special education–integrated general math classes to calculus) in Virginia, Texas, and Utah.

Perhaps I come to SEL with a rather unique perspective. I didn't know the formal language of SEL until joining the Yorktown High School staff 5 years ago; however, having both a teaching and counseling background made SEL part of my beliefs intrinsically. As I learned more, it totally made sense to me that SEL skills are vital for both our students' success in the classroom and in life.

In my role as a resource teacher, I work with the teachers of the advanced classes in supporting the different needs of their students. One concern I had prior to coming to this position was the huge amount of stress that our higher ability students in high school are under as they take as hard a class load as they can to challenge themselves and prepare for college. I truly believe that our SEL focus at Yorktown helps support these students and helps them achieve at a higher level. It is so important that our students understand their own abilities to self-motivate, persevere during times of heavy workloads, and also have the self-discipline to take care of themselves in other areas of their lives. Understanding and knowing how to foster these skills allows our teachers to help our students learn life lessons, not just advanced placement calculus or government.

Each time I work with a student or a teacher comes to me with a concern about a student, I try to focus on the SEL skills and specific areas in which students may need to strengthen their abilities. In addition, as a school, we have had several days in which the entire school focused on building community and communication skills, with students interacting with others whom they did not know prior to that day.

I firmly believe that we owe it to our students to help them be knowledgeable in various subject areas but also to be caring, competent members of their communities, wherever these may be. Having SEL as a part of our dual focus, along with academic excellence, allows us to achieve this goal. What a great gift it will be to our students in the future when they realize that the skills that they needed to succeed both in terms of work and interacting with others were taught and strengthened both implicitly and explicitly while they were at Yorktown.

Christopher Lommerin

SEL remains one of the most important aspects of a child's education. Without a solid grasp of oneself and the skills to interact among fellow human beings, children—and all adults, for that matter—will have difficulty establishing positive and productive futures.

Children can only hold so much information. If a glass can hold 8 ounces of water and it is full, attempts to put in more liquid will only make a mess and waste water. Picture that glass being a child filled with stress and emotional baggage due to parents fighting, parents not being present, peer pressure, legal problems, poverty, bullies at school, and so forth. If a child's glass is filled with all of these issues, a teacher cannot be expected to add more in the form of education.

By infusing SEL into classrooms and schools, teachers can learn to empty their students' glasses to make room for new knowledge. I have observed positive academic growth at our school, which is in a challenging urban area marked with many difficulties, over the past 7 years. This is partially due to the implementation of an established social-emotional program of the kind described in this section.

Jacqueline Norris

As a professor of education who has also been a classroom teacher, principal, and district administrator, I see so many of my colleagues teaching about constructivist approaches to teaching. We teach methods that call for hands-on and minds-on learning, but there are few of us who teach hearts-on learning. We want to engage students' minds as if they were just brains sitting in those seats. How do we reach their hearts so that they see teaching as a "moral imperative," as Michael Fullan would say? I work with preservice teachers who want to teach people who look like them and learn the way they learn. I try to build empathy in them so that they grapple with and persist in reaching people whose life experience is foreign to theirs.

Since No Child Left Behind, I have found that the easiest way to do this is to demonstrate how emotions affect learning. The biggest help with teachers during training workshops has been to show them that I am not asking them to do something new. I show them that they can modify their strategies a little using the content they are bound by the standards to teach. I have them tell me lessons that they love to teach, and then I show them how they can revise the lesson adding an SEL strategy. They really appreciate the new approach and feel less threatened because the core of the lesson is familiar. The classroom examples in this section of the book will allow teachers to see how they can move from where they are to greater involvement with SEL.

Suzanne Evans is a Gifted Services Resource Teacher and Chair of the SEL Steering Committee at Yorktown High School in Arlington, VA.

Christopher Lommerin was the principal at the Stillman Elementary School in Plainfield, NJ, at the time of this writing. He has been in the field of education for 15 years and an administrator for 10.

Jacqueline A. Norris has been a teacher and administrator in New Jersey public schools for more than 30 years. She is presently Assistant Professor of Education at the College of New Jersey.

10

I Can Problem Solve

An Interpersonal Cognitive Problem-Solving Approach for Children

Myrna B. Shure

One child nags, demands, and cries.

Another hits other children and takes away their toys.

A third does not listen to people or pay attention in class.

There are lots of ways to handle behavior problems in the classroom. Modeling, coaching, telling children what and what not to do, and even explaining why are often observed. But these techniques have one thing in common. They are all doing the thinking for the child. My research colleague, George Spivack, and I set out to find a different way to guide the behavior of children. We learned that we could guide behavior by engaging children in the process of thinking about what they do and considering how their actions affect their own and others' feelings, what might happen next, and how else they can solve the problem at hand. We learned that as early as age 4, children who behave differently, think differently.

First, we identified a set of problem-solving thinking skills that could distinguish competent from less competent youngsters as early as age 4—skills we called "Interpersonal Cognitive Problem Solving," and we also identified behaviors that accompany those skills (Shure, 1993; Spivack & Shure, 1974). (For description and references of measures of these skills, see Appendix at the end of this chapter.)

GOOD AND POOR PROBLEM SOLVING: A CONTRAST

Here are how three children the same age, 5, differ in their behaviors and in how they negotiate their interpersonal worlds:

Benjamin gets what he wants by hitting others. A teacher asked him what happened when he hit another child to get a toy. His answer: "He hit me back, but I don't care."

If Benjamin getting what he wanted truly mattered more than the consequence of getting hit back—perhaps even hurt—would he even think about the impact of his behavior at all? Can children who do not care, or who endure their own pain when they are 3, 4, or 5 years old, possibly be able to develop empathy for the victims they might hurt (physically or emotionally) later on? Caring about oneself is an extremely important ingredient to later problem solving, as Goleman (1995) suggested when he said, "The key to sounder personal decision-making [is], in short: being attuned to our feelings" (p. 54). In light of escalating substance abuse (a form of hurting oneself) and violence (a form of hurting others), perhaps children who say "I don't care" should make us take special pause.

Martha, a timid, fearful child, has a skill that Benjamin does not. She is able to appreciate how people feel when provoked. But, like Benjamin, Martha is unable to think of solutions to her problems, and she also does not think much about what might happen next if she does find herself in conflict with someone. Although awareness that she might have made another person angry is a step ahead of lack of such sensitivity, her inability to reduce that anger may only heighten her anxiety and make her more timid and fearful. She has learned it is safer to simply avoid people and problems she cannot solve.

Now let's look at Rafael, who wanted a shovel that Steven was playing with. When refused after a request for the shovel, he did not grab the shovel or hit Steven. He tried a different way. "Why can't I have it?" he asked. "Because I need it. I'm building a castle," answered Steven. Now Rafael offered, "I can help you build a castle. We can build a castle together." And Rafael and Steven happily worked together in the sand.

Rafael was applying skills of highly sophisticated thinking. With a variety of options available to him, he was meshing his needs with those of Steven's. No teacher had to intervene, explain the virtues of sharing, or take the shovel away so neither could have it. Instead of feeling anger and frustration, Rafael felt proud, and both children were happy with how the problem was solved.

To test whether engaging children in the process of thinking about what they are doing could reduce or prevent early high-risk behaviors in the classroom, we created an intervention to teach children age-appropriate pre-problem-solving and problem-solving skills.

THE INTERVENTIONS: AN OVERVIEW

Interventions for preschool through Grade 6, originally called Interpersonal Cognitive Problem Solving, now called I Can Problem Solve (ICPS; Shure, 1992a, 1992b, 1992c), consist of two parts: Through carefully sequenced activities, children are taught pre-problem-solving and problem-solving skills in game form, and problems with hypothetical characters. After each new concept or set of concepts is introduced, teachers guide the children to use the concepts during the day, in real life, to help them associate how they think with what they do and how they behave.

Pre-Problem-Solving Skills

ICPS Word Pairs

Children in the preschool through the primary grades are first taught a series of word pairs that they may already know but that are associated with fun then applied in new ways to later help them settle disputes. For example, playing the word pair *is/is not*, 6-year-old Crystal pranced around the yard at recess chanting, "This is a swing; this is not a slide." Giggling, she then added silly things as, "This is not a giraffe, this is not a house, this is not a bogey man." How could her teacher use these words to help her resolve a real-life problem? When Crystal tore a child's paper, on purpose, and thought that was funny, her teacher asked, "Is tearing someone's paper a good idea or not a good idea?" Crystal smiled. She understood. A very simple start.

Crystal's teacher added a new word pair the next day—*same/different*. After asking, for example, whether "tapping my knee and stamping my foot are the same or different," two of Crystal's classmates gave their teacher a way to use these words when a real conflict arose. Both insisting that "he hit me first," she asked, "Do you two see what happened the same way or a different way?" These two words proved to be very helpful for Crystal too, when a classmate told her, "Your hair is ugly, you got braids." Checking her natural inclination to give her a good, swift kick, Crystal simply replied, "My hair is different from yours."

Starting at age 5, children enjoy the "Two Things at the Same Time" game. After thinking of two things they can do at the same time, such as "I can clap my hands and talk at the same time," they can then think of two things that they cannot do at the same time, such as "I cannot clap my hands and roll my arms at the same time." One child said, "I cannot hold my nose and breathe at the same time." His teacher found this useful when one child started talking to a neighbor during a lesson, by asking, "Can you talk to your neighbor and listen to me at the same time?" Recognizing the emphasized phrase from the ICPS games, the child smiled, and no more needed to be said.

Playing with the words *before/after*, such as "I brush my teeth after I get out of bed in the morning," or "I cannot brush my teeth before I get out of bed," helps teachers find out what is on children's minds when they are in conflict. Instead of asking the accusatory question, "Why did you hit him?"—usually responded to with shrugged shoulders, an "I don't know," or a lie, an ICPS teacher asked, "What happened before you hit him?" When children associate the emphasized word with ICPS games, they are more likely to talk.

Feelings, Listening, and Paying Attention

Sensitivity to one's own and other's feelings, and listening and paying attention to others are important for problem solving because they open up more options from which to choose. Building on the earlier ICPS word pairs, for example, a child can appreciate that if one way to make someone feel happy is not successful, it is possible to try a different way. Children learn to distinguish happy from proud and angry from frustrated. They learn to ask how other people feel when, for example, they grab a toy or hit a child, and then to identify how they themselves feel. All of these skills are important first steps for later problem solving. In the later grades, children focus on more sophisticated feeling words, such as *disappointed, worried*, and *relieved*.

An activity children enjoy to help sharpen listening skills is what I call the "Silly Skits." Beginning in kindergarten, and building in complexity in the later grades, children are asked to tell what is funny about the conversation between two characters (played by puppets or live actors). For example, in the kindergarten, children hear the following:

A: My knee is bleeding.

B: I like strawberries.

A: I need a Band-aid.

B: Today's my birthday.

A: My knee really hurts.

B: Why does your knee hurt?

A: Because I fell.

B: Oh, you fell.

The skit is re-created, only this time the children are asked to raise their hands when they notice the other character is listening and responding accordingly. Children excitedly raise their hand when they hear B ask, "Why does your knee hurt?" and again, when they hear, "Oh, you fell." Children can make up their own silly skits, and older students write them out, then perform them for the class.

The word pairs, feeling words, and Silly Skits can help a teacher in real life when children are noisy, all talking at once, and not listening when she is trying to settle them down to start a lesson. One ICPS teacher asked, "How do you think I feel when you are all talking and not listening?" Another asked, "Can you all talk to each other and listen to me at the same time?" And a third surprised her class by referring to the Silly Skits when she said, "My knee is bleeding." The children giggled, knew what she was referring to, and quieted down.

Helping children learn to wait is a key ingredient to later social competence and mental health (Goleman, 1995). To help children learn this skill, they enjoy thinking of good and not-good times to do things, such as ask for something—when someone is sleeping, in a bad mood, or coming down from a plane in a parachute. After making up their own good and not-good times to act, children think about, "What can I do while I wait?"

Interpersonal Cognitive Problem-Solving Skills

Alternative Solution Skills

With pictures, puppets, and role-playing techniques, children ages 4 and older name lots of different ways to solve hypothetical problems. The focus is on child-generated different ways rather than adult-valued good ways—to encourage a process of thinking, "There's more than one way to solve a problem. I don't have to give up too soon."

Consequential Thinking: When the children are comfortable generating alternative solutions, a new word pair is added, *might/maybe*, and children are guided to evaluate whether their solution is or is not a good one in light of what might happen next. Children create stories that include conflict situations, how each character feels, what they could do to solve the problem, what might happen next, and if needed, what else they could do so that would not happen.

Means-Ends Thinking: Beginning at age 8, children plan sequenced steps toward a goal (e.g., planning a party to make new friends). With fictional characters, children create a story describing each step and potential obstacles that could interfere with reaching that goal (e.g., it snowed so hard no one could come) and recognize that it might take time to reach the goal (e.g., "He'll wait for better weather and have the party another time.").

Teaching children ICPS skills in isolation is not enough. Our research has shown that to impact behavior, children have to associate how they use their newly acquired ICPS skills when real conflicts come up (e.g., see Shure & Spivack, 1982). We have seen that children do not listen when they are being yelled at, and often they do not even listen to more positive approaches, such as suggesting what they do or even explaining why. Perhaps children already know what we are telling them, so they tune out. Perhaps they do not have the skills to absorb what we say. In any case, suggesting how to solve a problem (e.g., "Why don't you share your toys?") and explaining why (e.g., "You won't have any friends if you grab toys.") is doing the thinking for the child. Placed in the role of passive recipient, children often tune out and do not hear a word we say.

Our approach is different. The children are active participants. They are part of the conversation. Because they are asked to respond, they have to listen; by their response, we know how well they have learned to think the problem-solving way. To do this, teachers are taught how to engage the child through a process I call "ICPS dialoguing." Here is how an ICPS teacher dialogued with Sarah, age 6, who was arguing with a classmate during indoor recess.

Teacher:	What happened? What's the matter? [eliciting the child's view of the problem]
Sarah:	She always goes first!
Carrie:	No, she always goes first.
Teacher:	Sarah, how do you feel about this?
Sarah:	Mad.
Teacher:	And what might happen if you two argue like this? [eliciting consequential thinking]
Sarah:	She won't be my friend.
Teacher:	What can you do so you both won't feel mad and you can still be friends? [eliciting solution thinking]
Sarah:	You go first now; I'll go first later. [using another ICPS word pair]

Teacher: Is that OK with you, Carrie?

Carrie: Yeah.

Teacher: Good thinking. You solved this problem all by yourselves.

What a different outcome than might have occurred had this teacher put the game away, suggested what to do, or even explained why. And in the spirit of ICPS, this teacher did not praise the content of Sarah's solution, but rather, the process. Now Sarah would not be stuck on a solution her teacher liked, should another child refuse the same solution that Carrie embraced.

After the teacher and children are comfortable with the ICPS dialoguing process, they can shorten it to one question, "Can you two think of a different way to solve this problem?" or, still shorter, "Let's ICPS this."

Integration of ICPS Skills Into the Academic Curriculum

To create an association of the ICPS lesson games with academic activities, the interpersonal concepts have been integrated into academic areas, such as math, science, and reading. For example, the feeling words are incorporated into age-appropriate concepts: "Would you feel happier with a whole piece of pizza or half a piece?" "Would you feel more frustrated if your basketball team lost by 222 divided by 111 points minus 75 points, or if they lost by 2 times 60 points minus 105 plus 4 points?" The concept "What might happen next?" is incorporated into science with such questions as "What might happen if you don't feed and water the plants for a month?" and into social studies with such questions as, "What might have happened if George Washington's men didn't show up at the Delaware?" Stories are read with ICPS dialoguing questions, such as "How did (character) feel when . . .?" "How did they solve the problem?" "What happened when they did that?" "Could they solve the problem a different way?" and so forth.

Impact of the ICPS Curricula

From preschool through Grade 6, ICPS curricula could enhance the trained problem-solving thinking skills, reduce and prevent the emergence of impulsive and inhibited behaviors, and promote positive caring and sharing behaviors (Shure & Glaser, 2001; Shure & Spivack, 1982; Spivack & Shure, 1974)—and for those trained in kindergarten and first grade, could create behaviors that were still apparent 3 years after training, in Grade 4 (Shure, 1993). Benjamin, who at age 5 told us, "I don't care" if he got hit, replied, in Grade 4, "I feel sad when I hurt someone. I can try a different way." ICPS-trained youngsters also improved in standardized achievement test scores. Evaluating his own social problem-solving program, Elias et al. (1986) found that trained fifth graders reported less stress and better adjustment to middle school in both the interpersonal arena and in their adjustment to academic requirements. With some integration of interpersonal concepts into the academic arena, it is also possible that perhaps youngsters who are failing in math do not really need more math. Perhaps they need to free themselves of any stress that is preventing them from focusing on the math they are getting.

BUILDINGWIDE CLIMATE TO PROMOTE SOCIAL-EMOTIONAL LEARNING (SEL)

We have found it most effective to start with one or two enthusiastic teachers at the same grade level—a procedure less overwhelming than trying to train a whole school at once. The principal, as well as the school counselor, school psychologist, and other student support personnel who work individually with high-risk children, can apply the ICPS dialoguing process to complement the style of talk the teacher is doing in the classroom. ICPS drawings and stories can be displayed in the hallways or in a school newsletter, which can also provide a vehicle for any adult participating in ICPS to relay his or her successes and failures. A school can select an ICPS Kid of the Day to relay a brief story of how he or she feels or how he or she solved a problem on the loudspeaker in the morning. In this way, the whole school can be included as classrooms fold into the formal training process.

When I asked children why we do ICPS, one sixth grader said, "We have to learn to think for ourselves. People won't always be around to help us." Perhaps SEL programs such as ICPS can lay the groundwork to help children think about problems that are important to them when they are very young, so they can think about problems that are important to them when they reach middle school, junior high, high school, and beyond.

APPENDIX

Samples of ICPS Evaluation Measures (Ages 4 to 7)

The Preschool Interpersonal Problem Solving (PIPS) Test (Shure, 1992d)

Using pictures and standardized probing techniques, the PIPS measures a child's ability to name different, relevant alternative solutions to two types of problems: (a) how to obtain a toy another child has, and (b) how to avert his or her mother's anger after having damaged an object. To maintain interest, different toys are shown after each relevant solution is offered (minimum of 7) and damaged objects are used (minimum of 5). Each child is tested individually for approximately 30 minutes.

The What Happens Next Game (WHNG; Shure, 1990)

Using stick figures and pictures, the WHNG measures the child's ability to name multiple consequences to two types of interpersonal act: (a) grabbing a toy from a peer, and (b) taking an object from an adult without first asking. As in its sister test, the PIPS, different toys and objects taken from an adult are shown after each relevant consequence to maintain interest (minimum of 5 for each situation). Each child is tested individually for approximately 30 minutes.

The Hahnemann PreSchool Behavior (HPSB) Rating Scale (Spivack & Shure, 1971)

The HPSB describes seven teacher-rated interpersonal behaviors, divided into three factor clusters: impulsivity, inhibition, and prosocial behaviors. Youngsters who are rated above the "average child" compared with children who are the same age and gender on impatience (nagging and demanding of adults, inability to wait turn, grabbing of toys from children), emotionality (anger or distress with peers and adults), and dominance-aggression (physical aggression, bossiness, etc.) are classified as impulsive. Youngsters rated at the extreme low end of the scale are classified as inhibited, the rationale being that behaviors that manifest so rarely may signify excessive control of behavior or of feelings, or too much timidity to display even normal amounts of assertiveness. Youngsters not classified as either impulsive or as inhibited are placed into the adjusted category. Positive prosocial items include the degree to which the child is liked by peers and displays awareness or concern for others in distress.

Children's Interpersonal Problem Solving Test (Shure & Spivack, 1985a)

Children are given three interpersonal problem situations (e.g., how to get a friend to stop pestering or bugging the child while he or she is trying to do his or her homework) and asked to list different solutions (maximum of 10 per problem given). Tested individually, each child takes approximately 30 minutes.

Multiple Consequences Test (Shure & Spivack, 1985b)

Children are given solutions to three problem situations (e.g., one child was mad at a friend and decided to tell him or her off) and asked to list different consequences to this act (maximum of 10 per solution given). Tested individually, each child takes approximately 30 minutes.

Means-Ends Problem Solving Test (Spivack, Platt, & Shure, 1985)

Children are given the beginning of a story and the end of the story with an interpersonal goal (e.g., making friends in a new neighborhood) and are asked to "fill in the middle." Scored are the number of different sequenced steps to reach that goal, potential obstacles that could interfere with reaching that goal, and evidence of time (how long it will take) or timing (a good time to act).

Teacher Rating Scale (TRS; Spivack & Shure, 1985)

The TRS consists of 28 items divided into five factors: impulsivity, inhibition, two prosocial factors—one of items describing peer acceptance, the other, quality of peer interaction—and listening and acceptance of another's point of view.

The Parent Component (ICPS for Families)

Based on a series of research studies (Shure, 1993; Shure & Spivack, 1978), the *Raising a Thinking Child Workbook* (Shure, 2000) has been created to provide an interactive set of exercises and games for parents to conduct with their children ages 4 to 7, exercises that teach the same skills the ICPS program teaches at school. Pages for parents are provided with an "ICPS ladder" to easily compare and contrast how they handle problems between themselves and their child (e.g., the child will not clean his or her room), and between two children (e.g., brother torments sister for any reason). Parents can see whether they are on Rung 1 (power techniques—threats, demands, punishment), Rung 2 (positive alternatives/suggestions—"Why don't you ask your brother for what you want?"), Rung 3 (explanations—"You're making your brother angry when you yell at him"), or Rung 4 (problem-solving style of talk—"Can you think of a different way to talk to your brother?").

This workbook, along with the trade book *Raising a Thinking Child* (Shure, 1996) or as a stand-alone, can be used by parents directly or by parent educators. School guidance counselors have found this workbook to be an excellent resource for integrating a parent-involvement initiative in their schools (meeting with a small group of parents once a week for 4 to 6 weeks)—ideal if those children are also receiving ICPS in the classroom.

REFERENCES

Elias, M. J., Gara, M., Ubriaco, M., Rothbaum, P. A., Clabby, J. F., & Schuyler, T. (1986). Impact of a preventive social problem solving intervention on children's coping with middle-school stressors. *American Journal of Community Psychology, 14,* 249–275.

Goleman, D. (1995). *Emotional intelligence: Why it can matter more than IQ.* New York: Bantam Books.

Shure, M. B. (1990). *The What Happens Next Game (WHNG): Manual* (2nd ed.). Philadelphia: Drexel University.

Shure, M. B. (1992a). *I Can Problem Solve (ICPS): An interpersonal cognitive problem solving program (Preschool).* Champaign, IL: Research Press.

Shure, M. B. (1992b). *I Can Problem Solve (ICPS): An interpersonal cognitive problem solving program (Kindergarten/primary grades).* Champaign, IL: Research Press.

Shure, M. B. (1992c). *I Can Problem Solve (ICPS): An interpersonal cognitive problem solving program (Intermediate elementary grades).* Champaign, IL: Research Press.

Shure, M. B. (1992d). *Preschool Interpersonal Problem Solving (PIPS) test: Manual* (2nd ed.). Philadelphia: Drexel University.

Shure, M. B. (1993). *Interpersonal problem solving and prevention: A comprehensive report of research and training* (#MH-40801). Washington, DC: National Institutes of Mental Health.

Shure, M. B. (1996). *Raising a thinking child.* New York: Pocketbooks.

Shure, M. B. (2000). *Raising a thinking child workbook.* Champaign, IL: Research Press.

Shure, M. B., & Glaser, A. (2001). I Can Problem Solve (ICPS): A cognitive approach to the prevention of early high-risk behaviors. In J. Cohen (Ed.), *Caring classrooms/intelligent schools: The social emotional education of young children* (pp. 122–129). New York: Teachers College Press.

Shure, M. B., & Spivack, G. (1978). *Problem solving techniques in childrearing.* San Francisco: Jossey-Bass.

Shure, M. B., & Spivack, G. (1982). Interpersonal problem solving in young children: A cognitive approach to prevention. *American Journal of Community Psychology, 10,* 341–356.

Shure, M. B., & Spivack, G. (1985a). *The Children's Interpersonal Problem Solving (ChIPS) test.* Philadelphia: Drexel University.

Shure, M. B., & Spivack, G. (1985b). *Multiple Consequences (M-CONS).* Philadelphia: Drexel University.

Spivack, G., Platt, J. J., & Shure, M. B. (1985). *Means-Ends Problem Solving (MEPS) test.* Philadelphia: Drexel University.

Spivack, G., & Shure, M. B. (1971). *The Hahnemann PreSchool Behavior (HPSB) rating scale.* Philadelphia: Drexel University.

Spivack, G., & Shure, M. B. (1974). *Social adjustment of young children.* San Francisco: Jossey-Bass.

Spivack, G., & Shure, M. B. (1985). *Teacher Rating Scale (TRS).* Philadelphia: Drexel University.

11

Teaching Preschool Children Coping Skills for Stress Management

Gloria S. Elder and Jennie C. Trotter

In today's fast-paced society, preschool children are faced with more stressors than ever before. They must cope with child neglect, parental difficulties, negative community environmental conditions, and frightening images of war and violence in the media. When stress is overwhelming, children seek relief. One child may act out negatively, whereas another may turn inward. The inability to effectively manage stress can eventually lead to alcohol and other drug abuse, as substance abuse is in part a learned response to stress. Therefore, it is very important to equip children early with skills that help them to cope effectively with the stress in their lives. The results of the lack of positive coping skills for young children can carry over to later years, when statistics indicate a sharp rise in substance abuse, crime, violent acts, and suicide.

The Pre-School Stress Relief Project (PSSRP) is designed to teach children coping skills early so that they are ready to deal with life's stressful events in a healthy manner before the children start to exhibit unhealthy behaviors. PSSRP is an early childhood education program for mental health, coping skills, violence prevention, and substance abuse prevention. It was developed to provide training, consultation, and educational resources in stress management for Head Start, day care, prekindergarten, and public school teachers. The project's goal is to enable teachers to instruct preschool children and primary school students in developing positive coping skills to deal with stress and related changes in their lives. Program procedures have been adapted for use with children with disabilities. The project also provides workshops for parents on stress reduction techniques for families.

Primary prevention is defined as lowering the incidence of emotional disorders by reducing stress and promoting conditions that increase confidence and coping skills (Albee & Gullotta, 1992). However, it is difficult to eliminate stress; what can occur is to teach coping skills to positively deal with it. This incorporates teaching developmentally appropriate skills necessary for forming positive self-images and learning strategies for coping. By teaching decision-making and problem-solving skills and their building blocks, we can help young children more effectively handle the stressors they encounter.

PRESCHOOL THROUGH GRADE 2

The PSSRP curriculum is divided into six lessons and uses videos, hands-on activities, and puppets, including Copee Bear, the mascot for this model program. Copee Bear teaches the children how to cope with feelings, body changes, and stress in their lives. Copee is featured in practically all of the supplemental materials, such as posters, videos, and songs, which make him a favorite of the children.

The curriculum lessons are as follows:

Lesson 1—I Am a Good Person

Lesson 2—Feelings and You

Lesson 3—Your Body Changes With Stress

Lesson 4—Good Ways to Get Anger Out

Lesson 5—Deep Breathing and Relaxation

Lesson 6—Yoga Exercises

The objective of Lesson 1, "I Am a Good Person," is to encourage children to say good or positive things about themselves. Teachers encourage children to think positively and use positive statements, such as "I am smart," "I can pass my test," and "I can control my temper." This helps them visualize a mental picture of what they want to happen, not what they fear.

The objective of Lesson 2, "Feelings and You," is to encourage children to express themselves verbally by using feeling words in a sentence, such as "I felt angry when you broke my toy," "I feel sad when no one plays with me," "I feel scared when I go to the dentist," and "I feel happy because I am having a birthday party."

The objective of Lesson 3, "Your Body Changes With Stress," is to help children recognize how feelings cause changes in the body. In this lesson, children are taught to name and demonstrate a body change. For example, the teacher shows a picture of a sad face and says, "When you feel sad, you might cry, and your eyes get red and swollen, and you make a frown." Then, the teacher demonstrates sad feelings for the children to see; next, the children imitate the sad feeling. Children learn how their body changes when they are happy, sad, scared, or mad and that the latter three are what is meant by "stress."

The objective of Lesson 4, "Good Ways to Get Anger Out," is to encourage children to practice good ways to get anger out. The lesson shows children that they can punch a pillow, count to 10, talk to someone about their angry feelings, go for a walk, or take time out to rest and relax. Positive releases of anger give children time to cool off and let anger out on things, not people.

The objective of Lesson 5, "Deep Breathing and Relaxation," is to help children learn three different kinds of body relaxation: (a) deep breathing, (b) muscle relaxation, and (c) guided imagery relaxation. Children are taught relaxation exercises to use when they feel uptight. The children participate in exercises to relax their bodies through deep breathing, muscle relaxation, and imagery relaxation. Numerous breathing exercises are supplemented with art, science, and manipulative activities, as well as dramatic plays that have children involved in role playing and deep breathing when they are sad, mad, scared, and happy. Age-appropriate muscle relaxation exercises have been developed for children and are demonstrated for children to follow. The relaxation exercises are fun and easy to do and have been integrated into familiar games like Simon Says and Follow the Leader. It is easy to teach children to do positive imagery relaxation because they have great imaginations.

The objective of Lesson 6, "Yoga Exercises," is to teach children exercises that help the body feel better. Children practice different sitting and standing yoga exercises at different times during the day to get stress out of their bodies. For example, children needing to calm down after outdoor play can do the "Monkey" and the "Rooster" exercises.

All of these lessons are of vital importance to stress management, and to reinforce the concepts for the children, supplemental materials to the curriculum include musical puppet videos, songs, puppets, stickers, posters, worksheets, home activity sheets, and story and coloring books. Original songs are included in the lessons to reconfirm the need to take time each day for oneself and the importance of getting plenty of sleep and eating fruits and vegetables.

ADAPTATION FOR USE WITH CHILDREN WITH DISABILITIES

The PSSRP is a process that is flexible and can be modified to be responsive to every child's individuality. The U.S. Department of Education has funded this project to be adapted for use by teachers and parents of children with disabilities. This model project has new and major implications for helping children with disabilities understand stress, how their bodies react to it, and how to positively cope with it. All children are in desperate need of learning constructive ways to cope with stress. Children with disabilities have additional challenges. The PSSRP model helps children with disabilities become stress resilient and have the experience of managing their stress successfully. The significance of this model is the reduction of risk factors and increased positive factors for children with disabilities.

The PSSRP adapted its curriculum to provide stress management training and educational materials to teachers and parents of preschoolers with disabilities to increase their resiliency factors. This revised curriculum is designed to address the application of developmentally appropriate practices related to stress management instruction for children with disabilities. According to standards of the National Association for the Education of Young Children as presented at their Web site (www.naeyc.org), judgments about developmentally appropriate practice must be constructed by teachers in relation to a specific group of children in a specific social and cultural context. Hence, special adaptations for children with disabilities are necessary.

Teachers will need to know their children well, including their learning style, interests and preferences, personality and temperament, skills and talents, successes, and challenges and to provide both individualized and group instruction. The use of various strategies, a variety of materials, and many different learning opportunities suited to the needs of the individual child are desirable.

The objectives, strategies, and materials provided in the PSSRP curriculum form the foundation of skill development. Activities can be modified or enhanced to ensure that objectives of the project are met for all child participants. The goal is to ensure congruence between daily practices and PSSRP activities. Furthermore, current classroom practices, such as deep breathing, positive anger releases, and yoga, that are familiar and effective should be maintained to reinforce children's mastery of concepts.

This model builds a vocabulary for feelings that can be spoken, signed, or presented in symbol form to children with limited language proficiency. In addition, children are impacted by the emotions and feelings displayed by their parents and teacher.

TEACHER TRAINING

A 2-day PSSRP teacher training is offered for preschool programs and elementary schools. It addresses the developmental stages of childhood (birth–12), pointing out to teachers that the age of the child is a factor in determining the child's ability to cope with stress. Other topics covered include understanding learning styles, the art of puppetry, practical application of the curriculum, and early referral for high-risk children.

Teachers see children handling stress in different ways. Two children may respond to a classroom visit from Smokey the Bear (a person dressed up in a bear costume) in different ways. One may be fascinated, and the other terrified. In this situation, the first child might show outward emotions by a smiling face or by jumping up and down with excitement, whereas the other may withdraw and show signs of fearfulness or nail biting. Teachers can help children to understand their happy and scared emotions by talking with children about their feelings and concerns. Allow children to express their own feelings as you listen with an open mind. Let them know that you are concerned about their feelings.

PARENTING

Parent training is also offered, covering similar content and relevant parenting concerns. One parent described how her shy child was brought out and made to feel more confident when dealing with stressful situations after participating in the project. Another parent found the techniques were helpful at home. After attending the workshop, she realized that, at certain times, her son was reacting to stress while she felt he was being obstinate. She then began to cope with his behavior in a more positive way.

Young children are faced with many situations that may be stressful. They can be the excitement of going to a birthday party or receiving a new puppy, coping with family separations, or moving to a new place. These stressors can be positive or negative. Stressors can be the "spice of life," or they can be associated with life's pressures and tensions. Both good and bad stress can cause one's body to respond to change; parents need to understand that this is true even for their young children (and of course for themselves, as well).

Parents can help children learn to cope with stressful situations such as these by preparing the child for change whenever possible. This will give the child time to adjust. Children are sensitive and may sense that changes are occurring and worry even more if they are not properly informed and prepared for change. We remind parents that children are resilient; they can bounce back and handle situations a lot better than we give them credit for. When explaining stressful situations to the child, always be truthful, within what he or she is able to understand. Provide the child with extra security before potentially stressful situations.

We take time to show parents how to help their children to express anger positively. Children have a right to feel angry or upset. Parents need to allow them the opportunity to express these feelings. They can teach children positive ways to release anger, such as to punch a pillow (teaches children to punch soft things that do not hurt themselves or others), count to 10, talk to someone about angry feelings, go for a walk, or take time out to rest and relax. Releasing anger in a positive way gives children time to accept their anger and not hurt themselves and others in the process. The training programs for both teachers and parents also help them learn how to handle their own stress and become familiar with stress management techniques. This, in turn, allows these adults to serve as positive role models for children. Adults are encouraged to provide timely interventions (e.g., coaching and redirection when suitable) and reinforce appropriate child behaviors. Additional techniques taught to parents and teachers can be found in Table 11.1.

THE EVALUATION COMPONENT

Over a 5-year period, the PSSRP trained more than 300 teachers and teacher aides, approximately 600 parents, and more than 4,000 preschoolers in positive coping skills for stress reduction in Georgia's Head Start and metropolitan subsidized day care programs. An outside evaluation by Louis Anderson (1991) led to these results:

1. A significant reduction in symptomatic behaviors exhibited by preschoolers, such as:
   - nail biting,
   - yelling,
   - stomach aches,
   - headaches,
   - temper tantrums.

2. A significant increase in the recognition of different emotions by preschoolers.

3. A significant difference in the preschoolers' recognition of how stress affects the body.

4. An informal teachers' evaluation showed:
   - 100% felt the curriculum had helped the teacher in managing stress in the classrooms,
   - 95% felt that the PSSRP has helped the teacher in managing his or her own stress at school and at home.

5. An informal parents' evaluation showed:
   - 100% of the parents felt that the program had increased their coping skills for stress reduction in their personal lives.

Table 11.1   Additional Stress Relief Strategies That Adults Can Use With Children

Teachers and parents can help children learn to cope with stressful situations as follows:

- Talk with children about their feelings and concerns.
- Allow children to express their own feelings as you listen with an open mind. Let them know that you are concerned about their feelings.
- Praise children for their accomplishments and efforts. Help them develop a sense of self-worth.
- Show affection to reduce the stress in a situation. Remember to say "I love you" and other positive, affirming statements to the child regularly. For example, "You are a good person," "You are beautiful," "You are strong," and "You can do it."
- Examine your own coping skills. Be positive. Teachers and parents should be aware of what coping skills they are modeling for children when they are experiencing stress. When under stress, do you tend to drink more or talk to a friend?
- Plan activities carefully. Do not overschedule a child. Children need time to rest. Do not plan three activities like soccer, swimming, and dance close together.
- Find humor in stressful situations and laugh with the child. Tell jokes and encourage the child to tell jokes to release stress.
- Set clear and consistent limits for the child's behavior. Making rules and setting schedules can create order in a child's life. Following up with consequences makes rules work, and children learn that discipline equals caring.

When persistent, disturbing behavior continues, seek professional help. Asking for help when you need it is a sign of strength. When you are at your wits' end, outside help can be comforting to you and helpful to the child.

INDICATORS USED BY PSSRP TEACHERS FOR ASSESSING STUDENT PROGRESS

The following, from anecdotal reports of teachers and PSSRP staff consultants, have served as indicators of students' progress. They are all based on ongoing observation of children's verbal communication and behavior.

- Through observation, teachers are able to see and hear children talk about their feelings more, rather than yelling, crying, fighting, and so forth. Teachers may notice an increased use of feeling words as children communicate with each other and their teachers. Children's behavior changes include asking for things that they want, rather than taking them. For example, "I feel angry when you take my toy without asking me. I would like for you to ask me for my toy."

• Children should show increased use of the PSSRP supplemental materials during free-play activities. Teachers may display the animal and people puppets in the dramatic play area, for easy use by the children. Children are observed playing with or imitating what is happening with them and talking to the puppets about what is happening in their lives.

• In classes that have set up an "Anger Corner," using the anger bag and the "Nine Good Ways to Get Anger Out," teachers should see more use of these areas and less overt and out-of-control expressions of anger. For example, the Anger Bag contains a pillow for punching, Playdoh to mold and pound, a writing pad, newspaper to tear, rubber or sponge balls for squeezing, a bottle of bubbles for blowing out anger, and a plastic cup for screaming.

With regard to more formal indicators, the PSSRP used the Conners Reading Scale with children who participated in a research project. Teachers completed the scale on the children in the experimental and control groups. For more information regarding the project and the evaluation tools, please contact Carlyle Bruce, PhD, at (404) 299-9373 or e-mail wellsys@wellsyscorp.com.

CONCLUSION

The impact of stressors depends a great deal on our environment, attitudes, and thoughts. It is very important for adults to provide successful experiences for children. This can be accomplished by being aware of their individual differences, strengths, and weaknesses, and by helping them set realistic goals. This helps children build self-esteem, reduces stress, and increases successful coping skills. More important, adults must use the strategies with children throughout a child's period of growth. By starting early, teaching the skills of stress relief will have positive long-term benefits. We trust that you will use this information to help children cope with stress.

REFERENCES

Albee, G., & Gullotta, T. P. (1992). *Primary prevention works*. Thousand Oaks, CA: Sage.
Anderson, L. (1991). *Pre-School Stress Relief Project evaluation research*. Unpublished report. Atlanta: Georgia State University.

12

Morning Meeting

Teaching the Art of Caring Conversation

Roxann Kriete

THE RESPONSIVE CLASSROOM

In the spring of my first year as a teacher in a vocational secondary school, I got a letter from a student for whom I had a particular fondness, letting me know that she was dropping out of school. School was not making much sense to her, and little that she was being asked to learn held much interest. She wrote, almost apologetically, that school just was not a place she felt she belonged. More than 20 years later, her words still seem profoundly sad:

I will always remember how you said "Hi, Sue," as I walked into eighth period. It made me feel like it really mattered that I came.

It touched and pained me that something which seemed so small to me, an act I hadn't even been aware of, had meant so much to her. I vowed to learn something from it and quickly became dedicated to greeting my students. I would station myself by the door and try to say a little something to each one as they entered, or at least to make eye contact and smile at every student, not just the ones like Sue for whom I had an instinctive affinity.

Gradually, I realized how much I was learning at my post by the door. I observed who bounced in with head up and smile wide, whose eyes were red rimmed from tears shed in the girls' room at lunch, and who mumbled a response into his collar and averted his eyes every day for an entire semester. I did not know what to do about much of it, but at least I was learning how to notice.

I have learned a lot since then. It is good for students to be noticed, to be seen by their teacher. But it is only a start, not enough by itself. They must notice and be noticed by each other as well.

Years after I taught Sue, I joined the staff of Greenfield Center School, Northeast Foundation for Children's kindergarten through eighth-grade lab school. There, I saw teachers teaching students to greet each other, to speak to each other, and to listen to each other. I saw students start each day together in Morning Meeting, where noticing and being noticed were explicit goals. Today, children in kindergartens and elementary and middle schools around the country launch their school days in Morning Meetings—a particular and deliberate way to begin the school day.

All classroom members—grown-ups and students—gather in a circle, greet each other, and listen and respond to each other's news. We take note of who is present and who is absent, whether it is it still raining or not, who is smiling and buoyant, and who is having a hard time smiling. We briefly grapple with problems that challenge our minds and look forward to the events in the day ahead. Morning Meeting allows us to begin each day as a community of caring and respectful learners.

MORNING MEETING FORMAT

The Morning Meeting format was developed by Northeast Foundation for Children staff as part of an approach to teaching and learning called the Responsive Classroom. It is an approach informed by belief in seven basic tenets:

1. The social curriculum is as important as the academic curriculum.

2. How children learn is as important as what children learn.

3. The greatest cognitive growth occurs through social interaction.

4. There is a set of social skills that children need to learn and practice to be successful. They form the acronym CARES—cooperation, assertion, responsibility, empathy, self-control.

5. We must know our children individually, culturally, and developmentally.

6. All parents want what is best for their children, and we must work with parents as partners.

7. The principles of the Responsive Classroom must be practiced by educators in their interactions with each other, with the children, and with the parents.

Building on these principles, Morning Meeting is made up of four sequential components and lasts up to half an hour each day. Although there is much overlap, each component has its own purposes and structure. The components intentionally provide opportunities for children to practice the skills of greeting, listening, and responding; group problem solving; and noticing and anticipating. This daily practice in caring conversation gradually weaves a web that binds a classroom together.

1. *Greeting*: Children greet each other by name, often including hand shaking, clapping, singing, and doing other activities.

2. *Sharing*: Students share some news of interest to the class and respond to each other, articulating their thoughts, feelings, and ideas in a positive manner.

3. *Group Activity*: The whole class does a short activity together, building class cohesion through active participation.

4. *News and Announcements*: Students develop language skills and learn about the events in the day ahead by reading and discussing a daily message posted for them.

Teachers who use Morning Meeting must believe in children's capacity to take care of themselves and each other as they learn social skills like respect and responsibility along with academic skills like vocabulary and algorithms. Morning Meeting creates opportunities for children to practice social skills just as they do academic skills. It helps teachers to model these skills and give children valuable feedback, provide practice in respectful behavior, and help children stretch the boundaries of their social world.

The sense of group belonging and the skills of attention, listening, expression, and cooperative interaction developed in Morning Meeting are a foundation for every lesson, every transition time, every lining up, and every upset and conflict, all day and all year long. Morning Meeting is a microcosm of the way we wish our schools to be—communities full of learning that are safe, respectful, and challenging for all.

The following section features Greeting, one of the four components of Morning Meeting. We chose to feature this component because it is the simplest of all the components to implement and the first one taught when teachers are introducing Morning Meeting to their students.

GREETING: A FRIENDLY AND RESPECTFUL SALUTE

"Good morning, Morgan." Hector speaks seriously and earnestly, for that is who Hector is. He looks directly at Morgan, who sits on his left, and offers his right hand.

"Good morning, Hector!" returns Morgan. She grins widely and grasps Hector's hand with exuberance. Morgan's "good mornings" are always punctuated with invisible exclamation points, for that is who Morgan is.

Shannon, on Morgan's left, shifts a bit and sits up taller, ready to receive the enthusiasm of a greeting, Morgan-style. And here it comes. "Good morning, Shannon!" "Good morning, Morgan!" Her teacher smiles, pleased with Shannon's strong voice and firm handshake. Shannon had entered the third-grade classroom in September with a tentative air. Everything about her seemed designed to help her escape the notice of her peers—the acceptable, regulation clothes in quiet colors, her fade-into-the-chair posture, her barely audible voice at meetings. Now, 4 months and more than 70 Morning Meetings later, here she is, wearing a smile almost as broad as Morgan's above her bright purple and red-striped turtleneck, a shirt which will not fade into any school woodwork, her hand extended and waiting for Morgan's.

And so it goes around the circle. Greeting takes slightly less than 3 minutes. Every member of the circle—children, teacher, assistant teacher, and Matthew's mother, who is visiting this morning—has been greeted by name, with a handshake and eye contact.

PURPOSES AND REFLECTIONS

Morning Meetings begin with Greeting. Even on days when there is not time for a full Morning Meeting, teachers convene the circle and make sure Greeting takes place. It is that important because of the tone it sets and the way that tone carries into the rest of the day.

Some mornings, Greeting is simple and straightforward. Variations might be simple, such as students tossing a ball to the student whom they are greeting, or substituting a high five for the handshake. Other mornings, the greeting process is more elaborate or complex, perhaps fanciful. It might be a call-and-response greeting, or a greeting that requires students to offer an adjective describing themselves and beginning with the same letter as their name. Some greetings work with all ages; others have features that make them appropriate only for younger grades or have complex steps better suited to older students.

Long or short, dignified or playful, greetings share four common purposes that are explored in the sections that follow:

- Set a positive tone
- Provide a sense of recognition and belonging
- Help children learn names
- Give practice in offering hospitality

Greeting Sets a Positive Tone for the Classroom and the Day: To greet, according to the Houghton Mifflin, is to "salute or welcome in a friendly and respectful way" (Answers.com, n.d.). Welcoming, friendly, respectful—those are attributes that characterize the climate in exemplary classrooms. Beginning Morning Meeting with a greeting helps create such a climate.

The fact that there is a designated Greeting each day is important. Although there is great room for individual personality to infuse the greeting—Hector's "good morning" is different from Morgan's, which is different from Shannon's—there is also an equity and a safety in having a structure for the greeting. It is unlike the spontaneous, informal way we greet our friends and acquaintances according to our immediate feelings: Our close friends get warm and enthusiastic smiles, maybe even a hug; acquaintances get more neutral hellos; those with whom we struggle to get along may get only a perfunctory nod or perhaps an averted glance.

The goal in Morning Meeting Greeting is for *all* to greet and be greeted equally. In a classroom community, starting a day by hearing your name spoken with respect and warmth is not a privilege that lands on just the popular few. It is, instead, a right to which all are entitled. When we make time for Greeting every morning, no matter how full the schedule, we make a statement as teachers that we expect respect and equity and that we will make sure it happens.

Being Greeted Provides a Sense of Recognition and Belonging That Meets a Universal Human Need: In *The Fifth Discipline Fieldbook* (Senge, 1994, p. 3), Peter Senge tells of the most common greeting among the tribes of Natal in South Africa. The greeting, "Sawu Bona," translates literally as, "I see you." The standard reply is "Sikhona," literally, "I am here." The order of these phrases is important and not variable. One cannot be there until one is seen. The truth of this extends beyond linguistic convention.

My student Sue (whom you met in the beginning of the chapter) went ungreeted and unseen for seven eighths of her day. Unseen, she felt she was not there. Because she was old enough to do something about it, she chose to physically remove herself. Sadly, our classrooms have too many other children who, although physically present, walk through their days feeling unacknowledged and unseen. They feel they are not really there.

I think of the old expression "neither here nor there." It means "unimportant and irrelevant," the opposite of how we want our students to feel. We want them to feel important and relevant. For them to be *here*, they must feel seen. The act of intentional greeting ensures and reinforces our seeing and being seen.

Greeting Helps Children Learn and Use Each Other's Names: To know someone's name and to feel comfortable using it provides powerful options. It lets us call on each other. It is a way we get each other's attention, enabling us to ask a question, to recognize one another in a discussion, to request help, to offer congratulations, or to whisper an apology.

We cannot assume that because students are grouped together that they will learn each other's names. Last year, a colleague returned from meeting with a group of middle school teachers who had asked him to come and speak with them about Responsive Classroom strategies at the middle school level. With fewer than 200 students comprising the seventh and eighth grades, this regional school was not large, although students from several adjacent towns met for the first time in seventh grade. The faculty really wanted to build a sense of community among their students and teachers and had been using a heterogeneous, team-based approach to organize their school for several years.

One of the teachers mentioned in conversation that just the day before he had asked a student in his math class to hand back a set of papers and she could not do it. Why? She did not know all of her classmates' names—could not match the names at the top of the papers with the faces of her peers. It was mid-January, and this was a team of students who had been together in many classes using cooperative learning strategies since September.

A student who does not know her classmates well enough to hand them their work is unlikely to feel familiar enough with them to offer her dissenting opinion about a character in a short story, or admit that she does not quite get this business of "3 is to 21 as x is to 28," or share a poem she wrote about her grandmother. And what a loss that is for her and for her classmates.

Much of our learning happens through social interaction. Knowing names is a fundamental building block for those interactions. It is why name tags at workshops are such a help and one of the reasons why substitute teachers, faced with 25 students they may have never seen before and cannot address by name, often feel so powerless. Naming is often the beginning of knowing.

Hearing our name is also a reminder of our identity, our individuality in the group. As members of a community, we regularly identify with larger groups. Although it is very important that we feel a part of a larger community, it is essential that we retain a sense of ourselves and other group members as individuals as well. Hearing our name lets us know that someone values speaking to us as an individual and wants our attention. Our name allows us to claim authorship when we are proud of what we have created, a stamp that lets the world know we exist and that what we have done matters.

Greetings Give Children a Chance to Practice the Art of Offering Hospitality:

> Hospitality is always an act that benefits the host even more than the guest. The concept of hospitality arose in ancient times when this reciprocity was easier to see: in nomadic cultures, the food and shelter one gave to a stranger yesterday is the food and shelter one hopes to receive from a stranger tomorrow. By offering hospitality, one participates in the endless reweaving of a social fabric on which all can depend. (Palmer, 1998, p. 50)

Welcoming each other to our classroom each day is an act of hospitality. The offering of that welcome, one to another, affirms that we are caregivers of each other in that community. Being a host also implies, builds on, and strengthens a person's ownership and investment in that place.

We practice daily the skills of welcoming with each other—the clear voice, the friendly smile, the careful remembering that Nicholas likes to be called Nick, the firm handshake. When guests visit and are part of our circle, we extend a welcome to them as well, although it can feel a bit awkward at first. "Should we call her Carol or Mrs. DiAngelo?" whispers Andy to his teacher when he notices that his friend Matt's mother is coming to Morning Meeting today. "Could you check with her and see which would feel more comfortable to her?" replies his teacher.

Several important messages are conveyed in that suggestion. First, there is no one right answer to that question in our culture these days. Some parents prefer that children use their first names; others deem it disrespectful. Second, the role of a host is to make the guest feel most respected and comfortable. And third, asking a polite and direct question is a very fine way to get an answer that you need. It is practice in assertiveness seasoned with courtesy, not an easy blend to get right at any age.

Kindergarten teacher Eileen Mariani of Montague, Massachusetts, is proud of a January morning in her room:

The habit of greeting in the Morning Meeting circle had been well established. On that particular morning, it was Isaac's first turn to be Morning Meeting leader. Isaac was a shy boy and had not wanted to be leader for several months after the other children were comfortable with that role. Eileen watched carefully, ready to help if Isaac seemed worried at any point. But, no need, he was doing splendidly.

He had chosen "Good morning, friends" for the Greeting, and it had been clapped and stamped with a nicely modulated glee around the circle, just returning to Isaac, when Isaac glanced up and stood abruptly, heading for the door. Eileen, whose view of the door was blocked by a bookshelf, also rose to survey what was going on. There stood Isaac, framed by the doorway, hand extended to a distinguished-looking visitor who was entering the room with the principal. "Good morning, Mr. . . . uh . . . I'm sorry, what is your name please?" Isaac proceeded to shake the visitor's hand before walking gravely back to his place on the rug to continue the meeting.

The months of modeling and practicing, the discussions of "What can you do if you don't remember someone's name?" had taken hold and enabled Isaac to extend graceful hospitality, not just beyond Morning Meeting with classmates, but even to a stranger at the door. Isaac's extended hand was a true act of welcome and hospitality.

Table 12.1 contains a summary of the highlights of Greeting. The next section provides some practical guidelines for beginning to use Greeting in your classroom.

Table 12.1 Highlights of Greeting

- Ensures that every child names and notices others at the outset of the day
- Allows the teacher to observe and "take the pulse" of his or her group that day
- Provides practice in elements of greetings such as making eye contact and shaking hands
- Requires students to extend the range of classmates they spontaneously notice and greet
- Helps students to reach across gender, clique, and friendship lines that form at particular ages
- Can employ strategies that challenge the intellect (patterns, acquisition of foreign language phrases, set making, calculating fractions)
- Encourages clear and audible speech

GETTING STARTED

Begin by Introducing Greeting

Choosing your language carefully when introducing Greeting establishes expectations from the outset. "We are going to learn to do lots of different *friendly* and *respectful* greetings," states the teacher, before going on to model what she means by those two adjectives.

The teacher turns to Sara and greets her, then asks the class, "What did you notice?"

"You said her name."

"You looked at her."

"You took her hand."

"Sara, what did you notice about the way I held your hand?"

Specific behaviors are noted and named, becoming part of a classroom lexicon. You might write on the chart as you summarize, "So, a friendly greeting means saying a person's name, looking at them, and shaking their hand in a gentle way."

As always, language and focus will vary with the age of the children in the group. With older children, focusing on the "respectful" aspect is often more useful. Even the most entrenched adolescents who argue that who they choose as friends is their own business will acknowledge that all of us are entitled to respectful treatment.

Always begin by modeling and practicing the positive ways of greeting. Then, depending on the makeup of your class, you may want to insert some of the more subtle gestures that children frequently try out. You might mumble a person's name, pump a hand exaggeratedly, or look at the clock while greeting a child. "How did I or didn't I show respect?" The details matter. We know that; they know that. Modeling and discussion helps them know that we know.

Keep Greeting Simple at First

When first introducing Greeting to a group, or at the year's start when a new group is getting to know each other, simple, direct greetings work best. The teacher models Greeting, calling attention to important qualities of the greeting—names spoken clearly, greeter and greeted looking directly at each other, and friendly handshakes and voices. When students are able to fluently go around the circle saying "Good morning" to each other, then it is time to introduce various other greetings.

This example illustrates how Sandra Norried of Washington, DC, a masterful and experienced third-grade teacher, offers her class just the right amount of choice:

For the first weeks of school, Ms. N. had chosen the greeting and now, in October, is beginning to hand that choice over to students. She knows from her years of teaching, however, that too many choices can be as limiting as too few, especially when the year is young. So for this week, the leaders will not choose the greeting itself, but one element of it—a rhythm instrument. Each instrument has been introduced, one per day, and now there are six to choose from.

"Today Sienna will lead our Greeting. Sienna, what will you use?"

Ms. N. hands Sienna a blue crate containing an assortment of rhythm instruments. Sienna studies the possibilities intently for a moment before reaching in to make her choice. Gently, with the slightest of jingles, she produces a tambourine and holds it aloft for her classmates to see. A collective grin spreads around the circle. The tambourine is clearly a favorite of these third graders.

The greetings move clockwise around the circle. After each "Good morning," the greeter shakes the tambourine before passing it to the greeted. Some shake it tentatively and softly; others brandish it above their heads, with extended and elaborated rhythms involving their whole bodies.

This kind of boundary setting helps to define space for learning, something teachers do constantly in their planning—deciding how far apart to place the cones on the play yard for tag games, which books to set out on the Choice Reading Shelf, how many choices to make available for greetings. Ideally, we set boundaries far enough apart that they allow ample room for exploration and experimentation, but not so wide that they allow students to get lost.

Help Students Learn Each Other's Names

Name tags, either prepared ahead by the teacher or made by students, are a great help in the early days of a new group. There are also many games and activities that focus on learning names and are very helpful in the early days. With young children, starting the year with chorus greetings in which everyone says or sings the names together can help the children feel comfortable and help them learn each other's names. When the children are ready to say names individually, making pairs ahead of Greeting so that each is prepared to say a partner's name can help boost children's confidence.

Anticipate and Help Students Handle Awkward Moments

Many greetings require students to choose the person they will greet, rather than simply proceeding around the circle in order. This requires participants to pay attention to remember who has and has not been named. Teachers can help by modeling what to do in those inevitable moments when, despite their best efforts, students cannot remember a name or who has already been greeted. "What can you say if you forget someone's name?" "What can you say if you forget who has been named?" Some teachers work out a signal—such as thumbs up until you are greeted—with their class to help the last few greeters who may be struggling to remember who remains to be greeted.

Implementing and Assessing Progress

The following lists can be used as a guideline for teachers in implementing and assessing Greeting activities in the classroom. Teachers should ensure that they

- organize space in the room so that there is adequate space for a meeting circle,
- teach a variety of age-appropriate greetings,
- model aspects of warm and respectful greetings,
- make sure children use friendly and appropriate words and body language,
- give students opportunities to choose and lead Greetings.

Teachers should also see to it that students

- choose different classmates each day to greet;
- wait for their turn;
- use a clear, audible voice;
- use friendly and appropriate body language and tone of voice.

CONCLUSION

The skills developed by Greeting and by many other components of the Responsive Classroom contribute to students' achievement in a number of ways. Second-grade teacher Barbara Knoblock of New Sarpy Elementary School in Destrehan, Louisiana, speaks specifically of the effects she has seen in her classroom as a result of implementing Morning Meeting for 3 years:

> I think the biggest impact has been on my students' attitudes toward one another. Morning Meeting has made my students much more aware of their language—verbal and body—and how it affects others. Because of this increased awareness, cooperative group activities are more successful now than in the past. The children help each other more willingly, share materials more easily, talk more nicely, and work together more cooperatively to complete an activity. They also like working together. As a result I find that I plan for group work more often. I also notice that the positive and caring atmosphere created by Morning Meeting has given my students the courage to become risk takers. Because they feel safe and known, they are taking more risks in their learning. What more could a teacher want for her students, but to be more positive learners and willing to try new experiences!

More formal evidence is summarized in the Collaborative for Academic, Social, and Emotional Learning's (2003) *Safe and Sound* document at www.CASEL.org. But the message for classroom teachers is the same: Building students' social-emotional skills creates marvelous learning opportunities and deepens the positive experience that schools can and should be for students.

Author's Note: Ongoing information about all aspects of Responsive Classroom and the Northeast Foundation for Children can be found at www.responsiveclassroom.org.

REFERENCES

Answers.com. (n.d.). *Greet*. Available from http://www.answers.com/to%20greet

Collaborative for Academic, Social, and Emotional Learning. (2003). *Safe and Sound: An educational leader's guide to evidence-based social and emotional learning programs*. Chicago: Author.

Palmer, P. J. (1998). *The courage to teach: Exploring the inner landscape of a teacher's life*. San Francisco: Jossey-Bass.

Senge, P. (1994). *The fifth discipline fieldbook*. New York: Doubleday.

13

Raising Healthy Children

School Intervention Strategies to Develop Prosocial Behaviors

Kevin Haggerty and Carol Cummings

Raising Healthy Children is a collaborative project between the Social Development Research Group and 10 elementary schools in a suburb north of Seattle, Washington. Its purpose is to increase protective factors that bond students to school and family. Over the last 30 years, research has documented factors that increase the risk that students will become involved in problem behaviors, as well as those factors that enhance resilience. Longitudinal studies have identified factors that increase the likelihood of these adolescent problems, often called risk factors, and factors that mediate or moderate these risk factors, often called protective factors (e.g., Dryfoos, 1990; Hawkins, Catalano, & Brewer, 1995; Maguin & Loeber, 1996; Newcomb, Maddahian, & Bentler, 1986; Yoshikawa, 1994). Protective factors include social and emotional competence skills, strong bonds to positive socializing influences, and healthy beliefs and clear standards.

We know that teaching social-emotional skills can have a long-term positive effect on academic achievement (Elias, Gara, Schuyler, Branden-Muller, & Sayette, 1991; Hawkins, Smith, & Catalano, 2004). We also know that single-focused skills training programs are not enough (Ennett, Tobler, Ringwalt, & Flewelling, 1994). Programs that teach social-emotional competence in the context of the broader school environment are most effective (Elias et al., 1997; Payton et al., 2000; Zins, Elias, Greenberg, & Weissberg, 2000). As described later, our research suggests that our integrated, broad-based approach to teaching social-emotional skills reduces children's risk of developing problems in adolescence. In this chapter, we provide examples of the essence of Raising Healthy Children, based on classroom process observations of teachers' implementation, and we present ways to use our approaches in your classrooms.

BACKGROUND

We began our project in 1993 with 1,040 first- and second-grade students from 10 elementary schools randomly assigned into either a program or comparison school condition. Project students are currently in 11th and 12th grades. Raising Healthy Children strategies included staff development, parenting workshops, home-based services, and student activities. Raising Healthy Children's comprehensive strategy is briefly outlined in Table 13.1.

Teaching staff at program schools participated in a series of five one-day workshops using a standardized curriculum with five instructional strategies: (a) proactive classroom management, (b) use of effective instructional techniques to motivate at-risk learners, (c) social-emotional skills training, (d) active involvement strategies, and (e) reading strategies. Students were exposed to teachers trained in these techniques throughout Grades 1 through 7.

Staff development was expected to directly increase teachers' skills and, as a result,

- increase students' involvement with teachers and other students,
- increase students' perceived rewards for involvement with school,
- increase students' social and cognitive skills, and
- increase students' bonding to school.

Furthermore, teachers' skill improvement was expected to decrease students' risk factors of early and persistent antisocial behavior, academic failure, and low commitment to school.

Box 13.1 Research Design

This study, conducted by the Social Development Research Group at the University of Washington, compares students from 10 schools that were matched and randomly assigned to program or comparison conditions, resulting in 562 students in the program group and 478 in the comparison group. Teachers, students, and parents were interviewed each year. In addition, teachers were observed twice yearly, and school records were collected.

Teachers participated in three one-day workshops during the year. In addition, teachers met several times during the year to share "hot tips" for teaching and to share where they have experienced success using the strategies from the trainings. Finally, program teachers were visited monthly and received reinforcement for using project-teaching practices. The intervention also provided parent and student intervention strategies that were explicitly designed to reduce risk factors and enhance protective factors. The Raising Healthy Children comprehensive strategies are briefly described in Table 13.1.

Table 13.1   Raising Healthy Children

Comprehensive Program Intervention Components

Intervention Strategy	Intervention Delivered by Whom	Intervention Target
Staff Development Strategy		
Proactive classroom management workshop	Project staff development coordinator, assisted by SHCs	Teachers, assistants, school staff
Social skills teaching		
Reading		
Active involvement		
Motivation		
1:1 teacher coaching visits		
Monthly booster "hot tips" sessions		
Parent Strategy		
Raising Healthy Children—proactive family management (5 two-hour sessions focused on teaching families family management practices)	SHCs and teacher	Parents of first through fourth graders.
How to Help Your Child Succeed in School (5 two-hour sessions focused on effective strategies to help with school success)	SHCs and teacher trainer	First- through third-grade students and their parents
Preparing for the Drug-Free Years (5 two-hour workshops focused on strengthening family bonds)	SHCs and teacher	Fourth- through sixth-grade students and their parents
Moving Into Middle School (5 two-hour sessions focused on social-emotional transitions to middle school	SHCs	Parents of sixth- and seventh-grade students
Building Respect and Responsibility (3 two-hour sessions focused on using the language of respect and emotion coaching)	SHCs	Parents
Home-based services (12 weeks of 90-minute visits using the curricula components listed above as the content base)	SHCs	Parents and students
Monthly *FamilyGram* newsletter	SHCs	Parents and students
Student Strategy		
Social skills training—Using the Get Alongs curricula in Grades 1–4 and integrating them into the literature curricula in Grades 5–7	Project teachers	Students
Summer camp (2-week, half-day sessions focused on social, emotional, and reading skills)	SHCs and school assistants	Students
Tutor training (2 weeks of training for seventh-grade students to prepare them to tutor fourth-grade students	SHCs	Students
Bimonthly *Connections* newsletter	Project staff and students	Students

Note: SHC = school home coordinator; approximately 80% full-time employed for each project-building parenting workshops, staff coaching and support, and home-based services.

A VISIT TO RAISING HEALTHY CHILDREN CLASSROOMS

Perhaps the best way to understand Raising Healthy Children (RHC) is to imagine you visited the classrooms of teachers who have been involved in staff development to learn to better promote a positive social-emotional learning environment in their classrooms. These workshops focus on classroom management practices, social skills teaching, active involvement practices, reading, and motivation. Here is what you might have seen:

Proactive Classroom Management

During the first month of school, as we visited teachers who had attended the RHC staff development training sessions, we found teachers focusing on bonding and connecting activities with their students:

Donna developed a wall mural with every third-grade student's name listed next to information on his or her pets, hobbies, favorite recess activities, favorite foods, and so forth.

Brenda had each of her sixth-grade students create a desk-size, three-dimensional stage. Each day of the first week of school, students brought something from home that introduced themselves to the class, placing the object on their stage. One day they brought something that told about their families; another, something they liked to collect; another, something of which they were proud. Students then did a "gallery tour," walking around and observing the stages of their peers.

Jonathan had seventh-grade students writing in a journal at the beginning of each period, reflecting on his or her "thought for the day." On our visit, students responded to the quote, "You don't have to blow out my candle to make yours burn brighter." Jonathan was working to establish prosocial skills and clear norms for behavior.

These examples demonstrate how the teachers in the study tried to distance themselves from the old cartoon stereotyping of the "brick wall" philosophy of classroom management: "Good morning, children. My name is Miss Applegate. One false move and I'll kill you!" Instead of trying to "win over them," we are trying to "win them over." What sets these classrooms apart from traditional classrooms of past years is the time teachers are spending connecting and bonding with their students. Teachers learned strategies to create a warm, inviting classroom. In addition, teachers developed a plan to teach a proactive management system. This includes identifying the skills students need to know to be successful in their classroom and planning when and how to teach these skills during the first month of school. As one teacher stated, "I found by spending more time teaching management, I've had the best year ever." Proactive classroom management strategies were aimed at establishing a learning environment that both promoted appropriate student behavior and minimized disruption to classroom activities.

Emphasis on work requirements was another common strategy teachers implemented during the first week of school, based on the staff development sessions. Students were taught how to keep an assignment sheet, and all assignments were posted in classrooms. Specifically:

Students in Steve's sixth-grade classroom recorded their pretest and posttest scores in their own three-ring binder. This served as a reminder that "success is improvement, not perfection."

After Jalynn taught her management system to her seventh-grade students, their first quiz was on class expectations. "What happens to your grade if your dog eats your homework and you don't turn it in?" "What is the first thing you do at the beginning of every class?"

In Linda's sixth-grade classroom, notebooks were checked weekly, and points were awarded for organization.

During staff development sessions, teachers learned that bonding and connecting applied to parents as well. Strategies to connect with parents and broaden support of expected behaviors outside the classrooms were practiced by project teachers. We observed one of our middle school core teams that sent home a *Core Team Times*. The first issue asked parents to answer questions designed to help the team provide the best possible learning experience for their child. Questions included: What do you see as your student's strengths in school? What do you see as your student's greatest challenge? How can we help in these areas? What goals or expectations do you have for your student in the seventh grade?

To maintain close contact with parents, Trish and Dean invited the parents of their sixth graders to a monthly meeting at which curriculum issues, adolescent behavior issues, and general questions were addressed.

Social-Emotional Skills

To promote the integration of social-emotional skills teaching in the classroom, units developed for eight social-emotional skills were made available to teachers at staff development sessions. The units were designed to assist in direct instruction, practice, reinforcement, and generalization of skill use in the classroom. The units were used with the Get-Alongs (Cummings, 1996), a series of interpersonal and problem-solving skills books for children in the primary grades that were integrated with reading units. The unit components and activities, however, are applicable to the upper grades as well. Each unit takes approximately 1 month to teach: 45 minutes for the first day and 5 to 10 minutes of short practice activities for the following days. The eight units included listening, problem solving, tattling versus reporting, sharing, learning anger management, giving compliments (put-ups), recognizing feelings, and learning manners.

As students develop, interpersonal and problem-solving skills were integrated into literature and social studies. When selecting readings, teachers chose from a variety of great literature that provided models of self-discipline, problem solving, respect, and responsibility. Their reading material provided the opportunity to reinforce what appropriate behavior looked like and how to recognize it in context. Extension activities helped students apply the lessons and behaviors to their own lives. Each of the project schools used readings from William Bennett's *Book of Virtues*. The book provides relevant literatures organized around themes.

Assessing student skill level was an important task for teachers. We invited teachers to assess students in their skillful behavior (see Figure 13.1). This provided teachers the opportunity to identify and prioritize which skills they would emphasize and directly teach. Teachers assessed the percentage of class members demonstrating specific skills. Those classrooms with less than 50% of the students demonstrating the skill had a need for priority direct instruction.

Figure 13.1

Social-Emotional Learning Skill	Not Developmentally Appropriate for My Grade Level	No Students Have This Skill	Less Than 50% Have This Skill	More Than 50% but Less Than 80% Have This Skill	80% or More Have This Skill	Skill Was Taught Directly	Skill Is Frequently Reinforced	Ranking
Listening and following directions								
Recognizing feelings								
Working together and sharing								
Having manners and civility								
Giving compliments and encouragement								
Problem solving								
Using anger management								
Refusing								

Report Card

This report card has a place for both teacher and student evaluation. It provides the opportunity for both to rate students' behavior and skills. Students rate themselves with 1 = *I'm developing this area*, 2 = *I am good at this*, or 3 = *I am skillful at this*.

Behavior	Student	Teacher
I express my emotions appropriately.		
I use anger control strategies.		
I have a positive attitude.		
I plan carefully.		
I am able to resist impulsive behavior.		
I show concern for others' feelings.		
I am helpful to others.		
I get along with my classmates.		
I contribute and do my share of group work.		

SOURCE: Adapted from Cummings (2000).

Cummings (1996) suggested that a typical lesson for teaching a skill is similar to teaching other content areas and includes the following:

- Mental set (providing the objective and reason for learning); some call this the WIFM (What's In It For Me?)
- Input (providing the necessary information students need about the skill and breaking the skill into small steps)
- Model (provide an example of what the skill looks like)
- Guided practice and check for understanding (providing opportunities to role-play skillful behavior in a variety of situations)
- Independent practice (students perform the skill without direct teacher supervision in the classroom and on the playground)

Listening was the social skill picked by most of our teachers for the first month of school. "Before you can listen to learn, you must first learn to listen." Teachers at Cedar Way Elementary posted a chart with the mnemonic we provided for the steps in active listening:

F = Face the speaker

O = Organize (what is being said)

C = Connect (what is being said to what you already know)

U = Use questions (if you are confused or do not understand)

S = See a picture (of what is being taught)

As they move further into the school year, Cedar Way teachers would simply request, "Focus, please" and students knew both the physical and mental components of active listening.

Creative room arrangements find students facing the teacher for directed instruction, yet facilitate easy transitions into partner or group work when necessary. Dana, a science teacher, commented that her students found rows easiest during "lecturette" time, and then shifting desks into foursomes worked best for lab work. It was easy for students to engage in distracting side conversations when they were always in a team, some with their sides or backs to the teacher. During independent seat work, "privacy screens" were created by students at Cedar Way to help them focus. Again, teachers were surprised at how many students preferred to use their screen when working alone to filter out distractions.

Active Involvement

Following staff development workshops in October, visits to teacher's classrooms highlighted active involvement strategies. Idealistic as it may seem, the goal was for 100% active involvement consistently in the lesson. In addition to learning cooperative structures in staff development sessions, teachers learned that meaningful involvement includes movement, novelty, and purposefully engaging the emotions. Students were taught questioning strategies that produced deeper levels of comprehension.

In lieu of questioning that begins with "Who can tell me the answer to this question?" teachers were trying a "think-pair-share" strategy. Jalynn said she consciously redesigned her seventh-grade daily-oral-language work with this in mind. Now her students correct the sentences on their sheet (think), explain their corrections to a partner (pair), and then share the correct answers with the whole group.

Working diligently on their pumpkins, Anne had seventh-grade students demonstrate their understanding of longitude and latitude by drawing lines on a pumpkin—much more exciting and realistic than using a two-dimensional worksheet!

Jamie enhanced vocabulary study by having seventh-grade students act out the vocabulary word (from a list of action verbs) while the rest of the class picked the word and wrote it on their think pad.

Donna combined social skill study with an involvement strategy called "carousel brainstorming." Every 4 minutes, teams of sixth-grade students rotated to a new station to brainstorm answers on large chart paper. Questions included "How do you deal with anger?" "How can you disagree in a nice way?" "How can you encourage others?" "How do you listen to others?"

Reading Strategies

Because reading is strongly related to verbal skills and, consequently, academic success (Slavin, 1990), effective reading strategies were taught. Systematically assisting students with basic reading skills has been shown to improve reading performance while decreasing disruptive classroom behaviors and improving students' social-emotional skills (Coie & Krehbiel, 1984).

Using literature clubs to turn reading into a social event was a favorite strategy for many of our intermediate teachers. Students in Claudia's fifth-grade class wrote letters to her describing the types of books they liked to read. Clubs were organized around like interests. Students prepared for their meeting using Post-it notes to locate certain pages that they wanted to share with their peers.

Although Claudia's clubs met at the same time daily, Margaret had one club meet at a time. She used this time for minilessons and assessment while the remainder of the fifth-grade class used the time to read and prepare for their club meeting. Completion of the reading assignment was the "admission ticket" to the club meeting. District standards were satisfied with the assignment of roles for each club meeting: the story mapper, the word finder, the performer, and the question writer.

The teaching of reading not only provided opportunities to increase bonding and practice social skills, it was also a natural catalyst for the integration of social-emotional skill teaching. In addition to the direct instruction of social-emotional skills, characters in novels were analyzed for their social competence.

Students filled out report cards for the characters Matt and Attean (in *Sign of the Beaver*), grading both characters on self-motivation, empathy, self-awareness, mood management, and general social skills.

Analyzing problem-solving skills used by the characters in *The Cay* produced rich classroom discussions.

Word walls featuring "emotional" words found in students' readings were developed in several classrooms to build social-emotional vocabulary.

Motivation

Teachers incorporated instructional practices that motivated students from the staff development workshops. These practices included using strategies to provide content relevant to students' lives, providing more choices for students, and encouraging internal attributions for success. Teachers were challenged by the fact that some techniques may increase effort (motivation) for some students yet undermine motivation for others. We saw evidence of motivational teaching strategies when we observed the following:

Diane demonstrating her knowledge of the value of immediate and specific feedback by having her fifth-grade students self-correct their homework.

Trish having sixth-grade students work in numbered teams to solve problems related to the sundial using novelty and collaboration as motivational tools. Teams waited in anticipation to present their answer as she used a spinner on the overhead projector to select the next team to respond.

Teri's fifth-grade students worked daily with a reading buddy and practiced story retelling and "paragraph shrinking" with each other. Teri used a timer for each segment to increase focus and accountability.

SCHOOLWIDE IMPLEMENTATION

A schoolwide focus on staff development has encouraged many of the RHC schools to adopt a schoolwide "skill-of-the-month" to further enhance the implementation of social skills teaching. For example, at Hazelwood elementary, the student body representatives created videotaped vignettes of the skill-of-the-month. The vignettes were broadcast to each classroom as part of the direct instruction of the new month's skills. This schoolwide focus on social skills was designed to foster and support schoolwide change. The schoolwide focus created a climate of consistency across teachers and staff and provided wonderful opportunities for schoolwide reinforcement, from the classroom, to the lunchroom, to the playground. In addition, the focus on the monthly social skill clearly defined the standards of behavior for the entire school and reduced problem behaviors.

HOW TO APPLY THIS TO YOUR CLASSROOM

The work of RHC suggests a variety of ways you can systematically enhance social-emotional competencies in your classrooms:

- Use classroom management practices.
- Teach work requirements and self-management skills.
- Provide a safe and caring classroom community.
- Bond and connect with students.
- Use a responsibility, not obedience, model of discipline.
- Teach social skills.
- Directly instruct on social skills.
- Practice role-playing social skills.
- Integrate social decision making into the curriculum.

- Align social skills teaching with district goals.
- Use selected literature in the curriculum to reinforce and recognize skillful behavior.
- Reinforce and reward prosocial behavior.
- Teach active involvement and cooperative learning.
- Design strategies to consistently, not eventually, involve all students.
- Use cooperative structures to practice prosocial skills.
- Align involvement strategies with district goals to enhance academic achievement.
- Use reading strategies.
- Provide a balanced reading program.
- Teach reading skills at the appropriate level of difficulty.
- Improve reading skills by providing more time to read.
- Motivate students in differentiated ways.
- Provide more opportunity for student choice.
- Build internal attributions for success: "I worked hard and it paid off."
- Connect the curriculum to students' lives.

DOES THIS APPROACH WORK?

In our earlier research, we found that staff development in these topic areas resulted in significant changes in students who were exposed to teaching practices that enhance social-emotional learning. The significant changes included

- increased positive attachment to family and school,
- increased scores on standardized achievement tests,
- decreased aggression for boys,
- decreased suspensions and expulsions,
- decreased drug use initiation, and
- decreased delinquent behavior (Hawkins, Catalano, Kosterman, Abbott, & Hill, 1999; Hawkins et al., 1992).

Early research analyses from the RHC staff development program show promise for increasing social and emotional competence after 1.5 years of intervention (Catalano, Mazza, Harachi, Abbott, & Haggerty, 2003). We found that students in the program schools, compared with students in comparison schools, displayed significantly

- higher social competence,
- higher levels of social interaction,
- higher levels of age appropriate behavior,
- higher commitment to school,
- higher academic performance,
- more age appropriate learning, and
- less antisocial behavior.

In addition, independent teacher observations found higher levels of social skills teaching and reinforcement in experimental classrooms than control classrooms

(Harachi, Abbott, Catalano, Haggerty, & Fleming, 1999). Finally, not only have we seen the reduction of risk factors and an increase in protective factors for students in the early years, but as students have aged, we have also found a significant decrease in substance-using behavior in students from the program schools compared with students from the control schools (Brown, Catalano, Fleming, Haggerty, & Abbott, n.d.)

CONCLUSION

This chapter describes a social development approach to positive youth development and preventing problem behaviors. The elementary and intermediate school interventions seek to increase academic success and to prevent a variety of adolescent health and behavior problems by enhancing developmentally specific protective factors and reducing developmentally salient risk factors. The school intervention focused on what teachers can do in their classrooms to both enhance social-emotional learning and protection while reducing risks. We are encouraged by the early findings. The findings demonstrate again the importance of schoolwide, developmental prevention efforts. This research brings us closer to better understanding what specific teaching behaviors are needed to enhance positive youth development through social-emotional learning.

Authors' Note: Ongoing information about all aspects of Raising Healthy Children can be found at www.sdrg.org.

REFERENCES

Brown, E. C., Catalano, R. F., Fleming, C. B., Haggerty, K. P., & Abbott, R. D. (n.d.). *Adolescent substance use outcomes in the Raising Healthy Children Project: A two-part latent growth curve analysis.* Manuscript submitted for publication.

Catalano, R. F., Mazza, J., Harachi, T. W., Abbott, R. D., & Haggerty, K. P. (2003). Raising healthy children through enhancing social development in elementary school: Results after 1.5 years. *Journal of School Psychology, 41,* 143–164.

Coie, J. D., & Krehbiel, G. (1984). Effects of academic tutoring on the social status of low-achieving, socially rejected children. *Child Development, 55,* 1465–1478.

Cummings, C. (1996). *The get alongs.* Edmonds, WA: Teaching.

Dryfoos, J. G. (1990). *Adolescents at risk: Prevalence and prevention.* New York: Oxford University Press.

Elias, M. J., Gara, M., Schuyler, T., Branden-Muller, L. R., & Sayette, M. A. (1991). The promotion of social competence: Longitudinal study of a preventive school-based program. *American Journal of Orthopsychiatry, 61,* 409–417.

Elias, M. J., Zins, J. E., Weissberg, R. P., Frey, K. S., Greenberg, M. T., Haynes, N. M., et al. (1997). *Promoting social and emotional learning: Guidelines for educators.* Alexandria, VA: Association for Supervision and Curriculum Development.

Ennett, S. T., Tobler, N. S., Ringwalt, C. L., & Flewelling, R. L. (1994). How effective is drug abuse resistance education? A meta-analysis of Project DARE outcome evaluations. *American Journal of Public Health, 84,* 1394–1401.

Harachi, T. W., Abbott, R. D., Catalano, R. F., Haggerty, K. P., & Fleming, C. (1999). Opening the black box: Using process evaluation measures to assess implementation and theory building. *American Journal of Community Psychology, 27,* 711–731.

Hawkins, J. D., Catalano, R. F., & Brewer, D. D. (1995). Preventing serious, violent, and chronic juvenile offending: Effective strategies from conception to age six. In J. C. Howell, B. Krisberg, J. D. Hawkins, & J. J. Wilson (Eds.), *A sourcebook: Serious, violent, and chronic juvenile offenders* (pp. 47–60). Thousand Oaks, CA: Sage.

Hawkins, J. D., Catalano, R. F., Kosterman, R., Abbott, R., & Hill, K. G. (1999). Preventing adolescent health-risk behaviors by strengthening protection during childhood. *Archives of Pediatrics & Adolescent Medicine, 153,* 226–234.

Hawkins, J. D., Catalano, R. F., Morrison, D. M., O'Donnell, J., Abbott, R. D., & Day, L. E. (1992). The Seattle Social Development Project: Effects of the first four years on protective factors and problem behaviors. In J. McCord & R. Tremblay (Eds.), *Preventing antisocial behavior* (pp. 139–161). New York: Guilford.

Hawkins, J. D., Smith, B. H., & Catalano, R. F. (2004). Social development and social and emotional learning. In J. E. Zins, R. P. Weissberg, M. C. Wang, & H. J. Walberg (Eds.), *Building academic success on social and emotional learning: What does the research say?* (pp. 135–150). New York: Teachers College Press.

Maguin, E., & Loeber, R. (1996). Academic performance and delinquency. *Crime and Justice: A Review of Research, 20,* 145–264.

Newcomb, M. D., Maddahian, E., & Bentler, P. M. (1986). Risk factors for drug use among adolescents: Concurrent and longitudinal analyses. *American Journal of Public Health, 76,* 525–530.

Payton, J. W., Wardlaw, D. M., Graczyk, P. A., Bloodworth, M. R., Tompsett, C. J., & Weissberg, R. P. (2000). Social and emotional learning: A framework for promoting mental health and reducing risk behavior in children and youth. *Journal of School Health, 70,* 179–185.

Slavin, R. E. (1990). *Cooperative learning: Theory, research, and practice.* Englewood Cliffs, NJ: Prentice Hall.

Yoshikawa, H. (1994). Prevention as cumulative protection: Effects of early family support and education on chronic delinquency and its risks. *Psychological Bulletin, 115,* 28–54.

Zins, J. E., Elias, M. J., Greenberg, M. T., & Weissberg, R. P. (2000). Promotion of social and emotional competence in children. In K. M. Minke & G. C. Bear (Eds.), *Preventing school problems—Promoting school success: Strategies and programs that work* (pp. 71–99). Bethesda, MD: National Association of School Psychologists.

14

Social Decision Making/Social Problem Solving

A Theoretically Sound, Evidence-Based Framework for Social-Emotional Learning in the Classroom

Linda Bruene Butler and Victoria Poedubicky

Students stream into Mr. Ahmad's class after recess, and one of his fourth-grade boys approaches him and says that he needs to have a Sharing Circle. This amuses and intrigues Mr. Ahmad, who simply says, "OK. Go ahead."

In a serious manner, the boy and three of his classmates rally their class to place chairs in a circle. Sharing circle rules and feeling word lists are prominently displayed as the young boy begins asking the group, "What was the problem on the playground today?" Passing an object around the circle and not speaking until it reached them, children begin recounting the problem. Using the feelings list on the wall to find words to accurately describe what they are feeling, children then begin to share how the problem made them feel. Mr. Ahmad sees one boy stand and point to the words *upset*, *confused*, *disappointed*, and *angry*, and then sit down to say more.

The children move the problem into a goal, with a list of solutions to help them reach their goal. After some discussion of the pros and cons of their ideas, the boy who asked for the circle asks the class to vote on the solution that they want to try first. After about 10 minutes, the students get up and move their chairs back to their seats, and the boy who called for the Sharing Circle says to Mr. Ahmad, "OK, we're done."

Mr. Ahmad reflected later that he was delighted and amazed how students so young had the ability to transfer and use the skills and tools that they have been using in Social Decision Making/Social Problem Solving (SDM/SPS) lessons in real-life situations. "These students surpassed my expectations," he remarked. He added that this was a wonderful example of what can happen when we program for the internalization of skills through continuous, coordinated instruction. Because his students had been practicing these skills for more than 2 years—since they were in second grade—they are able to own and use these skills in real-life situations, and that has always been the goal.

How was Mr. Ahmad's class able to get to this point? What skills and lessons needed to be taught for his students to take such ownership? What would need to be put into place for this to happen? How can your students develop the skills needed to independently demonstrate good decision making and sound character in their daily lives?

To answer these questions, we will visit Mr. Ahmad's school. His school, which we will call Schuyler School, is a demonstration site for the New Jersey Center for Character Education, at the Center for Applied Psychology at Rutgers University. The district was chosen as a demonstration site because, before it was a designated a model, it had been engaged in a multiyear effort to develop and integrate curriculum-based programming to promote students' social-emotional skills and extend the application of these skills throughout all aspects of the school day. Before we begin our visit, let's get some background. What is the nature of social-emotional learning (SEL)/emotional intelligence programming? What does it take to put it in place?

THE FOUNDATION

The short answer to these questions is that the steps that need to be taken are those outlined in two publications: *Promoting Social and Emotional Learning: Guidelines for Educators* (Elias, Zins, et al., 1997) and *Safe and Sound: An Educational Leader's Guide to Evidence-Based Social and Emotional Learning (SEL) Programs* (CASEL, 2003). In practice, the pathway to students being able to achieve the social-emotional skill level that Mr. Ahmad's class has shown begins by a classroom or school adopting a research-validated SEL program as an organizing framework. In adopting methods with tested guidelines for implementation, Schuyler School began with an "informed base" for developing a program. The focus at the district and classroom levels is to adopt and adapt these tested tools to the unique priorities and needs of the student and community.

An SEL leadership team composed of administrators, teachers, special-education teachers, child study team members, and administration and parent representatives made a decision to adopt the SDM/SPS program. They chose this program because its objectives matched the mission of the school district to teach students sound character and critical thinking skills. They also liked the fact that the targeted skills could be applied flexibly to a wide range of problems and decisions that naturally occur in academic content areas and could address unique student and community needs. This flexibility allows staff to sustain programming despite administrative changes that inevitably occur.

SDM/SPS MODEL

The overriding goal of the SDM/SPS model is to provide students with experiences they need to develop the ability to think clearly and make responsible prosocial decisions, even when under stress.

For any skill or skill set to be accessible under stress, it must be "overlearned," or internalized to the extent that it becomes automatic (Elias & Bruene Butler, 1999). Research has found that best practices for teaching social-emotional competencies involve first using direct, formal, constructivist-oriented instruction and practice in a skill, and then combining this with ongoing opportunities to practice and apply the skills taught in many diverse situations (Elias, Zins, et al., 1997). The social-emotional and cognitive skills needed to make clear decisions in life are similar to any other complex and integrated skill area, such as driving a car, riding a bike, or participating in a competitive sport. Comparing this to the teaching of skills needed to play soccer or instrumental music, for example, players or musicians are taught various individual skills prior to applying skills in a game or in a concert. Players overlearn skills through repetition and drill, both off the field or stage and on. Social-emotional skills that are needed in the game of life also need this level of training if they are to be internalized to a point where they are accessible for use in new, complex, or challenging life situations.

A critical aspect of the SDM/SPS model is training teachers to combine curriculum-based skill-building lessons with plans for ongoing, infused opportunities for students to practice the skills being taught in academic content areas and life situations in and out of school (Elias & Bruene Butler, 2005). The latter is equivalent to soccer players or musicians putting their skills to work in the actual game or concert.

The heart of the instructional design of the SDM/SPS model is providing students with both direct instruction and repeated practice in an eight-step decision-making process with the mnemonic of FIG TESPN (identify **F**eelings, **I**dentify the problem, **G**oal setting, **T**hink of solutions, **E**nvision consequences, **S**elect the best solution, **P**lan it/try it, and **N**otice what happens—pronounced "Fig TESS-pin").

But, as with any other content area, the ability to think critically depends on content knowledge. For example, how can children think about the decisions that a president makes without content knowledge about how the laws and structure involved in a democracy work? The same is true for social and emotional literacy. Because of this, another critical component of the SDM/SPS model is systematic training on social-emotional skills. The social-emotional skills targeted were identified through research differentiating children with the ability to establish acceptable and productive relationships with other people from those who are not able to do so in their peer relationships.

Students first learn a set of concrete skills for working in a group and skills for identifying and regulating feelings in themselves and in others. These skills are tools that help them to be more rational and informed social problem solvers and decision makers.

Skills are systematically taught and labeled with skill prompts that provide a consistent language for calling on the skills and reinforcing their use in the classroom and throughout other aspects of the school day. First, we will visit a few classrooms to see what this looks like in action. Then we will take a look at how the program works at the school-building level to extend and deepen classroom-based skill-building efforts.

SYSTEMATIC SKILL BUILDING IN THE CLASSROOM

Let's start our visit by taking a look at Mr. Ahmad's class as he reviews a skill that he taught on the first day of class. He is reviewing the skill of *Listening Position*. Listening Position is a skill that teaches children to stay focused on the speaker and on task. By demonstrating the skill when asked, students become able to access the skill on their own at the appropriate time (during instruction or teaching time, etc.). Helping students to understand the "why" of a lesson is an important aspect of building a skill. Mr. Ahmad has now invited his class to play a round of Simon Says. Take note of the processing questions that follow the game.

"Okay class, we are going to play Simon Says. This is not a high-stakes game, so I'm going to ask that if you are out to please sit down. You may still play the game in your seat, but I'd like for you to sit down. Are you ready?" The game is played like Simon Says, with Mr. Ahmad saying "Simon says 'Pat the top of your head.' Simon says 'March up and down.' Simon says 'Pat your tummy.'" He says, "Do this," pointing to and doing a variety of movements. Students are reminded to sit if they "do" a movement when Simon didn't say. When there are about four students left, Mr. Ahmad asks them to sit and tells them the game is now over.

During the processing of the game, Mr. Ahmad asks his class "What did you need to do to stay in the game?" Children answer, "Keep my eyes on the teacher," "stay focused," "be quiet," and "listen for what Simon said to do." "OK, we are going to try the game again. This time, remember to use Listening Position and the other ideas you heard your classmates mention, to help you stay in the game longer."

Classes invariably do better the next time, and the time after that. With occasional repetition, listening improves in other areas of classroom life. After each practice, Mr. Ahmad processes and then makes connections to learning in class. He elicits from students the ideas that these are the very things they need to do to be good students. They need to be focused on the teacher or whoever is speaking, not talk, and remember the rules that apply to the situation. These questions answer the "why" questions many students have in regard to learning a skill or a subject area lesson. At various times during every school day, he ask students, "Are you in good Listening Position?"

Building a skill is a six-step process:

The first is to introduce the skill. "Today we're going to learn a skill called Listening Position."

Second, motivate the learners by giving them a reason why learning the skill will benefit them. Mr. Ahmad used the game of Simon Says to engage and motivate students in reviewing the skill of Listening Position.

Third, present and model the behavioral components of the skill and explore examples of not using the skill. Mr. Ahmad showed the class what a good

Listening Position looked like and what a poor one looked like. Through the processing of Simon Says, the students explored firsthand what might happen if they became inattentive (they would have to sit out the game).

Fourth, Mr. Ahmad provides opportunities for students to practice and provides performance feedback. He compliments students who demonstrate the skill properly and reminds those who do not of what they need to do.

The fifth step is to give the skill a prompt or cue phrase, which in this case is "Listening Position."

The sixth step shows Mr. Ahmad using the cues for practice at the start and end of each class, including allowing students to identify groups that are demonstrating good Listening Position as a criterion for who gets dismissed first.

Now, let us move down the hall to the health class, where we can observe another example of systematic skill building.

Ms. Brodka's Health Class

As we walk into this lesson, we find that students are learning to become self-aware of feelings triggered by stressful situations. Students are learning how to identify physical signs of feelings that signal that a strong emotion has been triggered (set off) by an event. The following line of questions lead children to understanding why this skill is essential. Ms. Brodka asks, "How do you feel when someone calls you a name?" "Upset," "angry," and "sad," different children respond, each taking turns holding a "Speaker Power" object. "Great! Where in your body do you feel upset, angry, and sad? For example, when I'm angry, my face gets hot or sometimes my head hurts." Once again, hands go up, and the object is given to a boy named Shaun. "I feel it in my hands—they clench up!" Another boy, Sal, waits to receive the object and then says, "I feel it in my head—it pounds!" "This is excellent," exclaims the teacher. "Now what do you do to make those physical signs go away and feel better?" Shaun says that he sometimes hits people with his clenched hands, and Sal says that he yells out mean things to people when his head hurts. "And do you feel better?" "No, I get in trouble."

Ms. Brodka next teaches the class a way to calm their emotions. It is a skill called *Keep Calm* from the SDM/SPS curriculum (Elias & Bruene Butler, 2005). She models the skill by breathing in for 5 seconds, holding for 2 seconds, and then exhaling for 5 seconds. She repeats the skill several more times, slower each time. Next, she asks the class to practice it with her. Handing the object once again around the class, she asks students to tell how they felt as they did the Keep Calm skill several times. Ms. Brodka then shows the class her Keep Calm area where students can go when they need to calm down.

Mrs. Fehn's Math Class

Looking in now on a fifth-grade class, we can see Mrs. Fehn preparing a class for a math test. She is standing before the class and is asking her students to take a deep breath, hold it, and then exhale. They are doing the same skill of Keep Calm, however this time, it is to prepare the students to take their test. Mrs. Fehn has found that many of her students freeze up on tests, and many perform poorly due to anxiety about test taking. Consistent practice—plus the fact that many of these students have learned and practiced this skill for at least 2 or 3 years—makes it easier for each student to become calm and more able to perform proficiently for tests. This is true for classroom unit tests as well as high-stakes standardized tests. Her class is beginning to transfer the skill of Keep Calm to academic situations in which they might become stressed.

OVERLEARNING SKILLS AND CONCEPTS IN THE CLASSROOM

In health class, two skills were demonstrated from the SDM/SPS curriculum. Speaker Power, which is a visual object passed to students to speak or share questions or answers in class, reinforces the character trait of respect. Speaker Power is controlled at first by the teacher. After practice and classwide success, the class may take control of the object, passing it among themselves, reinforcing the criteria for receiving the power to speak and developing respect for the speaker.

The other skill demonstrated in both the health class and in the fifth-grade class was Keep Calm. Keep Calm is a skill that helps children learn to regulate their emotions in stressful situations. When they are able to perform Keep Calm properly, they will become more rational decision makers and problem solvers in social situations, especially when under pressure. This skill is prompted on a regular basis by a teacher or any other adults in the building (or other students who are part of the "Keep Calm Force") when a child exhibits physical signs of upset feelings. As multiple adults in the school environment use and reinforce the same prompts and cues over time, students' overlearning of skills is more likely. This is likely what accounts for the SDM/SPS program's consistent findings of generalization to everyday academic and social behavior.

Once skills (in this case, Speaker Power and Keep Calm) are taught in the context of formal lessons, they are then integrated into many areas of a student's school day for continued practice. Speaker Power and Keep Calm can be applied while learning lessons in health, while learning in the regular classroom, when students are participating in group work, or even during a disagreement on the playground, cafeteria, or classroom.

All three of these classrooms give clear examples of how individual skills such as Listening Position, Speaker Power, Identifying Physical Signs of Feelings, and Keep Calm are taught, overlearned, and reinforced in the classroom. Now, let's see how some additional skills from SDM/SPS are integrated into other areas of academic content.

INTEGRATION OF SKILLS INTO ACADEMIC CURRICULUM FOR INCREASED PRACTICE OPPORTUNITIES

The next class you are about to visit will be integrating the readiness skill of "BEST" into a language arts class. BEST is an acronym for Body posture, Eye contact, Say appropriate words, and Tone of voice. This skill teaches children to monitor these four aspects of behavior so they can deal with other people in a respectful way.

Special emphasis is placed on helping students be appropriately assertive when confronting other people, rather than aggressive or passive. Students are taught to become aware of staying in their own space, holding eye contact, selecting their words carefully, and checking their tone of voice so that they do not repel the person they are trying to connect with.

The students have been reading a book called *Molly's Pilgrim*. As we enter, we see a role play with two students. Connie (playing the part of Molly) is walking up to Edward (acting the part of Molly's teacher) and saying in a very aggressive voice and moving into his personal space, "Those kids over there are making fun of me because I look different than they do! You'd better do something about it!" Edward says to the child, "I think you had better go back and try this again and use a better tone of voice." Connie comes back and tries it again, this time standing in her own space (B), looking into the teacher's eyes (E), putting the problem into words (S), and using a normal tone of voice (T). Edward, as the teacher, replies and reflects back what Connie said: "Thank you for telling me. Now, I will go over and talk to the children who were judging you by your outside rather than by your heart. I will let you know how it goes."

This teacher took the skill of BEST and used it to do three things: (a) to reinforce and provide an opportunity to practice the skill of BEST, (b) to allow students an opportunity to critique aggressive behaviors and consequences, and (c) to provide a forum for continued practice of a social skill through the use of literature. In other words, it put a social skill into an academic context. (It is also worth noting that during the role plays, other students in the class are assigned to watch the BEST behavior of the role players and give feedback afterward, thereby keeping everyone involved in skill building.) This can also be seen in the following social studies class.

Mr. Lerner is doing a unit on the civil war.

While each group is working on solving their group's problem, a young boy named Ben is seen walking over to an area set up in the back of the room. His head is down, and he is mumbling to himself. He sits down, pulls out a piece of paper that looks like a worksheet, and begins filling it out. When he is finished, he goes back to his group and is seen talking to his group using a normal tone of voice.

Ben has just filled out a *Problem Diary* in a Keep Calm area in the back corner of the classroom. A Problem Diary is a form that has each of the steps in the SDM/SPS decision-making process typed on it. A Problem Diary can be used in two ways: first, as a way to reflect on a poor decision already made, and second, as a way to head off a troubling situation by thinking ahead about positive solutions and consequences. In Ben's case, he knew he was feeling angry, and rather than saying or doing something that would get him in trouble, he decided to go to the Keep Calm area and figure out what his goal was and what solutions he could attempt to reach his goal, envision consequences, and select the best one. Filling out the Problem Diary also helped him defuse his emotions so that his solutions were not being controlled by angry feelings.

IMPLEMENTATION THROUGHOUT THE SCHOOL AND COMMUNITY

Now that we have observed a few examples of how some of the SDM/SPS skills are integrated in the classroom, let's take a walk through the halls of Schuyler School so that we can observe some other ways students are practicing their SDM/SPS skills beyond the classroom door.

Walking into the school counselor's office, it is obvious that SDM skills and activities are a central component of the comprehensive school counseling efforts in this building. Skill posters, problem-solving worksheets, and lists of problem-solving groups indicate that the skills are used in the context of individual counseling sessions and small-group counseling. The school counselor also relates that FIG TESPN as an eight-step thinking framework and other skill prompts are infused in lessons conducted by the counselor in classrooms addressing academic, personal, and social and career development topics.

The National Standards for School Counseling ideally position the school counselor as the SEL coordinator in a school building (Bruene Butler, Poedubicky, & Sperlazza, in press). The counselor in this building also coordinates other programs to support students in practicing social decision-making skills in unstructured situations such as in the cafeteria, on the playground, and in their relationships with their peers and teachers. The counselor also coordinates training and supervision (with the support of other teachers) of students participating in the Keep Calm Force, peer mediation, and safety patrol. The Keep Calm Force is a group of students who act as peer reminders to other students to use Keep Calm in stressful situations while on the playground or in other unstructured settings. Peer mediators use a variation of FIG TESPN to assist students in conflict to think through the problem and negotiate solutions.

The school counselor takes us across the hall to the SDM lab (SDML; Elias, Hoover, & Poedubicky, 1997; Poedubicky, Brown, Hoover, & Elias, 2000–2001). The SDML is a place where students are given a structured opportunity to apply their SDM/SPS skills to real-life situations that have resulted in the need for discipline or self- or teacher referral for an identified problem. The SDML is operated by trained facilitators from the local university, businesses, and community; volunteer teachers; and teacher's aides. Older students who have been through and benefited from the lab sometimes act as peer coaches during lunchtime hours. Students are taken through a problem-solving process through computer software (Elias, Friedlander, & Tobias, 2000; Friedlander, 1993).

As we leave the SDML, we walk pass the music room and the gym. We stop to talk to the teachers. Both the music and physical education teachers report that they use the SDM/SPS skills and prompts on a daily basis. For example, the music teacher has adapted Listening Position to *Singing Position* and incorporates Keep Calm as an integral part of all performances. The physical education teacher also uses the Keep Calm prompt continually to focus athletic performance, for example, prior to taking a foul shot in basketball or batting in softball. Also, BEST is used to enhance team sportsmanship. The physical education teacher also emphasizes BEST when students are in the role of referee.

We end our visit at the principal's office. There, we find out that the assistant principal and principal use these skills and skill prompts with students, staff, and parents in discipline situations with students, to provide support with strategies to parents, and at staff meetings, by using the FIG TESPN framework to develop plans related to professional development, curriculum, and school improvement. As we leave the school, we also notice a flyer announcing a workshop for parents. There, they will learn about ways that they can help coach their children and have demonstrations and practice opportunities based on *Emotionally Intelligent Parenting*

(Elias, Tobias, & Friedlander, 2000). A Web site is also posted at www.EQParenting .com to obtain further information.

CONCLUSION

As we bid a farewell to this short but informative visit to Schuyler School, we have a better understanding of what it takes for students to internalize social-emotional skills and use them in the service of good character. This is not something that is left to chance; programmatically and systemically, children are taught and provided opportunities to practice skills on a daily basis. In this school, it started in individual classrooms, with caring teachers such as those we visited. Over time and with collaborative effort and planning on the part of a team of educators, the entire school has become involved in building skills that will help children become productive adults who demonstrate good character. Many other schools have gone down this road, led by caring teachers. The same can happen to you.

Authors' Note: Ongoing information about all aspects of Social Decision Making/Social Problem Solving can be found at www.umdnj.edu/spsweb.

REFERENCES

Bruene Butler, L., Poedubicky, V., & Sperlazza, J. (in press). Promoting the emotional intelligence of students with special needs through comprehensive school counseling. In J. Pellitteri, R. Stern, C. Shelton, & B. Ackerman (Eds.), *Emotionally intelligent school counseling.* Mahwah, NJ: Erlbaum.

Collaborative for Academic, Social, and Emotional Learning (CASEL). (2003). *Safe and sound: An educational leader's guide to evidence-based social and emotional learning (SEL) programs.* Chicago: Author.

Elias, M. J., & Bruene Butler, L. (1999). Social decision making and problem solving: Essential skills for interpersonal and academic success. In J. Cohen (Ed.), *Educating minds and hearts: Social emotional learning and the passage into adolescence* (pp. 75–94). New York: Teachers College Press.

Elias, M. J., & Bruene Butler, L. (2005). *Social Decision Making/Social Problem Solving curriculum for grades 2–5.* Champaign, IL: Research Press.

Elias, M. J., Friedlander, B. S., & Tobias, S. E. (2000). *Engaging resistant children through computers: A manual for social-emotional learning.* Port Chester, NY: Dude/National Professional Resources.

Elias, M. J., Hoover, H., & Poedubicky, V. A. (1997). Computer-facilitated counseling for at-risk students in a social problem solving "lab." *Elementary School Guidance and Counseling, 31,* 293–309.

Elias, M. J., Tobias, S. E., & Friedlander, B. S. (2000). *Emotionally intelligent parenting.* New York: Three Rivers Press/Random House.

Elias, M. J., Zins, J. E., Weissberg, R. P., Frey, K. S., Greenberg, M. T., Haynes, N. M., et al. (1997). *Promoting social and emotional learning: Guidelines for educators.* Alexandria, VA: Association for Supervision and Curriculum Development.

Friedlander, B. (1993). *Personal problem solving guide computer software.* Morristown, NJ: Center for Child and Family Development.

Poedubicky, V., Brown, L., Hoover, H., & Elias, M. J. (2000–2001). Using technology to promote healthy decision making. *Learning and Leading with Technology, 28*(4), 19–21, 56.

15

Inside Open Circle

Beverly J. Koteff and Pamela Seigle

It is time for a multiplication facts test in Ms. Tosches's third-grade class. But instead of asking the children to clear their desks and get out a pencil, the teacher first leads them through calm breathing steps. "Breathe in slowly and deeply, filling your belly with air like a balloon," Ms. Tosches says. "Now, breathe out slowly. Let's do it two more times."

Out on the playground, a first grader comes running to his teacher. "He won't let me have a turn on the swing." Instead of intervening, the teacher asks the child if this is a "Double D." "No," says the child, realizing that nothing dangerous or destructive is happening. The teacher then coaches him on how to solve the problem himself. "What steps can you take if you can't get a turn on the swing?" his teacher prompts. "What are some of the things you can say to that person?" Soon, the child is happily swinging.

A first-grade girl has been having a terrible time at home in the morning getting dressed for school. The problem goes on for weeks, and the parent mentions it to her child's teacher. "Your daughter is a very good problem solver," says Ms. Jay, the teacher. "Why don't you let her help solve the problem?" So the next morning, the mother says to her daughter, "We have this problem, and Ms. Jay said you know how to problem solve." The minute the little girl hears this, she says, "I'll take care of it." She goes to her room and makes a chart of the steps she wants to take, including what she wants her mother to do and what her part of the bargain will be. If she gets dressed independently and on time, she will get a sticker. "After months of fighting in the mornings, the problem was solved that simply," says Ms. Jay, "because the child saw herself as powerful to solve it."

THE OPEN CIRCLE CURRICULUM

What do these three situations have in common? In each of them, the child's elementary school communities participate in the Open Circle Program, based at the Stone Center, part of the Wellesley Centers for Women at Wellesley College, and use the Open Circle curriculum (Seigle, Lange, & Macklem, 2003).

Open Circle, a year-long curriculum and approach for students in kindergarten through fifth grade, helps equip children with skills necessary to develop healthy, positive relationships. Students learn how to communicate effectively with each other, how to solve problems, how to listen, how to respect differences, and more.

Twice a week, students gather their chairs into a circle. "We form a circle because in that shape, you can see everyone, making it feel more welcome," explains Emily, a fifth grader. "Not wanting anyone to feel left out, we always leave in an extra space in case a guest walks in the room while we are in Open Circle." For 15 to 30 minutes, the classroom teacher and students discuss a lesson topic and do an activity, such as a role play or a game that reinforces a concept presented. By consistently coming together in a circle twice a week, a context is created that allows children not only to learn and practice social skills but also to bring issues to the circle that are important to them. These include issues such as problems from the playground, incidents in the cafeteria, or classroom interactions.

The Open Circle curriculum is grade differentiated. The same topics and concepts are presented in all six books, but at an age-appropriate depth. Each year a child participates in Open Circle, concepts are reinforced and skills are practiced, with fresh activities, assignments, and children's literature suggestions at each grade level.

The Open Circle curriculum contains 35 lessons in three sections. Lessons on creating a cooperative classroom environment include such topics as setting class rules, being a good listener, establishing nonverbal signals for the class, being inclusive, cooperating, dealing with teasing and discrimination, and speaking up. A second section of the curriculum gives students a six-step process for solving people problems. A third group of lessons on building positive relationships includes topics such as expressing anger appropriately, reading body language, and practicing positive self-talk.

INVOLVING THE ENTIRE SCHOOL COMMUNITY

Students are not the only ones who learn and practice the relationship skills presented in Open Circle. The entire elementary school community is included: classroom teachers, principals, parents, school support staff, and specialists.

Teachers who implement the Open Circle curriculum in their classroom for the first time attend four full days of training over the course of a year. A significant portion of their training involves experiential activities that give them an opportunity to reflect on their own social competency skills. The training encourages teachers to be aware of the extent to which they model the behaviors they are teaching their students. In addition, teachers learn and practice the skill of facilitation, which is central to the program. As a facilitator of children's learning, teachers assume the role of a conductor who focuses on the learning process and guides by asking reflective questions, giving feedback, listening, and helping to process group and individual experiences. Time in training is also spent reflecting on their teaching practices. Throughout the first year, teachers also receive coaching and consultation in their classroom.

Principals may attend a full-day workshop to learn about the program and the social competency concepts that children are learning in the classroom, or they may attend a year-long principal leadership program to explore in more depth how to support the program as a schoolwide initiative. They practice the skills and are encouraged to use them not only with the children in their buildings but also with staff and parents. Many principals hold staff meetings in an Open Circle format and use the six problem-solving steps to address staff and schoolwide issues.

School support staff and specialists have the opportunity to participate in a special training that gives them an overview of the program and allows them to capitalize on students' skill development as they work with them.

Parents, a vital link to the success of the program in a school community, receive training too. A five-session parent course led by a school psychologist or social worker who has been trained to run the workshops is offered at their children's school. Open Circle vocabulary and concepts are introduced, and parents practice skills such as giving and receiving compliments, being a good listener, and problem solving. Parents even get homework assignments, just like their children. Often, the assignment is to practice a social competency concept with their child and write a reflection on the results. "My child was surprised to hear me use the same language that he knows from school," said one parent. "This is providing the consistency that children need." In addition, sample family newsletters in English and Spanish are included with the curriculum. Teachers can send these letters home to let families know what their children are discussing in Open Circle. The newsletters include key vocabulary, children's literature suggestions, and ideas for activities parents can do at home to reinforce or extend the social competency concepts presented at school.

To ensure sustainability of Open Circle, school teams including teachers, principals, and other staff are invited to participate in a program that supports them in developing and implementing a plan over time to establish Open Circle as an integral part of their school culture. A leadership program for principals focuses on building an adult community that "lives" our expectations for children.

DEALING WITH DANGEROUS, DESTRUCTIVE, AND ANNOYING BEHAVIOR

Two lessons in the Open Circle curriculum that teachers find particularly helpful for students are "Dealing with Dangerous and Destructive Behavior" and "Dealing with Annoying Behavior." In the first of these two lessons, the objective is to understand when it is important to go immediately to a responsible adult for help, and the concept of Double Ds, or "dangerous and destructive" behavior is introduced. Dangerous behavior means that someone might get hurt. Destructive behavior means that something might get broken, damaged, or destroyed. Mean teasing and bullying are also examples of destructive behavior.

The teacher asks students for examples of dangerous and destructive behavior that may occur in school or on the playground. Students are reminded that they can always talk to a responsible adult about something that is important to them, but that it is especially important to tell an adult immediately if someone is doing something dangerous or destructive. The teacher asks, "Who is a responsible adult that you could talk to on the playground? in the lunchroom? on the bus?"

For homework, students are asked to be aware of and make a list of behaviors in three categories: dangerous, destructive, or annoying.

- At the next Open Circle meeting, students review the definition of a Double D and who to tell if they see a Double D behavior in class, at recess, or in the cafeteria. At the third-grade level, for example, the lesson proceeds:

  Ask students to give you some examples of annoying behaviors (copying someone's answers, cutting in line, etc.).

  Ask students how they feel when someone annoys them (angry, frustrated, etc.). Ask students what they usually do or say when someone annoys them. Have them evaluate the consequences of several ways of responding to annoying behavior:

  If they ignore the annoying behavior, what might happen?

  If they tell the teacher, what might happen?

  If they yell at the person, what might happen?

- Suggest that when someone is annoying you, it is helpful to use words in a positive and constructive way to tell the person what you do not like and what you would like them to do instead. For example, "It hurts when you poke me. Please stop." Or, "When you take my markers without asking, I don't know where they are when I need them. Next time, please ask me before borrowing something."

- Some steps for dealing with annoying behavior are as follows:

  Say what is annoying you and how it affects you or makes you feel.

  (It's annoying. It's distracting. It's disturbing you, etc.) You might use the statement, "I feel _____ when you _____."

  Say what you want to happen instead.

- Ask for two volunteers to do a role play for the class. Have one choose an annoying behavior and role-play it. Then have the other person respond to it by telling why the behavior is bothering him or her and what he or she would like to have happen. Have the first student respond. Call attention to tone of voice, body language, and so forth. Ask students whether they feel this response would work for them. What are the effective parts about it? What might not be as effective? Ask students what they can do if it does not work.

These two lessons equip children with the ability to decide when a situation needs immediate help from an adult. They also give children strategies for dealing with the many incidents of annoying behavior that happen daily at school. Yet students are assured that teachers and other adults in their school community are always willing to help if they cannot deflect annoying behavior by themselves. Beyond the children gaining effective interpersonal skills, the teacher also gains valuable time in the classroom to concentrate on instruction rather than dealing with episodes of annoying behavior.

Same Lesson Topic at Different Grade Levels

At the kindergarten and fifth-grade levels, these two lessons are similar to the third-grade lesson presented previously, in that they introduce and reinforce the Double D vocabulary and emphasize the importance of telling a responsible adult when dangerous or destructive behavior is involved. However, kindergartners hear a story about annoying classroom behavior and its effect on the classroom. They are asked to discriminate between Double D and merely annoying behaviors. Then they are presented with the strategy of using words rather than action to deal with annoying behavior. Volunteers are asked to role-play situations using words as a response to annoying behavior.

Fifth graders also use the Double D vocabulary and give examples of Double D and non–Double D behavior. However, the concept is expanded to include discussion of how difficult it can be to tell on a friend and what might happen after someone tells on a classmate. Each student is asked to name something he or she does that others might find annoying. The students discuss responses to annoying behavior and the consequences of those responses. Students are then presented with a three-step strategy for dealing with annoying behavior:

1. Describe the behavior that is annoying you.

2. State how you feel about it and how it affects you. ("I feel _____ when you _____.")

3. Say what you want to have happen instead.

Students are reminded that it is important to tell the person directly what he or she is doing that annoys you in a way that is respectful and constructive. After a volunteer role-plays about dealing with annoying behavior, fifth graders discuss whether the response would be effective, what they might do if the annoying behavior continues, and the responsibility of the annoyer to respond to a request to stop annoying behavior. Across the grade levels, students are presented with the same basic vocabulary and concepts. However, the concepts are explored in greater, age-appropriate depth as students progress through Open Circle grade levels.

A FORUM FOR CLASSROOM ISSUES

In addition to teaching children social competency skills, Open Circle serves as a forum for dealing with classroom issues. If there is a problem to solve or a group decision to make, such as how to prevent older kids from interfering with recess games or how to spend money that the class has raised, students and teachers can use Open Circle as a forum to discuss the issue. They know that twice each week, time will be set aside to deal with their issues. A school counselor commented, "Open Circle is a perfect forum for discussing difficult topics. The children have learned that it is a time to talk about things that are important to them but may not be easy to discuss, and a time when they feel safe and dare to take risks. A second-grade teacher and I called a special Open Circle to talk about muscular dystrophy." One of the students in that class who has muscular dystrophy was having increasing difficulty moving around the classroom and wanted his classmates to understand how he felt. So the counselor, teacher, parent, and student together planned a special

Open Circle to discuss the child's issues, especially his feeling of being different. It made a significant positive difference for everyone involved.

CLASSROOM CLIMATE

In addition to serving as a forum, Open Circle provides teachers with new strategies for creating a positive social climate in the classroom. "I was definitely a dictator before I began using Open Circle," says one third-grade teacher. "I now consider myself a sharer with the children. They trust me, and I trust them."

All teachers are encouraged to carry over social competency concepts from Open Circle into academic lessons and other parts of the school day. For example, a third-grade teacher regularly connects the six-step problem-solving process with literature. "Children often see in a story whether the characters use the problem-solving steps or not to solve their problems and maybe what went wrong with their problem solving," she said. "Did they use the steps appropriately? Did they keep trying when the first solution didn't work? Did they calm down before they acted? In the *Frog and Toad* series, for instance, frequently there is a problem. I use the language of Open Circle and relate what happens to the problem-solving steps."

EVALUATION RESULTS: POSITIVE CHANGES FOR CHILDREN AND TEACHERS, CLASSROOMS AND SCHOOLS

Since 1987, Open Circle has reached more than 200,000 children in diverse schools and communities in the Northeast and beyond. Over the years, the program has gathered evidence documenting the effectiveness of its curriculum and approach (Krasnow, Seigle, & Kelly, 1994). Particularly promising evidence emerged from two recent research studies. The first study (Hennessey, n.d.) involved fourth-grade students and their teachers in eight classrooms at four elementary schools. Four of the classrooms used the Open Circle curriculum. The other four did not use the curriculum and served as the control group for the study. In the fall, students in the Open Circle classrooms were found to be similar—both academically and socially—to those in the control classrooms. By the spring, students in the Open Circle classrooms were rated by teachers as having significantly greater social skills and demonstrating significantly fewer problem behaviors than the students in the control group. Furthermore, these differences were consistent when urban and suburban classrooms were compared separately.

The second study (Taylor, Liang, Tracy, Williams, & Seigle, 2002) focused on the effects the program has had on children as they enter middle school. Researchers found positive effects on middle school adjustment for both girls and boys. For example, the study found that girls who had participated in Open Circle for at least 2 years in elementary school showed, among other benefits, a significant increase in self-assertiveness compared with girls who had not participated. Boys with at least 2 years of Open Circle participation in elementary school reported higher levels of social skill and self-control and fewer problems with physical fighting when compared with nonparticipants. These findings lend support to the hypothesis that having 2 or more years of Open Circle in elementary school has an impact on social adjustment even after children are no longer exposed to the program in middle school.

Tools to Monitor Progress: The curriculum also includes tools to help teachers and students themselves assess their progress. Each new lesson begins with a review of homework from the last lesson designed to help students begin to apply the concepts they are learning. Also, each section of the curriculum ends with a lesson that gives students and teacher the opportunity to reflect on and evaluate what they have learned. They set class goals and individual goals for specific skills they need to work on. For example, at the end of the section "Creating a Cooperative Classroom Community," third graders complete the questionnaire in Table 15.1. Then together, students and teacher complete a summary for the entire class. (See Table 15.2.)

Teachers often report a growth in positive student behavior, a sense of responsibility students feel toward the class, and the development of a caring classroom community. Many teachers also tell us that the program has touched their lives, both professionally and personally, and allowed them to act in a more "authentic" manner in the classroom. They have found themselves to be better listeners and better at calming down in stressful situations and sharing control with their class. Other teachers say that they talk less and ask questions more often, and they have become more reflective and aware of the ways in which adult behavior fails to align with their expectations for children.

A special education teacher comments,

The most important benefit of Open Circle to me as a special education teacher is the acceptance that it fosters of the individual differences of the students. In Open Circle, it does not matter who cannot read or spell. A level playing field is provided, where what matters is the person, and every student is made to feel that he or she is an integral part of that classroom. Some of the brightest, most verbose students have to learn to listen and be patient, and the most reserved, least expressive students are heard.

Teachers consistently report that Open Circle creates an environment in which everyone can participate, regardless of their skills. Community-building lessons help create an acceptance and respect for each child in the classroom. Often, children who previously were scapegoats or directly blamed for poor social behavior are encouraged by their classmates, who become allies with the teacher in supporting positive social behavior. Many special educators view Open Circle as an opportunity to reinforce in a group setting the concepts they teach their students individually.

A principal remarked that since Open Circle began in his school, "schoolwide, the number of children sent to me has gone way down, along with the severity of incidents." The program reinforces his view of discipline—that it is not about yelling or punishing. "I see my role as a disciplinarian is to help kids learn more about the mistakes they made and figure out strategies to prevent them from happening again. When I meet with students who have participated in Open Circle, I can remind them of the problem-solving steps they have learned with me," he says.

Table 15.1   Student Evaluation Tool

Name: _____

Date: _____

For each behavior listed below, either check **yes** if you are doing it, check **no** if you are not doing it, or check **sometimes** if you are doing it sometimes.

	Yes	No	Sometimes
1. Listening	_____	_____	_____
2. Using nonverbal signals	_____	_____	_____
3. Giving compliments	_____	_____	_____
4. Including others	_____	_____	_____
5. Encouraging others	_____	_____	_____
6. Cooperating	_____	_____	_____
7. Tattling	_____	_____	_____
8. Dealing with situations myself	_____	_____	_____
9. Dealing with teasing	_____	_____	_____
10. Speaking up	_____	_____	_____

List below the skills you would like to work on:

_____

_____

_____

_____

_____

_____

Table 15.2 · Class Summary Sheet for Student Evaluation

Teacher: _____

Number of students in class: _____

Grade: _____

Date: _____

	Yes	No	Sometimes
1. Listening	_____	_____	_____
2. Using nonverbal signals	_____	_____	_____
3. Giving compliments	_____	_____	_____
4. Including others	_____	_____	_____
5. Encouraging others	_____	_____	_____
6. Cooperating	_____	_____	_____
7. Tattling	_____	_____	_____
8. Dealing with situations myself	_____	_____	_____
9. Dealing with teasing	_____	_____	_____
10. Speaking up	_____	_____	_____

_____

_____

_____

_____

_____

CONCLUSION

The student-centered nature of Open Circle is best captured in the words of a fourth grader. This student once described Open Circle in terms of a toolbox: "The most important thing we've learned is how to deal with our problems in a peaceful and nonviolent way. That helps in the real world and especially on the playground. I guess what you're doing is getting supplies for your toolbox that you're going to need later in life to fix up the problems you have." Open Circle provides a structure for many significant adults in a child's life, as well as peers, to help fill that toolbox.

Authors' Note: Ongoing information about all aspects of the Open Circle Program can be found at www.open-circle.org.

REFERENCES

Hennessey, B. A. (n.d.). *Promoting social competency in school-aged children: The effects of the Reach Out to Schools social competency program.* Manuscript submitted for publication.

Krasnow, J. H., Seigle, P., & Kelly, R. (1994). *Project report 1990–1993: The social competency program of the Reach Out to Schools project.* Wellesley, MA: Stone Center, Wellesley College.

Seigle, P., Lange, L., & Macklem, G. (2003). *Open Circle curriculum, grades k to 5* (Rev. ed.). Wellesley, MA: Open Circle Program, Wellesley College.

Taylor, C. A., Liang, B., Tracy, A. J., Williams, L. M., & Seigle, P. (2002). Gender differences in middle school adjustment, physical fighting, and social skills: Evaluation of a social competency program. *Journal of Primary Prevention, 23,* 261–274.

16

Teaching Emotional Literacy in Elementary School Classrooms

The PATHS Curriculum

Carol A. Kusché and Mark T. Greenberg

• If you walk into Mrs. Lamkin's first-grade classroom at Demonstration School (DS) #34, you will hear her students giving each other compliments on a routine basis. They also give compliments to Mrs. Lamkin, because they know that she has feelings, too. At lunchtime, they thank and compliment the cafeteria personnel for fixing their lunches. Several parents have asked Mrs. Lamkin what she has been doing this year, because their kids are behaving so much better at home.

• Daniel, a first grader in Mrs. Lamkin's class, no longer bothers other kids when he gets angry. Instead he folds his arms and goes into his imaginary turtle shell to calm down. When Mrs. Lamkin sees this signal from Daniel, she praises his behavior and then talks to him about his problem and his feelings. Daniel takes his "angry," "frustrated," and "bored" feeling face cards out of his feelings box and shows Mrs. Lamkin how he feels. They dialogue about Daniel's problem and together devise an acceptable way to handle it.

- Out on the playground during recess, two girls get into a fight. The playground teacher sends them to the principal's office. The principal, Ms. Howen, has them use her Control Signals poster to calm down and then talks to them about their problem. They discuss how they are feeling and why. Then Ms. Howen asks each of them to fill out a Solving My Problem worksheet before sending them back to class. As they are leaving, Moe, the notorious fourth-grade bully who recently transferred from a neighboring school district, comes bursting in to exuberantly announce that he has gone a whole day without getting into trouble. Ms. Howen takes her "proud" and "delighted" feeling faces out of her feelings box and shows Moe how proud she feels about his success.

These events at DS #34 are all the result of a commitment that the teachers and administrators made 3 years ago to implement social-emotional learning (SEL) in general, and the PATHS (Promoting Alternative Thinking Strategies) curriculum (Kusché & Greenberg, 1994) in particular, on a schoolwide basis.

WHY TEACH EMOTIONAL LITERACY?

The impetus for this decision began with a back-to-school retreat in the autumn of that year. All of the teachers and administrators, including the district superintendent, had met for the day to discuss long-range goals for elementary education. The retreat facilitator had asked the group to consider two questions: "What competencies will your students need when they are adults in the year 2020?" and "What are you doing now to teach these skills?" It became clear from the resulting discussion that SEL would be crucial for future success and, at the same time, that this knowledge would be beneficial for current challenges as well (e.g., for increasing emotional intelligence, improving developmental assets, preventing violence and substance abuse, and promoting positive youth development).

During the retreat, the teachers learned about research that showed strong correlations between emotional distress, cognitive processing deficits, and poor academic achievement (Kusché, Cook, & Greenberg, 1993) and strong negative relationships between low levels of developmental assets and high numbers of risk behaviors (Benson, Galbraith, & Espeland, 1995). The high percentage of children suffering from emotional distress was also striking, but the teachers learned that even high achievers and well-adjusted children benefited from improved emotional intelligence. At the end of the retreat, the vote was unanimous: Emotional literacy and social competency training should be made an educational priority each year along with reading, writing, arithmetic, and computing.

A search committee was formed to determine which curriculum would be best to use to obtain the type of results that they wanted to see with their students. The choice felt overwhelming at first, because there were literally hundreds of programs to choose from. Many of the programs seemed relatively simple for teachers to implement, whereas others were much more involved. It was not easy to discern which of the programs would actually work. Indeed, after looking more closely at the available research, the committee members discovered that very few programs had documentation to demonstrate effectiveness. Some showed no significant effects, whereas many others had never even been evaluated. Only a handful had findings to verify significant improvement in the children who received the curriculum as compared with control children who did not.

WHY USE PATHS?

PATHS was one of the few SEL programs that had been well researched with a number of different populations of children (e.g., regular education, special education, deaf, emotionally disturbed, English as a second language). The search committee also found that PATHS was designed as a multiyear, universal prevention model and would be beneficial for all of the children in their school, not just for a select subset of students. Furthermore, effective outcomes with PATHS had been demonstrated with boys and girls from a large variety of ethnic groups (e.g., European American, African American, Asian American, and Hispanic, as well as those in other countries such as Great Britain, Canada, Australia, New Zealand, Holland, Norway, Belgium, Israel, and Germany). This was especially important for this particular school, because it served a diverse population of students.

In addition, the search committee was reassured to learn that numerous review panels had given PATHS high recognition and recommendations. For example, PATHS was rated as a Model Program (the highest possible rating) by the *National Registry of Evidence-Based Programs* (Substance Abuse and Mental Health Services Administration [SAMHSA], 2005), being 1 of only 12 SAMHSA Model Programs shown to have significant outcomes related to academic achievement and only 1 of 2 programs designed for elementary school–age children. Similarly, PATHS has received top ratings from a variety of other independent review panels including *Positive Youth Development* (Catalano, Berglund, Ryan, Lonczak, & Hawkins, 2002), the *Blueprints for Violence Prevention* project of 1997–1998 (Elliot, 1997–1998), the Office of Safe and Drug Free Schools (U.S. Department of Education, 2001), *Safe and Sound* (Collaborative for Academic, Social, and Emotional Learning, 2003), and the Centers for Disease Control and Prevention (2003).

Furthermore, the committee members learned that PATHS was one of the few curricula that emphasized emotional understanding as a primary goal and that targeted all of the key active ingredients identified by the W. T. Grant Consortium (1992) for effective prevention and emotional intelligence programs. These included identifying and labeling feelings, expressing feelings, controlling impulses, increasing communication skills, interpreting social cues, improving self-esteem, and teaching social problem solving (Goleman, 1995; Hawkins & Catalano, 1992).

The importance of SEL for daily functioning in general and for school performance in particular was also underscored. The committee learned that feelings affect motivation, learning, memory, attention, concentration, critical thinking, creativity, curiosity, empathy, problem solving, oral expression, written expression, interpersonal relationships, optimal brain integration, classroom behavior, school functioning, academic success, physical health, and other important domains of education (Kusché & Greenberg, 1998). Promoting social-emotional competence also assists with the prevention of violence, antisocial behavior, emotional distress, and substance abuse and with the enhancement of teacher-student relationships, classroom environment, the appreciation of school, and developmental growth. Finally, teachers generally do their best teaching when controlled emotional expression is encouraged in the classroom.

Based on research findings from various studies of PATHS (Conduct Problems Prevention Research Group, 1999; Greenberg & Kusché, 1998), the search committee ascertained that with a reliable implementation of PATHS, they could expect to see the following types of results with their students:

- Improved self-control
- Improved understanding and recognition of emotions
- Increased ability to tolerate frustration
- Use of more effective conflict-resolution strategies
- Improved cognitive flexibility and planning ability
- Decreased symptoms of sadness and depression
- Decreased aggression and other conduct problems
- Improved classroom atmosphere

The search committee also questioned whether time spent on PATHS might slow academic progress. They found, however, that compared with control children, the academic achievement scores of PATHS students were just as good, and in some cases, better. This was important because the committee had heard that in other cities, some parents had expressed the worry that social skills programs might take away from valuable classroom time and thereby interfere with academic progress. They were relieved that evidence existed, at least with PATHS, that showed this simply is not the case. Finally, the search committee was excited to see that current models of brain development had been used in the development of PATHS (see Chapter 2 for a discussion of the link of brain research to SEL).

THREE RECOMMENDATIONS

1. Schoolwide Commitment

Thus, after doing their homework, the search committee of DS #34 strongly endorsed the implementation of PATHS. The search committee also made three further recommendations, based on what they had learned. First, they felt that a schoolwide commitment was needed. To teach emotional literacy for 1 year would not make any more sense than to teach math or reading for only 1 year. Thus, teachers would need to coordinate the program from one year to the next, and lessons would need to advance as the children matured. Since PATHS was based on a developmental model, it would work well with the school's philosophy.

2. Administrative and Peer Support

Second, after talking to numerous teachers, it was apparent that they needed peer support, as well as the crucial support of the school principal and other administrative staff. Each teacher would need to value the time it took to teach PATHS on a regular basis (two to four times per week throughout the school year) and to use the generalization strategies during the classroom day. If the school leadership did not value the goal of emotional literacy, then most teachers would find it difficult to harness the motivation necessary to learn and use a new program such as PATHS. The teachers at

DS #34, like most teachers, had too much to do and too little time to do it, so priorities would be given to those areas that the leadership emphasized and reinforced.

3. Training and Consultation

Finally, the search committee noted the importance of teacher training and ongoing consultation, at least during the first 2 years of implementation. As with most schools, none of the teachers at DS #34 had any formal training in emotional literacy, so it was unrealistic to expect that they would know how to teach it. Thus, even though PATHS included all of the lessons, instructions, and materials that were needed for implementation, the search committee recognized that a 2-day training workshop with follow-up consultation would be very valuable for the teachers. In addition, the search committee wanted all auxiliary staff to receive training in ways in which they could also use PATHS concepts at school, including before and after-school personnel and school counselors.

THE 6-YEAR PLAN (GRADES K–5)

Thus, when the new school year began, all of the teachers at DS #34 had attended a 2-day training workshop and were ready to implement PATHS on a schoolwide basis. The kindergartners mastered a basic self-control program, practiced giving compliments, learned how to share (and why sharing is important), and discussed their feelings with one another. In first grade, Mrs. Lamkin built on what the children had learned the year before. She reviewed complimenting and basic feelings, continued with intermediate feelings, introduced a more sophisticated method for self-control that included informal problem solving, and taught a unit on manners and why they are important. Next year, the second-grade teacher will review these topics and introduce more advanced feelings, problem-solving skills, and relationship issues such as friendship and teasing. In the third, fourth, and fifth grades, the children will continue with advanced emotional intelligence, more complex relationship issues, problem prevention, and formal problem solving. Also, the teachers at DS #34 will continue to meet on a biweekly basis for peer support and to share experiences, exchange ideas, and coordinate classroom strategies.

INCLUDING PARENTS

In addition to PATHS lessons and generalization strategies used during the classroom day, the teachers wanted to include and inform parents as much as possible so that emotional literacy could generalize to the home. Parent letters and information summaries (included in PATHS materials) were sent home with the children to keep parents apprised and to provide suggestions for ideas that could be used at home. In addition, children were given homework assignments (provided in PATHS) to share with their parents, such as complimenting each family member or interviewing parents about a time when they felt proud when they were children. Mrs. Lamkin also invited parents to come to the classroom to watch the PATHS lesson when their child was the PATHS Kid for that day, and she showed a videotape of the class play of *The Turtle Story* during open house.

DIFFERENT MODELS FOR IMPLEMENTING PATHS

Our example of DS #34 does not refer to a single school but rather an amalgam of many of the different schools with which we have worked across the United States (and internationally). In our experience, we have found that two different paradigms have both worked very well. One involves direct training of teachers and other school personnel, who then implement PATHS in their classrooms with or without ongoing consultation. In the second model, outside consultants (e.g., counselors, master teachers) learn PATHS and then begin implementation as a joint effort with the classroom teachers. Over time, the consultants slowly withdraw from direct implementation, but remain available for consultation as the teachers take on increased responsibility for PATHS in their classrooms. There have also been many schools in which PATHS has been successfully implemented without any external support. This is not to say, of course, that PATHS implementation has never encountered difficulty. However, the collaborative process we have outlined, as well as a problem-solving orientation when obstacles are encountered, have helped the vast majority of settings that have embarked on PATHS to, if you will pardon the pun, follow a path to success.

FROM DS #34 TO YOUR CLASSROOM

One idea that you might like to try in your classroom involves discussing feelings in stories from the news, in history lessons, or from children's literature. Look around for a story or news article to read to the class that contains emotional content (they are everywhere). Choose one to read aloud to your class. After reading it, ask your students to discuss the feelings: "How do you think X felt when Y happened?" "How many of you think that you would feel that way, too?" "Who thinks that they might feel differently?" Similarly, history will become more relevant if you emphasize emotions (e.g., "How do you think the settlers felt when they faced the Oregon Trail?" "How did the colonists feel when the British government wanted them to pay taxes?").

Then ask your students if anything similar has ever happened to them, or if they have ever felt similarly; if so, ask them what happened and to say more about how they felt. Point out the similarities and differences between the various examples: All people feel the same types of feelings, but different people feel differently about different things.

Another idea from PATHS that you can use all year is called the PATHS Kid for Today. The objectives for the PATHS Kid paradigm include developing better self-esteem, improving children's sense of responsibility, using a systematic plan to achieve fairness, teaching self-respect and respect for others, and developing the concept and process of complimenting. This activity should be used on a regular basis (e.g., 2 to 5 times per week) at approximately the same time each day throughout the school year.

Find two large canisters (or boxes) with openings large enough for a hand to fit inside and label them "I have NOT had a turn to be the PATHS Kid" and "I have had a turn to be the PATHS Kid." Write the name of each child in your class on slips of paper (small "stickies" work well for this) and fold them in half so that the names do not show (which means, if you use stickies, that the name has to go on the sticky side, not the front side). Put all of the names in the first jar ("I have NOT had a turn"), as well as your own name and the names of any other adults who work regularly in your classroom (so you, too, can get a Compliment List).

To introduce the PATHS Kid paradigm, explain to your students that you want to have a class helper (every day, every Tuesday and Thursday, etc., as desired) to be your assistant (during class lessons, specified activities, etc., again as desired). Explain that to be sure that everyone gets a turn in a fair manner, you want to use an orderly plan. "Orderly means that we will do the same thing every time so that it will be fair to everyone." Show them the jars, and explain that everyone will have the same chance to get chosen, so that it is fair to everyone. You will draw the name of the first PATHS Kid, and from then on, the current PATHS Kid will draw the name of the next PATHS Kid. After a child has had a turn, his or her name will go into the second jar, and when everyone who wants a turn has had one, you will start over again. (If a child does not want to be PATHS Kid when his or her name is chosen, he or she can choose to have it put in either jar, although it is usually best to put it back into the "did not" jar so that the child can reconsider in the future.)

Explain that the PATHS Kid will help you during the day. You will need to decide how you want to use your PATHS Kid, but one thing that we have found to be very helpful for improving behavior is to have the PATHS Kid sit or stand next to the teacher in front of the class and help with classroom discipline. For example, if the class is becoming rambunctious, you can say, "Your class is getting out of control. What are you going to do to get them to pay better attention?" (In PATHS, we suggest using a technique we call the Three Steps for Calming Down, but any model that you are currently using can be substituted instead.) When confronted with this role reversal, children with attention difficulties or behavior problems get to experience disruption from the teacher's perspective, and they identify with the goal of attaining control. Shy children, on the other hand, get the chance to take a leadership position. It is very interesting to observe how this affects subsequent behavior for the better. Other suggestions would be passing out papers, calling on quiet students with raised hands to answer questions, holding up pictures, and so on.

Continue to explain to your class that in the afternoon, the class will make a Compliment List for the PATHS Kid, who will also get a special letter to take home to his or her parents. Say, "So, the first thing we need to do is to understand what a compliment is." Encourage discussion with your students, then summarize: "A compliment is a nice thing that we say to someone. We give compliments because we like something about that person and we want him or her to know it."

"There are many different kinds of compliments that you can give. Can anyone think of some examples?"

Elicit responses and record them on the chalkboard. Be sure to include the following five categories if your students do not think of them:

1. Ways people look (e.g., "I like your hair.")

2. Things people have (e.g., "I like your bicycle.")

3. Things people do (e.g., "You run very fast.")

4. The way people are (e.g., "You are a good friend.")

5. The way people behave (e.g., "I like how well you listen," "You're good at sharing.")

Add students' examples to categories as appropriate and add categories as needed. Review categories following class discussion.

Then continue with discussion of how people respond to getting compliments: "Most of the time when we get a compliment, it makes us feel happy, proud, and important. These are all comfortable feelings. But sometimes getting a compliment can make us feel shy, embarrassed, or even angry. Those are all uncomfortable feelings. Most of the time, though, compliments help people feel good about themselves."

"Sometimes when we get a compliment from someone, we do not know what to say back. 'Thank you' is one thing you can say, but you can say other things too."

Role-play giving an imaginary child a compliment. Then ask your students to exchange compliments with their neighbor or desk mate. Remind them to give compliments to others when they appreciate something that someone has said or done and to give compliments to themselves when they feel proud. Ask them to give compliments to the lunch or playground staff today, and as an optional homework assignment, ask your students to give compliments to their family members and write down or draw what happened (then discuss as a class the following day). The PATHS curriculum also provides a two-page parent information summary entitled "Increasing Self-Esteem" to be sent home, and you might want to consider doing something similar, or at least share with parents what you have done with the students.

Draw the name of the first PATHS Kid from the jar, and after appropriate applause, place the name on a poster or large sheet of paper labeled, "The Next PATHS Kid will be _____." There should also be space on the poster for a Compliment List (make copies of ours or one of your own design to use on an ongoing basis).

On the following day, have the PATHS Kid assist you during the day as desired. Remind your students to observe him or her closely so that they can give him or her really good compliments later that day. For example, think about things like the following: Is the PATHS Kid being helpful? Friendly? A good listener?

Near the end of the day, assemble the class to make the Compliment List (you might also want to invite the child's parents to come in at this time). Ask the PATHS Kid to pick one of the children raising their hands to give him or her a compliment. Have the PATHS Kid choose a second child for another compliment. Then you should give the PATHS Kid a compliment, and finally, the PATHS Kid should give a compliment to himself or herself. Record each compliment on the Compliment List as it is given. After the Compliment List is completed, read it aloud to the class, followed by applause. Then put the Compliment List up on the PATHS Kid poster under the child's name (a Tack a Note nonpermanent adhesive stick works great for this), ask the PATHS Kid to select the name of the next PATHS Kid from the jar, and put the new name up on the poster as well (kids love the anticipation). At the end of the day, give the PATHS Kid his or her Compliment List to take home (we recommend sending an accompanying note for the parents as well) and remind the child to get a compliment added by a parent. This paradigm should be repeated each specified day. Once everyone (including you) has had a chance to be the PATHS Kid, you can start again. You might also consider inviting the school principal and other staff members to come in to get a Compliment List.

At first, you can expect the compliments to be rather superficial in nature (e.g., "I like your shoes"), but as time progresses, you will see sophisticated compliments emanating from even the youngest students. Also, it should be noted that this procedure takes considerable time when you first begin using it, but it will only take a few minutes after several days. It is an excellent, upbeat way to provide a consistent ending to each school day.

This activity is extremely meaningful for children and can be adapted or tried outside of the context of the PATHS program, although it is most effective as part of the larger skill development process. Rarely do children say hurtful things, but if this happens, you can always remind your students that compliments are nice things we say to people. In general, we have been struck with how powerfully this model affects children, to the extent that their behavior often improves, as does self-esteem.

EVALUATING PATHS IN YOUR CLASSROOM

There are many ways to evaluate how well PATHS is doing in your classroom, including both informal observations and more formal quantitative or numerical data. Monitoring your goals should be an ongoing part of the implementation of PATHS (or of any new curriculum). By ascertaining the amount and quality of implementation and their effects on your students, you will be able to determine which goals and objectives have been met and what changes will be required to make further progress.

The first way to monitor the effects of PATHS is to observe incidents in which students have used or generalized these skills during the remainder of the school day. Noting incidents during the school day that indicate new ways of communicating feelings, managing difficult emotions, and resolving conflict will provide a portfolio of the daily influence of PATHS. You might also want to get feedback from extracurricular staff at school or from parents on changes they see at home.

A second way to assess the influence of PATHS is to complete measures on your students just prior to your use of PATHS and again near the end of the school year. You can then compare changes in behavior, emotional understanding, and so on. One measure that we recommend is the Teacher Child Rating Scale, as it captures many of the behavioral changes that are goals of the curriculum. Copies of this measure and scoring can be obtained at http://www.prevention.psu.edu/projects/PATHS/html. Another very simple measure is to ask each child to tell you the names of all of the feelings that he or she can remember. The average number on the lists obtained prior to implementing PATHS can then be compared with the mean obtained at the end of the year. Comparisons can also be made to assess the progress of individual students. This test, however, is not recommended for the subsequent years of PATHS, as the children are likely to begin the year with a high score from having learned the names of feelings during the previous year.

One can also assess the PATHS experience in a more detailed manner that will provide you with ideas for revision and innovation in future years. If you are interested in this type of evaluation, we recommend that you use a form that provides feedback on each lesson, such as the PATHS Lesson Evaluation Form. In addition, it can be useful to take a broader perspective, and one way to accomplish this is to rate the overall quality of the PATHS experience across the school year (e.g., by using the

PATHS End of the Year Rating Form). Both of these forms can be downloaded at http://www.prevention.psu.edu/projects/PATHS/html.

CONCLUSION

SEL is beneficial for students in numerous ways, all of which contribute to optimal youth development in general and to school success in particular. Furthermore, not only are these skills needed during childhood, but they are critical for successful adult functioning as well. In other words, emotional intelligence is now as important for adequate preparation for adult life as reading, writing, arithmetic, and computer skills. Thus, teaching curricula such as PATHS on a regular basis, every year, for children of all ages (as well as for their parents) is crucial, both for our students' present and for their future. Fortunately, this is also a subject area that is enjoyable for educators to teach and for children to learn. We hope you now feel inspired to discover this for yourself!

Authors' Note: Ongoing information about all aspects of the PATHS program can be found at www.channing-bete.com/positiveyouth/pages/PATHS/PATHS.html and http://modelprograms .samhsa.gov/template_cf.cfm?page=model&pkProgramID=24.

REFERENCES

Benson, P. L., Galbraith, J., & Espeland, P. (1995). *Proven, practical ways to raise good kids.* Minneapolis, MN: Free Spirit.

Catalano, R. F., Berglund, M. L., Ryan, J. A. M., Lonczak, H. S., & Hawkins, J. D. (2002). Positive youth development in the United States: Research findings on evaluations of positive youth development programs. *Prevention & Treatment, 5,* Article 15. Retrieved September 2, 2005, from http://journals.apa.org/prevention/volume5/pre0050015a.html

Centers for Disease Control and Prevention, U.S. Department of Health and Human Services. (2003). *Best practices in youth violence prevention program: Here's proof prevention works— PATHS—Promoting Alternative Thinking Strategies.* Retrieved April 18, 2004, from http:// test.rowsciences.com/modelPrograms/modelprogram_web/worddocs/FactSheets/PA THS.doc

Collaborative for Academic, Social, and Emotional Learning. (2003). *Safe and sound: An educational leader's guide to evidence-based social and emotional learning programs.* Chicago: Author.

Conduct Problems Prevention Research Group. (1999). Initial impact of the Fast Track prevention trial for conduct problems: II. Classroom effects. *Journal of Consulting and Clinical Psychology, 67,* 648–657.

Elliot, D. S. (Ed.). (1997–1998). *Blueprints for violence prevention.* Boulder: Institute of Behavioral Science, Regents of the University of Colorado.

Goleman, D. (1995). *Emotional intelligence: Why it can matter more than IQ.* New York: Bantam Books.

Greenberg, M. T., & Kusché, C. A. (1998). *Blueprints for violence prevention: The PATHS project.* Boulder: Institute of Behavioral Science, Regents of the University of Colorado.

Hawkins, J. D., & Catalano, R. (Eds.). (1992). *Communities that care.* San Francisco: Jossey-Bass.

Kusché, C. A., Cook, E. T., & Greenberg, M. T. (1993). Neuropsychological and cognitive functioning in children with anxiety, externalizing, and comorbid psychopathology. *Journal of Clinical Child Psychology, 22,* 172–195.

Kusché, C. A., & Greenberg, M. T. (1994). *The PATHS (Promoting Alternative Thinking Strategies) curriculum.* South Deerfield, MA: Channing-Bete.

Kusché, C. A., & Greenberg, M. T. (1998). Integrating emotions and thinking in the classroom: The PATHS Curriculum. *THINK, 9,* 32–34.

Substance Abuse and Mental Health Services Administration. (2005). *National Registry of Evidence-Based Programs and Practices.* Retrieved September 12, 2005, from http://model programs.samhsa.gov

U.S. Department of Education. (2001). *Exemplary and Promising Safe, Disciplined and Drug Free Schools program 2001.* Retrieved June 2, 2003, from http://www.ed.gov/offices/OSDFS/exemplary01/index.html

W. T. Grant Consortium on the School-Based Promotion of Social Competence. (1992). Drug and alcohol prevention curricula. In J. D. Hawkins & R. F. Catalano (Eds.), *Communities that care* (pp. 129–148). San Francisco: Jossey-Bass.

17

The Second Step Program

Social-Emotional Skills for Violence Prevention

Joan Cole Duffell, Kathy Beland, and Karin Frey

"Okay everybody, it's time to break into math groups." Mitch Rosenburg's third-grade class had an hour remaining before departing for a field trip to the zoo. His excited students popped in and out of their seats and ran around the clusters of desks. He raised his voice a notch.

"I said, please break into your small groups. Jeremy, find your group and take your seat. You too, Rachel." The children moved into their groups noisily. The volume in the classroom increased. "Okay, eyes front." Five of his 28 students sat attentively; others continued to chatter. Mitch felt his frustration rise.

"Pay attention!" Mitch slammed his math book down on a desk. The noise stopped. Several children looked at him with big eyes. Rachel looked like she was about to cry. Mitch glanced from Rachel to the Second Step anger management poster on the wall behind her.

Swallowing his pride and seizing the teachable moment, Mitch said aloud, "I've got to calm down. I'll take three deep breaths." After three audible intakes of breath, Mitch relaxed and spoke in even tones to his class. "I'm sorry I slammed the book down. I was feeling pretty angry and I guess I let my anger get control of me." He continued, "Now I need to solve the problem that had me feeling so angry." Mitch pointed to the first step listed on the Second Step problem-solving poster. "Who can tell me what the problem was?"

Several students waved their hands in the air.

"Jeremy?"

"You wanted to teach a math lesson, and we were messing around and not listening."

"Okay. Does everybody agree with that problem statement?" Heads nodded solemnly.

"Now let's look at the next step on the poster. What are some solutions to this problem?" Mitch's chalk raced across the blackboard as the children brainstormed suggestions.

Over the next 5 minutes, Mitch and his students followed the remaining sequence of problem-solving steps, which culminated in a new system (complete with consequences) for helping students attend more quickly. Mitch proclaimed, "Well, you've demonstrated great skill in solving this problem. Tomorrow we'll check in to see how our solution is working. Now let's tackle a few math problems."

Rosenburg (not his real name) recounted his story during a recent Second Step teacher training session. Mitch's story provides an excellent example of how Second Step lessons can be integrated into classroom life. Seeing their teacher use the anger management strategies they have been learning about has a profound effect on students. Mitch, on the other hand, was able to use the strategies to advance his academic goals. His willingness to model prosocial behavior in the classroom is reminiscent of Daniel Goleman's (1995) comment in his book *Emotional Intelligence*:

> Whether or not there is a class explicitly devoted to emotional literacy may matter far less than *how* these lessons are taught. There is perhaps no subject where the quality of the teacher matters so much, since how a teacher handles her class is in itself a model, a de facto lesson in emotional competence—or the lack thereof. (p. 279)

Goleman's (1995) observation captures a significant underpinning of social-emotional learning (SEL): Teacher behavior plays a critical role in children's prosocial development. Mitch's use of the Second Step problem-solving and anger management strategies demonstrates how a social-skills curriculum offers teachers the form and structure—indeed, the very language—they need to create a classroom climate that supports social, emotional, and academic learning.

SECOND STEP RESEARCH FOUNDATIONS

SEL is essential to lifetime success in school (Wentzel & Wigfield, 1998), family relationships (Dix, 1991; Gottman, Katz, & Hooven, 1996), and the workplace (Spencer & Spencer, 1993). Moreover, specific social-skill deficits are commonly found in children and adults who display antisocial behavior (Maiuro, Cahn, & Vitaliano, 1986; Spivack & Cianci, 1987).

Second Step: A Violence Prevention Curriculum was developed to teach social-emotional skills to children from preschool to Grade 9. Its first edition was published in 1988 by the nonprofit Committee for Children. The Second Step program is now actively used in an estimated 20,000 schools across the United States and Canada and is supported by Committee for Children's staff of trainers and implementation specialists. The program and training materials have also been translated into a dozen languages and implemented in thousands more schools by the Committee for Children's SEL partner organizations in Europe and Asia.

The Second Step program is based on research that suggests that the acquisition of key social competencies will decrease children's risk of engaging in destructive behavior and expand their repertoire of prosocial skills (Weissberg & Greenberg, 1997). The strategies Second Step employs to teach these skills are based on more than 40 years of research and theory in SEL (e.g., Bandura, 1973, 1986; Crick & Dodge, 1994; Eisenberg, Fabes, & Lasoya, 1997; Feshbach, 1984; Halberstadt, Denham, & Dunsmore, 2001; Kendall, 1993; Kendall & Braswell, 1985; Luria, 1961; Spivack & Shure, 1982).

FORMATIVE AND OUTCOME RESEARCH

Research on the effectiveness of the Second Step program ranges from small, formative pilot studies to rigorous outcome evaluation. In formative studies, preschool through middle school children's perspective-taking and problem-solving abilities improved significantly after participating in the Second Step program, whereas children in classrooms without Second Step lessons showed no improvement from pretest to posttest. Teachers rated the lessons as easy to prepare and incorporate into other subjects and very good for stimulating student interest (Beland, 1988, 1989, 1991; Moore & Beland, 1992). Middle school students who participated in the Second Step program were less likely to endorse the use of physical aggression, rumors and insults, or social exclusion (shutting someone out of the group). They also viewed prosocial behaviors as less difficult to perform following the program (Van Schoiack-Edstrom, Frey, & Beland, 2002).

A more rigorous outcome study published in the *Journal of the American Medical Association* observed student behavior on the playground, in the cafeteria, and in class in the fall and spring (Grossman et al., 1997). The study concluded that the Second Step curriculum led to moderate decreases in aggression and increases in neutral and prosocial behavior in school. In contrast, students at control schools (those not using the curriculum) became more physically and verbally aggressive over the school year.

A larger study looking at 15 schools showed that third- and fifth-grade students who were using the Second Step curriculum were more likely to resolve conflicts without adult intervention than control-group students. Their negotiation strategies were less aggressive and more collaborative (girls only). Second Step participants also had more positive social goals and reasoning, and greater satisfaction after negotiating, than children who had not gone through the program (Frey, Nolen, Edstrom, & Hirschstein, 2005).

SECOND STEP PROGRAM REVIEWS AND AWARDS

National policy research groups and SEL experts give the Second Step program top scores for effecting change in children and its user-friendly approach for teachers and parents. The program received the highest designation possible—a Collaborative for Academic, Social, and Emotional Learning (CASEL) Select Program Award—in a comprehensive evaluation conducted by CASEL in 2002. Second Step is also a winner of the prestigious "exemplary" award from the U.S. Department of Education's 2001 Panel on Safe, Disciplined, and Drug-Free Schools and was granted the same top rating in a review by the U.S. Department of Justice, Office of Juvenile Justice and Delinquency Prevention, in 2003. The White House (1998) *Annual Report on School Safety*, produced by the U.S. Departments of Education and Justice, featured the Second Step curriculum as "a model program" for school violence prevention.

CURRICULUM CONTENT

Empathy

Goleman (1995) placed empathy at the core of social competence:

Being able to put aside one's self-centered focus and impulses . . . opens the way to empathy, to real listening, to taking another person's perspective. Empathy leads to caring, altruism, and compassion. Seeing things from another's perspective breaks down biased stereotypes, and so breeds tolerance and acceptance of differences. These capacities are ever-more called on in our increasingly pluralistic society, allowing people to live together in mutual respect . . . these are the basic arts of democracy. (p. 285)

Studies confirm that empathy is positively related to children's offers to help others (Strayer & Schroder, 1989) and to their acceptance by peers (Fabes et al., 1994). Because empathic people tend to understand others' points of view, they are less likely to misunderstand and become angry over others' behaviors and more likely to develop social expertise (Hastings, Zahn-Waxler, Robinson, Usher, & Bridges, 2000).

The first unit in the Second Step program focuses on empathy and perspective taking because these skills provide the affective base for subsequent lessons in impulse control, social problem solving, and anger management. The empathy unit focuses on three skill areas (Feshbach, 1982):

- Identifying feelings through facial cues, body language, and situational cues.
- Taking the perspective of another person ("standing in another's shoes").
- Responding emotionally to another person.

In beginning empathy lessons, students view photographs of children displaying specific facial cues that provide clues to various emotional states (happy, sad, scared, and so on). The objective of these lessons is to help children identify physical characteristics that convey emotion. Later, the children practice detecting and displaying emotions through role play.

It is surprising how many young people have difficulty reading even the most basic emotional expressions. One Second Step teacher was amazed to see a usually disruptive and active boy sit spellbound as she displayed the emotion photographs. She later described him as someone who typically displayed little emotional expression himself and had difficulty understanding his peers. In a study on social-emotional competence, 5-year-olds with greater emotional understanding showed higher academic gains at age 9, even when compared with 5-year-olds with equal verbal abilities (Izard, Fine, Schultz, Mostow, & Ackerman, 2001).

Teachers have been ingenious in their attempts to make the empathy unit come to life for their students. One teacher had her students individually pose in various states of facial expression as she photographed them. Each student then had a group of photos from which to choose as he or she came to the circle for the Second Step lesson. At the beginning of each lesson, the teacher asked the children to show the group which photo best described their feelings that day. Those who could find no photo expression to illustrate their present state of mind were asked to draw a picture and show it to the class. Other teachers have used cartoonlike illustrations of facial expressions in the same way.

Subsequent empathy lessons teach about the roles of body language and situational cues in identifying and predicting feelings in others. The unit progresses to more sophisticated areas of empathy, covering such concepts as fairness, the possibility that feelings may change, and the fact that two people may feel differently about the same experience, such as riding on a roller coaster or encountering a large dog. Teachers often use the empathy lessons as springboards for rich discussion about children's cultural and family differences. This unit provides opportunities for spirited interaction with students, allowing them to link the classroom lessons with their lived experience.

Activity

Have you ever tried to talk with someone who obviously was not listening to you? A brief, 5-minute exercise presented during Second Step training for support staff illustrates how the lack of empathy skills (in particular, listening) leads to negative feelings and cognitive confusion on the part of the speaker. Adults as well as children are unable to think or communicate clearly when their listeners display inattention. Try this exercise with your class (recommended for third grade and older):

1. Involve your students in creating a list of poor listening skills (not looking at the speaker, doing something else while the person is talking, interrupting or introducing a different topic when the speaker is in mid-sentence, and so on). Post the list in a visible place. You may want to model this behavior in a role play that the class watches.

2. Ask each student to find a partner.

3. One partner will talk for 30 seconds about something he or she likes (a book, movie, vacation spot) while his or her partner demonstrates poor listening skills. Stop the activity and ask the students how they felt when their partners were not listening.

4. Create a list of active-listening skills (making eye contact with the speaker, nodding, showing empathic facial expression, asking questions pertinent to the speaker's topic). Again, you may need to conduct a model role play to demonstrate the behavior.

5. Repeat the activity using a different topic. This time, the listeners will use active-listening skills. Stop the activity and ask the students how they felt when their partners demonstrated listening skills.

PROBLEM SOLVING FOR IMPULSE CONTROL

Impulse control involves the ability to stop and think through consequences before taking action. This unit presents a five-step problem-solving strategy that is shown to contribute to socially competent behavior in children and youth (Kendall & Braswell, 1985; Spivack & Shure, 1982), combined with rehearsal of the behavioral skills required to put a solution into practice (Elliot & Gresham, 1993; Ladd & Mize, 1983; Michelson, 1987).

In learning problem-solving skills, students apply the five-step strategy to hypothetical, age-appropriate problem situations, and later, to real-life problems. The skill steps for problem solving require children to ask and respond to the following:

1. What is the problem?

2. What are some solutions?

3. For each solution, ask
   - Is it safe?
   - Is it fair?
   - How might people feel about it?
   - Will it work?

4. Choose a solution and use it.

5. Is it working? If not, what can I do now?

The steps are provided on posters for display in the classroom, in school hallways, on the playground, and in other areas of the school to encourage transfer of training through the course of students' normal daily activities. The parent component provides the same steps on refrigerator magnets to assist families in practicing and reinforcing the skills at home (see the Appendix at the end of this chapter).

Many educators make creative use of the problem-solving steps to encourage transfer of learning in real-life situations. Some Second Step schools integrate the problem-solving strategy with peer mediation. The student-peer mediators receive enriched training in the problem-solving steps and additional training in peer-mediation skills. These students look for opportunities to cue and coach their peers who are engaged in playground or lunchroom conflict. Because peer mediators coach students to use the same language and skill steps practiced in class, everyone is better prepared to move to a quick and just resolution of the problem.

Once students have practiced the problem-solving skill steps in various hypothetical situations, they rehearse application of their solutions through role play. Known among researchers as "behavioral social-skills training," this strategy has proven particularly useful when coupled with problem-solving steps (Marchione, Michelson, & Mannarino, 1984).

To illustrate how these two strategies work together, let's imagine that Heather wants to play with a toy that Lamar is using. In her attempt to solve the problem prosocially, Heather arrives at a creative solution: trading the desired toy with Lamar for another. However, executing a successful trade requires Heather to be proficient at putting her strategy into action. If unskilled in the strategy, Heather might grab the desired toy away from Lamar before handing the bartered item over to her now-defensive playmate. A fight ensues. Heather is mystified: "I picked a good solution! Why didn't it work?" Although she may have used the problem-solving steps correctly, her inept execution of an otherwise appropriate idea backfired. Rather than providing reinforcement of Heather's attempt at prosocial behavior, the consequence will likely work to its detriment.

In behavioral-skills training, a solution such as trading is practiced through role plays in which students learn to apply the strategies for negotiating a successful trade (Step 1: Consider an item for trade that the other child would find desirable, Step 2: Ask first if he or she would like to trade, and so on). Other examples of behavioral skills include interrupting politely, taking turns, apologizing, and resisting peer pressure. By practicing discreet social skills, children like Heather are more likely to be successful problem solvers in real life.

Suggested Activity

Use the problem-solving steps with your students to work through a problem shared by the whole class. For example, "When we go out to the playground, three groups of children want to play kickball and there's only one ball." Move through the steps together, including brainstorming and selecting solutions. Then move to Step 4, "Choose a solution and use it," the next time the class goes out for recess. Because your group may not possess the behavioral skills to put their solution into practice, an adult should be present to cue and coach the students as they attempt to implement their solution. Check back after recess and ask, "Did it work? If not, what can we do now?"

EMOTION MANAGEMENT

The Second Step program presents emotion management toward the end of the program because it is important that children first learn empathy and problem-solving skills. As students learn to regulate their emotions, such as anger, they are encouraged to solve the problem that first triggered the anger response. The anger management strategy has been successfully used with angry children (Nelson & Finch, 2000) and adolescents (Feindler, Marriott, & Iwata, 1984), and stress-reduction and anger management strategies have since been effectively implemented in numerous primary and secondary prevention programs (Lochman, Burch, Curry, & Lampron, 1984).

The emotion management steps help students recognize anger cues and triggers and use positive self-statements and stress-reduction techniques (e.g., counting to 10) to prevent the onset of uncontrollable angry feelings. Next, they apply the problem-solving strategy as a verbal mediation technique to solve the problem. Later, they reflect on the anger-provoking incident. The steps are as follows:

1. How does my body feel?

2. Calm down:
   - Take three deep breaths.
   - Count backward slowly.
   - Think calming thoughts.
   - Talk to myself.

3. Think out loud to solve the problem.

4. Think about it later:
   - Why was I angry?
   - What did I do?
   - What worked?
   - What didn't work?
   - What would I do differently?
   - Did I do a good job?

Like the problem-solving skills, the emotion steps are printed on posters. Educators are encouraged to display the skill-step posters in the hallways, lunchroom, classrooms, and outside areas. These steps are also sent home to parents to encourage family reinforcement.

Second Step educators demonstrate boundless creativity in reinforcing these skills throughout the day. One principal created small cards printed with the problem-solving steps on one side and the anger management steps on the reverse. Students carry the laminated business-sized cards in their pockets to encourage them to use the steps when confronted with a conflict. Playground and lunchroom supervisors and peer mediators carry the cards as coaching aids. Another school printed the steps on a laminated card attached to a key ring; students used their "keys to success" on the playground.

Beyond teaching the lessons, classroom teachers are well positioned to cue and coach students in their newfound skills as problems occur. Although transfer of learning is a critical aspect of SEL, it does not necessarily require intensive intervention. A teacher in Shoreline, Washington, sends his second graders to the "Second Step Corner" when they return from recess engaged in a conflict. The corner is a welcoming area in which the problem-solving and anger management posters are displayed with several photo cards from recent lessons. The students attempt to solve the problem themselves using the skills they have learned in class. He reports that they rarely need more direct intervention.

CURRICULUM STRUCTURE AND FORMAT

Preschool/Kindergarten Through Grade 5

At the early childhood and elementary levels, each of the units employs "photo-lesson" cards to teach the various skill lessons. Large, attractive photographs depict children at the appropriate grade level in various social or emotional situations. The reverse sides of the cards contain the lessons for the teacher to follow, lesson objectives, language-acquisition goals, notes to the teacher, role-play suggestions, transfer-of-learning ideas, and extension activities.

Teachers rate ease of use and minimum preparation time among the more attractive features of the curriculum. Each lesson suggests works of children's literature to help teachers integrate the Second Step program into their language arts curriculum. The program also provides video lessons, skill-step posters, and a Second Step Family Overview Video to engage parent support. The nonprofit creators of the Second Step program, Committee for Children (2004), have since developed a literacy and social-learning curriculum (titled *Woven Word: Early Literacy for Life*) designed to help early childhood educators integrate emergent literacy with Second Step lessons.

The most popular features of the preschool/kindergarten curriculum may be "Impulsive Puppy," "Be-Calm Bunny," and "Slow-Down Snail," the appealing stuffed puppets used to teach impulse-control skills. Children seem instinctively drawn to Impulsive Puppy, who, like them, needs help with such behaviors as interrupting politely, sharing, and taking turns. Impulsive Puppy mirrors the impish and sometimes aggressive enthusiasm of many 5-year-olds, but he learns from his friend Slow-Down Snail how to slow down, stop, and think before he acts. Over a series of lessons, children watch Impulsive Puppy change his behavior as he becomes more aware of the needs of others. His modeled transformation can be powerfully motivating to children as they struggle with similar changes in their own behavior. Be-Calm Bunny is passed from speaker to speaker in a preschool or kindergarten class to help teachers manage class discussion with young children.

Middle School and Junior High

The Second Step program for middle school and junior high is similar in content to the preschool/kindergarten through Grade 5 program, but it places stronger emphasis on student attitudes and beliefs about aggression. The format relies more on video, classroom activities, group discussion, and overhead transparencies for lesson instruction. The middle school curriculum presents a three-level format to encourage schoolwide implementation, accommodating schools that serve Grades 6 through 8 or 7 through 9.

The first module in the middle school/junior high series is referred to as Level 1: Foundation Lessons. This component contains 15 lessons and provides the foundation for the subsequent years. Level 1 introduces the basic Second Step skills and strategies and teaches a specific set of behavioral skills. Lessons in Levels 2 and 3 focus more on the motivation to act prosocially and the attitudes that contribute to those actions. The program contains lively video components that emphasize specific behavioral skills and address student attitudes and motivations.

SUSTAINING BEST IMPLEMENTATION PRACTICES

However good a program or approach may be, success over the long term depends largely on how SEL is lived out in the school. Based on a review of model sites of schools that were carrying out high-quality, empirically supported, prevention-oriented SEL programs, Maurice Elias and Patricia Kamarinos (2003) have outlined key features of programs that encourage sustainability over time:

- Intervention by program developers engages new administrators.
- Program consultation is offered to school staff.
- Training and professional development for staff needs to be constantly ongoing to respond to the evolution of staff and changes in school populations.
- They have deep involvement of teams of teachers.
- There is initial and continued involvement of invested role-model teachers.

- Programs are integrated into the whole-school scope and sequence.
- Districts develop capacity to assume some of cost.

Several of these key factors are addressed in the Second Step implementation steps outlined in the following.

SECOND STEP TRAINING FOR EDUCATORS

However well conceived, classroom lessons provide only half of the SEL equation. As Goleman's (1995) opening comment suggests, the way in which teachers impart these skills may be just as important as the lessons themselves. Second Step training is designed to give educators the information and skills they need to teach and reinforce social-emotional skills in the classroom and throughout the school.

Some educators receive intensive training as Second Step trainers, gaining skills, tools, and resources (including a set of training videos and a fully scripted trainer's manual) that enable them to train their school staff to teach the curriculum to students. The training-for-trainers model is beneficial because the school or district localizes its resources and creates an infrastructure that supports initial and long-term training needs. A deeper level of understanding of the Second Step program's pedagogy and theoretical underpinnings achieved by this higher level of training can allow educators to adapt the program to local needs and mandates while retaining the integrity of the core program.

Committee for Children provides models for refresher or booster training sessions designed to keep the program fresh, particularly as it continues over a period of school years. The organization also sends out a quarterly implementation support e-newsletter to educators with articles focused on implementation issues keyed to the time of year. For example, articles in the fall e-newsletter focus on themes such as "getting started" or "gaining buy-in from staff and parents," whereas spring articles might offer ideas for transferring social skills to the playground or planning training and implementation needs for the next school year. Committee for Children maintains a staff of highly trained educators turned implementation support specialists, who consult individually with Second Step administrators, trainers, and teachers by telephone or e-mail to support use of the program. Elias and Kamarinos (2003) suggested that outside consultation, as well as a school commitment to prioritizing SEL, makes it more likely that a program will endure in the face of change or crisis.

In the Milwaukee public schools, the district's school psychologists formed a cadre of trainers who participated in a 3-day Second Step training for trainers. The psychologists in turn provided onsite staff training to their schools (including teachers, administrators, and support staff) and ongoing Second Step implementation support. In subsequent years, the trainers provided follow-up trainings in the schools, met with principals about effective implementation strategies, and provided technical assistance to educators using the materials with special-needs students in inclusive classrooms. Throughout the years, Committee for Children's training and implementation support staff provided support to these trainers and district leaders, assisting them with ongoing program and training issues.

SCHOOLWIDE IMPLEMENTATION: FOSTERING A CLIMATE FOR CHANGE

The Second Step program is designed to be presented to students by their core class-room teachers. Although the need to train teachers in lesson presentation skills is somewhat obvious, school climate is more likely to improve if parents and all staff—bus drivers, playground supervisors, administrators, and other adults—receive training as well. Children will benefit far more from the classroom instruction if the adults in their lives consistently cue and coach them to use their newfound skills across the school curriculum and throughout their day.

Implementing the program schoolwide is likely to foster more positive outcomes than single-classroom or partial-school implementation (Elias et al., 1997). A school-wide approach offers educators—and particularly school administrators—the opportunity to transform the school climate. More than telling children which behaviors are and are not allowed, schoolwide implementation of the Second Step program teaches them how to enact those behaviors, whereas staff and parent training gives everyone—teachers, principals, support staff, and parents—similar language and strategies for reinforcement.

CONCLUSION

A well-conceived, research-based curriculum is an important ingredient for SEL, but not the only one. The Second Step program's success lies largely in the hands of the educators who use it. The degree to which lessons are consistently well conducted, the amount teachers and administrators cue and coach students to practice the strategies, and whether adults provide daily models for the very skills they strive to impart—these factors may play as important a role in effective social learning as the curriculum content. How the skills children and teachers learn are sustained over time is a crucial matter that needs more attention, both from program developers and those who implement the program, from administrators to classroom teachers and trainers.

In Goleman's (1995) words:

> The classes themselves may at first glance seem uneventful, much less a solution to the dramatic problems they address. But that is largely because, like good childrearing at home, the lessons imparted are small but telling, delivered regularly and over a sustained period of years. That is how emotional learning becomes ingrained; as experiences are repeated over and over, the brain reflects them as strengthened pathways, neural habits to apply in times of duress, frustration, hurt. And while the everyday substance of emotional literacy classes may look mundane, the outcome—decent human beings—is more critical to our future than ever. (p. 261)

APPENDIX

Parent Education: A Family Guide to the Second Step Program

Although research has demonstrated the Second Step program's effectiveness in changing children's behavior at school—even in the absence of parent education (Frey et al., 2005; Grossman et al., 1997)—there is reason to believe that without parent training, these changes are unlikely to transfer to other domains of children's lives (Ramsey, Patterson, & Walker, 1990; Simon & Johnston, 1987). In an effort to mend this gap, Committee for Children developed *A Family Guide to the Second Step Program* for preschool through Grade 5.

The family guide is intended for use with parents of students receiving Second Step instruction in school. In its entirety, the family guide consists of a series of six facilitator-led, video-based instruction modules. Throughout the six sessions, parents and caregivers discuss and practice the same concepts and strategies their children learn through the Second Step program. Video vignettes showing how parents can use the skills at home often elicit humorous self-reflection; one parent viewer was heard to quip, "I've been in that exact situation before. I 'lost it,' just like the mom in the video."

In some schools, family guide sessions are led by the school counselor or social worker. Other schools train a cadre of parents to conduct outreach and copresent the sessions. This is especially useful in schools with diverse immigrant populations. Parent attendance is supported by the provision of child care, refreshments, and most of all, the lively, interactive presentation style of the facilitators. Nonetheless, some parents may not attend the meetings. A take-home videotape (included in the curriculum) will provide a general overview of the Second Step program for families who do not attend.

REFERENCES

Bandura, A. (1973). *Aggression: A social learning analysis.* Englewood Cliffs, NJ: Prentice Hall.

Bandura, A. (1986). *Social foundations of thought and action: A social cognitive theory.* Englewood, NJ: Prentice-Hall.

Beland, K. (1988). *Second Step grades 1–3 pilot project.* Seattle, WA: Committee for Children.

Beland, K. (1989). *Second Step grades 4–5 pilot project.* Seattle, WA: Committee for Children.

Beland, K. (1991). *Second Step preschool-kindergarten pilot project.* Seattle, WA: Committee for Children.

Committee for Children. (1988). *Second Step: A violence prevention curriculum* (1st ed.). Seattle, WA: Author.

Committee for Children. (2004). *Woven word: Early literacy for life.* Seattle, WA: Author.

Crick, N. R., & Dodge, K. A. (1994). A review and reformulation of social information–processing mechanisms in children's social adjustment. *Psychological Bulletin, 115,* 74–101.

Development Services Group. (2003). OJJDP model programs guide. Retrieved September 12, 2005, from http://www.dsgonline.com/mpg2.5/TitleV_MPG_Table_AllProgramByTitle.asp

Dix, T. (1991). The affective organization of parenting: Adaptive and maladaptive processes. *Psychological Bulletin, 110,* 3–25.

Eisenberg, N., Fabes, R. A., & Lasoya, S. (1997). Emotional responding: Regulation, social correlates, and socialization. In P. Salovey & D. J. Sluyter (Eds.), *Emotional development and emotional intelligence: Educational implications* (pp. 129–163). New York: Basic Books.

Elias, M. J., & Kamarinos, P. (2003, August 8). *Sustainability of school-based preventive social-emotional programs: A model site study.* Presentation at the meeting of the American Psychological Association, Toronto, Canada.

Elias, M. J., Zins, J. E., Weissberg, R. P., Frey, K. S., Greenberg, M. T., Haynes, N. M., et al. (1997). *Promoting social and emotional learning: Guidelines for educators.* Alexandria, VA: Association for Supervision and Curriculum Development.

Elliot, S. N., & Gresham, F. M. (1993). Social skills interventions for children. *Behavior Modification, 17,* 287–313.

Fabes, R. A., Eisenberg, N., Karbon, M., Bernzweig, J., Speer, A. L., & Carlo, G. (1994). Socialization of children's vicarious emotional responding and prosocial behavior. Relations with mothers' perceptions of children's emotional reactivity. *Developmental Psychology, 30,* 44–55.

Feindler, F. I., Marriott, S. A., & Iwata, M. (1984). Group anger control training for junior high school delinquents. *Cognitive Therapy and Research, 8,* 229–311.

Feshbach, N. D. (1982). Studies of empathic behavior in children. In N. Eisenberg (Ed.), *The development of prosocial behavior* (pp. 315–318). New York: Academic Press.

Feshbach, N. D. (1984). Empathy, empathy training, and the regulation of aggression in elementary school children. In R. W. Kaplan, V. I. Konecni, & R. W. Novaco (Eds.), *Aggression in youth and children* (pp. 192–208). Boston: Maninus Nijhoff.

Frey, K. S., Nolen, S. B., Edstrom, L. V., & Hirschstein, M. K. (2005). Effects of a school-based social competence program: Linking behavior, goals, and attributions. *Journal of Applied Developmental Psychology, 26,* 171–200.

Goleman, D. (1995). *Emotional intelligence: Why it can matter more than IQ.* New York: Bantam Books.

Gottman, J. M., Katz, L. P., & Hooven, C. (1996). Parental meta-emotion philosophy and the emotional life of families: Theoretical models and preliminary data. *Journal of Family Psychology, 10,* 243–268.

Grossman, D. C., Neckerman, H. J., Koepsell, T. D., Liu, P. Y., Asher, K. N., Beland, K., et al. (1997). Effectiveness of a violence prevention curriculum among children in an elementary school: A randomized controlled trial. *Journal of the American Medical Association, 277,* 1605–1611.

Halberstadt, A. G., Denham, S. A., & Dunsmore, J. C. (2001). Affective social competence. *Emotional Social Development, 10,* 79–119.

Hastings, P. D., Zahn-Waxler, C., Robinson, J., Usher, B., & Bridges, D. (2000). The development of concern for others in children with behavior problems. *Developmental Psychology, 36,* 531–546.

Izard, C., Fine, S., Schultz, D., Mostow, A., & Ackerman, B. (2001). Emotion knowledge and social behavior. *Psychological Science, 12,* 18–23.

Kendall, P. C. (1993). Cognitive-behavioral therapies with youth: Guiding theory, current status, and emerging developments. *Journal of Counseling and Clinical Psychology, 61,* 235–247.

Kendall, P. C., & Braswell, L. (1985). *Cognitive behavioral therapy for impulsive children.* New York: Guilford.

Ladd, G. W., & Mize, J. (1983). A cognitive social learning model of social-skill training. *Psychological Review, 90,* 127–157.

Lochman, J. E., Burch, P. P., Curry, J. F., & Lampron, L. B. (1984). Treatment and generalization effects of cognitive-behavioral and goal-setting interventions with aggressive boys. *Journal of Counseling and Clinical Psychology, 52,* 916.

Luria, A. (1961). *The role of speech in the regulation of normal and abnormal behaviors.* New York: Liberight.

Maiuro, R., Cahn, T. S., & Vitaliano, P. (1986). Assertiveness deficits and hostility in domestically violent men. *Violence and Victims, 1*, 279–289.

Marchione, K., Michelson, L., & Mannarino, A. (1984). *Cognitive-behavioral treatment of antisocial behavior.* Unpublished manuscript, University of Pittsburgh, Pittsburgh, PA.

Michelson, L. (1987). Cognitive-behavioral strategies in the prevention and treatment of antisocial disorders in children and adolescents. In J. P. Burchard & S. N. Burchard (Eds.), *Prevention of delinquent behavior* (pp. 275–310). Newbury Park, CA: Sage.

Moore, B., & Beland, K. (1992). *Evaluation of Second Step preschool-kindergarten: A violence prevention curriculum kit. Summary report.* Seattle, WA: Committee for Children.

Nelson, W. M., III, & Finch, A. J., Jr. (2000). Managing anger in youth: A cognitive-behavioral intervention approach. In P. C. Kendall (Ed.), *Child and adolescent therapy: Cognitive-behavioral procedures* (pp. 129–170). New York: Guilford.

Ramsey, E., Patterson, G. R., & Walker, H. M. (1990). Generalization of the antisocial trait from home to school settings. *Journal of Applied Developmental Psychology, 11*, 209–223.

Simon, D. J., & Johnston, J. C. (1987). Working with families: The missing link in behavior disorder interventions. In R. B. Rutherford, C. M. Nelson, & S. R. Forness (Eds.), *Severe behavior disorders of children and youth* (pp. 447–460). New York: Wiley.

Spencer, L. M., & Spencer, S. M. (1993). *Competence at work: Models for superior performance.* New York: Wiley.

Spivack, G., & Cianci, N. (1987). High-risk early behavior pattern and later delinquency. In J. D. Burchard & S. N. Burchard (Eds.), *Prevention of delinquent behavior.* Newbury Park, CA: Sage.

Spivack, G., & Shure, M. B. (1982). The cognition of social adjustment: Interpersonal cognitive problem solving thinking. In B. B. Lahey & A. E. Kazdin (Eds.), *Advances in child psychology* (pp. 323–372). New York: Plenum.

Strayer, J., & Schroder, M. (1989). Children's helping strategies: Influences of emotion, empathy, and age. In N. Eisenberg (Ed.), *Empathy and related emotional responses* (pp. 85–105). San Francisco: Jossey-Bass.

Van Schoiak-Edstrom, L., Frey, K. S., & Beland, K. (2002). Changing adolescents' attitudes about relational and physical aggression: An early evaluation of a school-based intervention. *School Psychology Review, 31*, 201–216.

Weissberg, R. P., & Greenberg, M. T. (1997). School and community competence-enhancement and prevention programs. In W. Damon (Series Ed.), I. E. Sigel, & K. A. Renninger (Vol. Eds.), *Handbook of child psychology: Vol. 5. Child psychology in practice* (5th ed., pp. 877–954). New York: John Wiley & Sons.

Wentzel, K. R., & Wigfield, A. (1998). Academic and social motivational influences on students' academic performance. *Educational Psychology Review, 10*, 155–175.

White House. (1998). *Annual report on school safety.* Available from www.ed.gov/pubs/AnnSchoolRept98/

18

Fostering Caring, Character, and Responsibility in Schools

Susan Carroll Keister

Social and emotional skills come alive when adults and young people experience and demonstrate caring, character, and responsibility with one another in respectful learning environments.

Welcome to four different schools that share a common concern that the social and emotional well-being of their students not get left behind under the guidelines of No Child Left Behind legislation being enacted in America's schools. All four found a common solution: They turned to evidence-based social-emotional learning (SEL) programs developed by Lions-Quest as the way to meet their students' needs. The author of this chapter has worked with these schools and numerous others to help them implement SEL efforts. As the forthcoming stories and quotes from educators reflect, one need not sacrifice educational excellence in the name of interpersonal goals. Indeed, the two are interdependent.

At Summit Elementary School outside of Columbus, Ohio, the entire staff has been trained in the Lions-Quest positive youth development model. As a result, school staff, parents, and community members convene regularly to dialogue about how they are going to help bring the school's mission statement to life for their children. Similarly, Principal Kathy Erhard holds regular meetings with teachers and students to "listen more, ask more" about how they want to teach and learn. Teachers model caring and collaboration as they engage their students in establishing guidelines for respect and safety that make genuine conversations, cooperative learning, and teamwork flourish in their classrooms.

In a Lions-Quest Skills for Growing program for Grades K through 5, in Raleigh, North Carolina, children go out on the playground, set up a game, agree on the rules, and settle disputes without adult intervention. School staff and students have been discussing and practicing ways to communicate their needs and solve problems in a positive, helpful way. Program coordinator Barry McMillion commented,

> I overheard two third graders discussing what bugged them. One said, "I really don't appreciate it when you do that." The other said, "I didn't know that bothered you. I'm sorry." An exchange like this would have been very unusual before Skills for Growing.

Using an approach that combined social consciousness with solid information and prosocial skills, Jack Terry's students in his Lions-Quest Skills for Adolescence middle school class in Westfield, Indiana, concluded their study of drug prevention skills by marching nearly a mile from their school to present a store owner with a petition signed by more than 500 students that asked for the removal of pro-drug publications. Students Brian Schenberg and Molly Ehmer read the following to the store owner:

> We, the members and friends of the Westfield Middle School Lions-Quest class, a class that deals with drug prevention, do hereby respectfully submit the following petition to your store. We do hereby request that you cooperate with the war on drugs by withdrawing the magazines, *Living High* and *High Times,* and other such magazines from your store. This type of magazine promotes and encourages the use of drugs.

The same day, the manager removed the magazines from the stands and applauded the young people for standing up for their beliefs.

Students at Bishop Ford Central High School in Brooklyn, New York, worked with several community agencies on several violence-prevention service projects as part of their participation in the Lions-Quest Skills for Action program. After learning skills in class and applying them through service, seniors facilitated 8-week sessions to orient freshmen to conflict resolution. In an interview with the author, teacher Karen Musicaro noted, "The combination of the in-depth materials on violence with direct service made students appreciate how much skill it takes to resolve real community conflicts and make peace."

THE IMPORTANCE OF RESPECTFUL RELATIONSHIPS

In each of these stories, young people, teachers, and other caring adults are working together in the teaching and learning of social-emotional competencies. We continue to ask ourselves, "What quality of relationships between teachers and learners characterize these situations? What characterizes learning environments that bring self-discipline, responsibility, good judgment, the ability to get along with others, and the ethic of service alive in young people?"

The programs of the Lions Clubs International Foundation (n.d.), called Lions-Quest,

> are based on the philosophy that to become healthy, capable adults, children must develop healthy behaviors, communication and decision making skills, and strong attachments with those who hold positive standards. They need meaningful opportunities to contribute to their family, school, and community and the means to develop critical thinking and interpersonal skills.

The mission is based on a simple premise: The quality of young people's lives is determined by meaningful relationships with significant adults in their lives—parents, extended family members, teachers, caregivers, coaches, youth workers, mentors, and friends. Lions-Quest's programs engage families, schools, and community members in working together to promote young people's healthy development and reduce conditions that put them at risk for problem behaviors. This means

1. strengthening the bonds between youth and their families, peers, school staff, and the community;

2. ensuring that all youth feel cared for, valued, and supported;

3. teaching the social, emotional, intellectual, physical, and ethical competencies that promote healthy behaviors, positive relationships, and a sense of purpose;

4. encouraging healthy aspirations and achievement;

5. providing meaningful opportunities for youth participation and contribution;

6. creating clear standards for behaviors and strong norms against violence and illegal drugs.

FIVE ESSENTIAL PROGRAM ELEMENTS

Lions-Quest offers K through 12 programs, educational materials, training, and services in the areas of essential life skills, character development, service learning, and positive prevention of health-compromising behaviors. Our programs include five main components that we believe are essential elements in a schoolwide climate that promotes SEL.

Professional Development and Follow-up Support

We believe that to effectively teach social-emotional competencies, educators themselves must embrace and model the essence of caring, character, and responsibility in their own behaviors. This requires that professional development accompany the implementation of Lions-Quest programs—powerful interactive experiences that include immersion into and dialogue about the programs' philosophy and program components along with hands-on practice in the teaching and learning strategies. We also recommend that an implementation team consisting of an administrator, teachers, and parent and community representatives attend the workshop. This way, everyone supporting the program in the school hones their social-emotional skills in (a) creating a safe and trusting classroom climate, (b) asking open-ended questions that spark divergent thinking, (c) listening carefully to truly understand others, (d) responding in ways that communicate genuine interest and acceptance, (e) leading discussions that generate authentic conversations, (f) facilitating groupwork that builds cooperation and leadership skills, (g) reflecting about learning in ways that generate personal meaning for students, and (h) validating young people's efforts in specific ways that promote transfer of learning.

K Through 12 Classroom Curriculum

The classroom curricula provide multiple strategies for teaching, integrating, and reinforcing specific personal, social, emotional, and thinking skills and program concepts across the disciplines and at home. Lesson plans follow a constructivist approach to teaching and learning (see the "Teaching Strategies for SEL" section for details) and focus on the following social-emotional competencies:

1. Building self-discipline, responsibility, and awareness of abilities and talents

2. Communicating effectively and cooperating with others

3. Celebrating diversity and respecting the unique contributions of others

4. Managing attitudes and emotions, with special emphasis on anger management

5. Strengthening positive relationships with family and peers

6. Learning and developing skills in solving problems, resolving conflicts, and making healthy decisions

7. Resisting negative peer pressure, drug use, and violence

8. Thinking critically

9. Setting goals and following through

10. Providing service to others

Service learning is central to all Lions-Quest curricula as a way for students to learn and apply the personal and social skills being taught in the program. Through ongoing service experiences and reflection, they develop compassion, tolerance, and perseverance along with communication and conflict resolution skills by working with diverse populations and meeting real needs in the school and community. Service learning provides the practice and application phase of SEL.

Positive School Climate

Brain and mind research indicates that learning is optimized in a low-threat environment that promotes relaxed alertness. This involves establishing real relationships, developing shared classroom agreements, co-leading class meetings, engaging in cooperative group work, influencing the content of the curriculum, making group decisions, implementing service-learning projects, and reflecting together about their learning. School climate is enhanced through a school climate team of parents, students, community members, and teachers who work together to develop a series of schoolwide events related to key skills, themes, and concepts in the program.

Family Involvement

Families play a vital and active role in shaping young people's learning experiences in Lions-Quest's programs. For example, parents receive five student-family activity booklets at each grade in Skills for Growing that reinforce the skills and concepts being taught in the classroom. Opportunities to participate on the advisory team and parent forums are encouraged in Skills for Action. Parents and community members participate on the implementation teams, engage in shared homework assignments, participate in prepared parent meetings, attend the professional development workshops, mentor the service-learning projects, and become a resource to the program in the classroom or school.

Community Involvement

Members of organizations such as Lions Clubs International, businesses, law enforcement groups, youth-serving organizations, and religious institutions consistently participate in the programs' implementation by attending workshops, participating on the school teams, helping with service-learning projects, volunteering as a classroom resource, and co-leading parent meetings. Lions in particular contribute regularly to the ongoing financial support of the program.

TEACHING STRATEGIES FOR SEL

To effectively teach social-emotional competencies, the teachers themselves must embrace a teaching and learning philosophy that models the attitudes, feelings, and behaviors we aim to teach. Our teaching and learning practices are rooted in this belief system: (a) All young people are full of potential—social, emotional, intellectual, physical, and ethical—and bring all parts of themselves to the learning situation; (b) adults who acknowledge and honor the full potential of young people communicate deep respect and a willingness to join as partners in learning; (c) young people join with adults in a learning community of reciprocal relationships; and (d) reciprocal relationships and safe environments allow young people to participate in the high challenge–low threat learning experiences that ignite learning and unleash potential.

The Lions-Quest four-phase lesson design optimizes SEL by teaching, modeling, and reinforcing the essential life skills that are the content of the Lions-Quest curricula. The phases are described in the following:

1. *Discovering* initially what learners already know about a topic through questioning, engaging in a variety of search strategies on the Internet (also known as *Webbing*), and brainstorming techniques in whole group experiences;

2. *Connecting* their current knowledge to new information and skills through research, hypothesis, presentations, discussions and dialogue, modeling,

guest speakers, and graphic organizers in individual, small, and whole group activities;

3. *Practicing* the new information or skills in a meaningful context through role playing, skits, creative writing, games, simulations, and questioning strategies in individual, small group, or whole group activities; and

4. *Applying* new knowledge to other subject areas, such as language arts, health, science, math, music, or art using all the strategies and groupings listed previously, or to meeting real needs through service learning. (See Sample Lesson, "What Bugs You?" in the Appendix at the end of this chapter.)

LESSON CONTENT AT THE MIDDLE AND HIGH SCHOOL

The essential life skills in Lions-Quest programs are developmentally sequenced so that they may be implemented as a continuous, comprehensive skill-building curriculum throughout Grades K through 12. For example, the skill of communicating a need in an honest and respectful way in the sample lesson is also included in Grades K through 2 and Grades 3 through 5 in Lions-Quest Skills for Growing in a developmentally appropriate way.

Similarly, at the middle school level, the skill takes the form of a lesson titled, "Communicating With What, Why, and How Messages," in the Lions-Quest Skills for Adolescence program. In this lesson, students explore their collective perceptions about why it is important to tell others how their behavior is affecting them. They learn about What, Why, and How messages and practice, through role playing and journaling how to communicate strong emotions such as anger or frustration in a positive and constructive way. The skill steps follow:

- Name *what* behavior is bothering you.
- Explain *why* it is bothering you and how you feel about it.
- Say *how* you would like the other person to behave instead.

After student volunteers practice with the teacher in front of the large group, pairs pick situations and refine their messages until they are clear and honest, free of put-downs and blame. After sharing and discussing them, students read an article, "Understanding and Handling Your Emotions," in their *Changes and Challenges* book and write a notebook entry about how they may apply What, Why, and How messages to situations they are likely to confront.

Similarly, Lions-Quest Skills for Action, and the topical program Teens—Alcohol and Other Drugs for Grades 9 through 12, continue this skill sequence with a series of lessons in the Skills Bank on interpersonal communication, specifically several related lessons on "communicating our needs." Instead of the skill being taught primarily as a self-contained lesson, it is taught through three application options: teach, reinforce, and enrich.

These options are used in conjunction with the service-learning experiences that characterize the high school curricula as a way to teach, reinforce, enrich, and reflect on skills that are needed to carry out service work. For example, one of the options has students describing in writing a situation they experienced in their service-learning work when they had to share a difficult need or feeling with others. They explain how they handled it then and how they would handle it now. Students share their experiences with the group and reflect on what communication style often results in arguments and hurt feelings, how to focus on the behavior and not the person, and how to be honest without threatening others. They examine how communication styles can vary from culture to culture and how important it is to check for understanding. At the end of the lesson, they prepare for new situations in which this skill may lead to more understanding and closer relationships with others they know. In this way, the skills are being taught in a real-world context at the time when they are genuinely needed.

FAMILY AND COMMUNITY INVOLVEMENT

In the "What Bugs You" lesson from Skills for Growing, families are invited to participate in the lesson through the *Together Times* student-family activity booklets that accompany all five units at Grades K through 5 (see Sample Lesson, Appendix). In "Communicating With What, Why, and How Messages" from Skills for Adolescence, families receive a letter introducing the skill that is being taught in the class, and parents are invited to attend the parent meeting on What, Why, and How messages provided in the *Supporting Young Adolescents* parent-meetings guide. They are also encouraged to read the accompanying article about healthy and honest communication with teenagers in the *Surprising Years* parent book.

Skills for Action and Teens—Alcohol and Other Drugs invite parents to attend student-led family forums to discuss the topics being addressed and experienced in these programs. In all programs, the Lions Club members and other interested community people are invited to attend all parent meetings and forums and read the parent activity booklets and books that accompany the programs.

EVIDENCE OF POSITIVE OUTCOMES

In evaluation results from more than 60 research studies, the Lions-Quest comprehensive programs, Skills for Growing (K–5) and Skills for Adolescence (6–8), have demonstrated effectiveness in strengthening the attitudes, feelings, and behaviors that promote positive social behaviors and protect young people from harmful, high-risk behaviors. These findings, conducted by independent agencies and Lions-Quest's own research and evaluation staff and audited by Pennsylvania State University, indicate that Skills for Growing students demonstrated significant improvements in their perception of the risks of harmful substances, their knowledge of peer relationships and decision-making skills, their feelings of positive self-concept, and their ability to make decisions without peer pressure.

Skills for Adolescence students had higher perceptions of expectations for success in school; significant improvements on the nationally normed California Achievement Test in both reading and mathematics; significant improvements in their attitudes and awareness of the harm of alcohol and other drugs; significantly improved knowledge about the risks of alcohol and other drugs; lower uses of beer, liquor, and chewing tobacco; and significantly lower intention to use beer and liquor in the next 30 days.

Skills for Action students maintained a low risk of dropping out of school and significant attitudinal gains in positive community values and interpersonal competence, such as responsibility and empathy for others, working effectively with others, and belief in getting things done. Students also showed perceived gains in communication skills, dealing with diversity, and showing concern for the well-being of others.

CONCLUSION

Social and emotional intelligence is vital to educating the whole person. Research in learning and human potential shows that young people flourish in high challenge–low threat learning environments in which respectful and caring relationships among young people and adults are consistently modeled, taught, and honored. When this mutual respect is communicated and upheld, teachers and learners alike are safe enough to reach inside themselves, try new things, take risks, and discover the depth of their own innate intelligence and creativity. As new skills, abilities, and talents emerge, people feel good about themselves and show a greater tendency to acknowledge and celebrate the progress and successes of others. This creates a genuine learning community of reciprocal relationships that brings forth the potential of every learner. When adults and young people embody the social-emotional competencies of self-awareness and discovery, respect and empathy for others, positive social behaviors, and motivation to be their best as a new way of being together, strong character and academic achievement soar. The classroom and school become places where people consciously provide for each other every opportunity to unlock, reveal, and share the full potential and intelligence in each of them.

Children benefit from positive youth development programs that provide dynamic teaching tools and experiential learning opportunities in social-emotional skills, service learning, active citizenship, character development, and the prevention of health-compromising behaviors. They also require a curriculum supported by processes that enhance positive classroom and school climate, build meaningful parent and community involvement, and encourage professional development for adults in how to embrace and model these competencies. In this way, young people are nourished by a caring and informed network of adults. When all partners become skilled in creating safe learning environments and modeling caring, character, and responsibility in respectful relationships, they cannot help but transform themselves and their schools.

Author's Note: Ongoing information about all aspects of the Lions-Quest program can be found at www.lions-quest.org.

APPENDIX

Sample Lesson

Included in the following is a sample lesson from the Lions-Quest Skills for Growing curriculum. This lesson provides an example of how Lions-Quest's programs address multiple learning styles with a variety of teaching and learning strategies designed to promote divergent thinking, cooperative group work, individual and group reflection, and transfer of learning to new applications. The lesson is also relevant to the issues in children's lives and provides practice in essential social-emotional competencies for self-discipline, responsibility, good judgment, and the ability to get along with others.

What Bugs You?

Skills for Growing, Grade 3, Unit 2, Lesson 3: "What Bugs You?"

Purpose

To help students learn to give helpful feedback when others are annoying them.

Lesson Objectives

The student will be able to do the following:

1. Explain how to respond when the behavior of a classmate irritates him or her.

2. Demonstrate responding in a positive way to annoying behaviors.

Preparation and Materials

Prepare the chart shown in Phase 2. Write the "bugging" situations listed in Phase 3, Number 2, on separate cards, making one card for every two students.

Phase 1: Discovering

1. The students name behaviors that bug them.

   Write "Behaviors That Bug Me" on chart paper. Ask the students to name some things classmates do that bug or bother them at school. Caution them not to mention any names. List their responses on the chart.

2. The students think about how they feel when someone bugs them.

   Tell the students you will read a list of different ways people sometimes feel when someone bugs them. Then ask them to think about their own feelings when someone bothers them.

   When someone bugs me, I usually feel one of the following ways:

   - Afraid to say anything because I might hurt that person's feelings
   - Worried that if I say something, others will get mad at me
   - Angry because someone is bothering me
   - Unsure what to do or say

3. The students think about things they do when someone bugs them.

Now ask the students to think about what they often do when someone bugs them as you read another list. Ask the students what might happen as a result of these reactions.

When someone bugs me, I usually do one of the following:

- Yell at them to stop bothering me
- Act as if everything is okay
- Tell my friends what I don't like about the person who made me mad
- Ignore the person and act rude
- Make a joke about it and hope the person gets the hint

Phase 2: Connecting

1. Explain the purpose of the lesson.

Explain that as we work and play together, there will be times when the behavior of others will upset us. Sometimes our feelings are hurt, or we get angry. These feelings are normal, but what we say and do when we are upset can either make the situation worse or help solve the problem. The purpose of this lesson is to discover ways to work out the problems so we can get along with each other.

2. Explain helpful ways to take care of "bugs."

Show the class the chart you have prepared and explain each part.

When Someone Bugs You:

Name the behavior that is bugging you.

Say what you want to happen instead.

- Name the behavior that is bugging you.

One way to begin solving the problem is to let the person know exactly what he or she is doing that annoys you. This is called attacking the problem, rather than attacking the person with mean words such as "You jerk!" and "You're so dumb." When you attack the person, you make the situation worse.

- Say what you want to happen instead.

What would you like the person to do or stop doing? Is there something you would both do together that would solve the problem?

Note: Clarify that there is not any right order to their responses. The important thing is to include both parts.

3. Provide examples of two ways to respond to bugging behaviors.

Read the following situations to the students. Ask them to put thumbs up if they think the reaction to the problem is helpful. Ask them to put thumbs down if they think the reaction is going to make the situation worse.

Situation: Someone borrows your paste without asking.

- "When you borrow my paste without asking, I don't know where it is. Next time, please ask before you borrow things from me."

Situation: Someone says your idea is dumb.

- "Well, I don't like your idea either. I don't even like you."

Situation: Someone keeps telling you what to do.

- "Who do you think you are, the boss? I can do this myself without your help. Why don't you just shut up?"

Situation: Someone borrowed your new colored pens several days ago and has not returned them yet.

- "I need my pens back now so I can work on my art project. I'd appreciate it if you'd return the things you borrow from me."

4. Check for understanding.

Pick three of four behaviors from the "Behaviors That Bug Me" chart from Phase 1 and ask the students to think of helpful ways to respond. Guide them in their answers and review the process, if necessary.

Phase 3: Practicing

1. Assign partners.

Help the students find partners, perhaps by drawing names two at a time from a container.

2. Explain the activity.

Explain that now the students will practice telling a partner in a helpful way about a bugging behavior. (Make sure the chart from Phase 2 is posted.) Give each pair a card with one of the following situations on it:

Situations

- A person in your group keeps poking you with a pencil and laughing when you get upset. What can you say?
- A girl in your group says she doesn't care what you draw for your picture. When the rest of you decide to draw a city, she gets mad. What can you say to her?
- You and a classmate are using markers to draw a picture. Your classmate keeps writing on you with the markers. What can you say?
- If it is your turn to answer a question, but someone else shouts out the answer, what can you say?
- Every time you have a good idea, someone in your group says it is no good and suggests something else. What can you say to this person?
- You just saw someone whispering to another classmate and looking at you. They were both laughing. What can you say to them?

Explain that the partners will read the card together and decide who will be the first to respond. Partners will respond in a helpful way to the bugging behavior described on the card. Then the partners will exchange cards with another pair. After reading the new situation, the second partner will respond in a helpful way.

3. Model the activity.

Select one of the cards, read it to the class, and respond in a helpful way.

4. The students work with partners to practice responding.

As the partners work together, circulate among the students and listen to their responses. If any partners are having difficulty, review the chart from Phase 2 and clarify the activity, if necessary.

5. Have volunteers demonstrate their responses for the class.

Read various situations aloud, and invite volunteers to stand up and demonstrate a response. Then ask others in the class to explain how well they think the response addressed the bugging behavior.

Closure (with students still in pairs)

- Did you find it difficult or easy to practice responding in helpful ways?
- Stand up if you thought it was easy. Raise your hand if it was difficult.
- Ask several students to explain their answers.
- "How do you think this lesson will help us get along as we work and play together? Raise your hand if you would like to share what you are thinking."
- "What will you do the next time someone bugs you? Tell a neighbor."

Phase 4: Applying

Select one or more of the following activities to help your students apply the lesson objectives to a new situation.

1. *Together Times*, **the Student-Family Activity Booklet**

Place the students into pairs and pass out the *Together Times*. Ask students to write their own responses on the backs of the bugs in the picture. Ask them to write about behaviors that bug them at school without mentioning the names of other students. Partners can help each other with ideas, but everyone will complete his or her own work. When the class is finished, ask volunteers to share some of their responses.

2. **Language Arts**

Working Out the Bugs

Have the students work in groups of three to make up skits showing how to respond in a helpful way when someone is bothering them.

After the skits are planned, have each student cut out one finger puppet, draw a face on it, and tape it to a finger. When the puppets are ready, ask the groups to decide who will be Puppets 1, 2, and 3. Puppet 1 will be the "botherer," and the other two will respond in a helpful way. If possible, use a large box as a stage or have students kneel behind a table or desk. Have the groups take turns presenting their skits to the class. Encourage the audience to tell what they liked about each skit.

3. A Buggy Bulletin Board

For this activity, ask students to write about a behavior that bugs them at school and what they can say to help solve the problem. (Caution them not to use the names of classmates.) When the papers are completed, have students display them on a bulletin board along with their own buggy creations made from a variety of art materials such as scrap paper, yarn, pipe cleaners, and glitter. You may want to include the chart from Phase 2 and the tickler poem "Bug Control" on the bulletin board as reminders of how to respond appropriately to bugging behaviors.

Closure

- "Think about what happens when people call others names instead of saying what is bothering them. Tell your neighbor one thing that could happen."
- "What are some times when responding in a helpful way might come in handy outside of class? Tell your neighbor one example."
- "Why do you think people who work together need to know how to talk to each other when something is bugging them? Raise your hand if you know a reason."

REFERENCE

Lions Clubs International Foundation. (n.d.). *Lions-Quest programs*. Retrieved September 12, 2005, from www.lions-quest.org/content/OurPrograms/OurPrograms.htm

19

Teaching Life Skills in the Schools

Steven J. Danish and Tanya Forneris

To be successful in life, it is not enough to know what to avoid; one must also know how to succeed. To succeed requires learning how to be competent. By *competent*, we are referring to the ability to do life planning, be self-reliant, and be able to seek help from others (Danish, D'Augelli, & Ginsberg, 1984). With the increasing emphasis on raising academic standards, many have come to view learning the three R's as *the* passport for future success. However, without the concomitant life skills, this passport is likely to be little more than a piece of paper symbolizing unrealized potential. As Comer (1988) has so aptly noted, schools have a responsibility for the total development of their students.

The Going for the Goal (GOAL) program (Danish, 1997, 2002a, 2002b) was developed to teach adolescents how to think about and develop confidence in their future, as well as how to acquire a sense of personal control over themselves and their environment so that they can make better decisions and ultimately become better citizens. To teach students to be self-directing, we must empower them. Empowering them involves enhancing their well-being by promoting healthy choices, including learning how to set personal goals, learning how to achieve these goals in the immediate future, and believing in their future. Part of the process we use to help empower participants is to teach planfulness. For example, one sixth grader who participated in GOAL reported that not only should he have a goal about his future, but he needed to start now: "This year, it's, like, more serious, 'cause you've got a whole lot of work, and you've got to try harder. I've got the future to think about now." Other students discussed the importance of choosing friends who had similar goals and were doing well in school. Other behaviors that students mentioned were "getting to bed earlier and getting up in the morning" and "coming to school every day whether I want to or not." A sixth-grade girl said, "Last year, I spent a lot of time trying to impress everybody else and not being me—no more." Another girl said, "Studying before a test doesn't help me; I got to spend a whole week." In other words, these students were telling us that they needed to learn life skills.

Life skills are those skills that enable students to succeed in the different environments in which they live, such as school, home, and their neighborhoods. Life skills can be behavioral (communicating effectively with peers and adults), cognitive (making effective decisions), interpersonal (being assertive), or intrapersonal (setting goals). Environments vary from individual to individual, thus the definition of what it means to succeed will differ across individuals, as well as across environments. Individuals in the same environment are likely to be dissimilar from each other as a result of the life skills they have already mastered, their other resources, and their opportunities, real or perceived. For this reason, the needed life skills are likely to be different for individuals of different ages, ethnic or racial groups, or economic status. Although it is necessary to be sensitive to these differences, it is important to recognize that there is a core set of life skills that all individuals need to know and that many individuals can effectively apply life skills learned in one environment to other environments as appropriate (Danish, 1997). In the GOAL program, both the core set of skills and how to transfer skills across setting are taught.

THE GOAL PROGRAM

In GOAL, students are taught how to (a) identify positive life goals, (b) focus on the process (not the outcome) of goal attainment, (c) use a general problem-solving model, (d) identify health-promoting behaviors that can facilitate goal attainment, (e) identify health-compromising behaviors that can impede goal attainment, (f) seek and create social support, and (g) transfer these skills from one life context to another.

There are 10 one-hour, skill-based workshops. After the first workshop, each subsequent workshop begins with a review of what has been taught in the previous workshop. In seven of the workshops, the review precedes a brief skit introducing the material to be covered. Skits feature the "Goal Seeker," a student who wants to become a computer programmer; "Goal Keeper," an individual who helps the student learn how to set and reach goals; and "Goal Buster," someone who is always trying to look for ways to block the student from reaching a goal. During the workshops, students play the roles of the characters during the skits. In each workshop, the Goal Seeker faces some sort of obstacle to goal attainment. By using the skill taught in the workshop that day, goal attainment becomes more certain.

In the first workshop, "Dare to Dream," the participants and the leaders, who are older peers, get to know each other. Students learn the importance of dreams and how to dream about their future. There are two major activities in this workshop for the students: (a) to identify goal keepers and goal busters in their lives and (b) to dream about their future and identify their *best* future 10 years hence in four areas—house and car, friends and family, career, and hobbies. Identifying their best future is emphasized so that the students do not settle for what they think they can reach—something too common for many students, especially those who have never or rarely experienced life successes.

In the second workshop, "Setting Goals," students learn that a goal is defined as a dream they work hard to reach. They learn the value of goal setting and the importance of setting reachable goals. The four characteristics of a reachable goal are that it must be stated positively, elaborated specifically, important to the goal setter, and under the goal setter's control. The activities in this workshop revolve around learning how to distinguish goals that are reachable (have the essential four characteristics) from those that are not.

In Workshop 3, "Making Your Goal Reachable," students apply what they learned in the second workshop. They are asked to write a reachable goal to be attained in the next 6 weeks and to make sure that it meets the four essential characteristics. The goal we ask them to set should be related to their job or career dream. An example of a goal statement for a student who wanted to be a computer programmer might be "to want to earn a B in math during this marking period by completing and turning in every homework assignment during the next 6 weeks." Following the construction of their goal statement, students receive feedback from their leaders and peers to make sure their goal statement adheres to the four characteristics of a reachable goal. By the end of the session, students have a goal statement that they work with for the rest of the program.

In the fourth workshop, "Making a Goal Ladder," students learn how to make a plan to reach their goal. They put their goal at the top of the goal ladder, identify at least six steps (all of which must meet the characteristics of a reachable goal), and then place them in the order needed to reach the goal at the top of the ladder. Finally, the students identify target dates by which each step or rung will be completed and sign a statement making a commitment to work hard to reach the goal. One of the steps on the ladder is to be completed during the upcoming week. For example, for the student whose goal was to earn a B in math by completing all the math assignments on time during the next 6 weeks, a goal ladder might be (a) write down the assignment each day, (b) ask questions in class when he or she does not understand, (c) bring home the math book every day, (d) set aside a time each day to do the assignment, and (e) ask the teacher questions about the homework items that are not understood.

In the fifth workshop, "Roadblocks to Reaching Goals," students learn how to identify roadblocks and their effect on goal attainment. They learn how various roadblocks such as drug abuse, teen pregnancy, violence, dropping out of school, and lack of self-confidence can prevent them from reaching their goals in life. They read brief stories of others who encounter roadblocks and identify some of their own possible roadblocks to their current goals.

In the sixth workshop, "Overcoming Roadblocks," students learn a problem-solving strategy called STAR (Stop and chill out, Think of all your choices, Anticipate the consequences of each choice, and Respond with the best choice). They practice using STAR in a number of simulated situations that they may encounter at school, after school, or at home.

In the seventh workshop, "Seeking Help from Others," participants learn the importance of seeking social support to achieve goals. Two types of help, "doing" help and "caring" help, are described. Their activities include engaging in a game that requires helping each other, identifying a "Dream Team" of 10 individuals (e.g., family members, friends they trust, and adults such as teachers, coaches, ministers, and youth group leaders) who can help them reach their goals by providing caring and doing help, and practicing how to ask for help in several simulated situations.

In the eighth workshop, "Rebounds and Rewards," students learn how to rebound when a goal or a step on the goal ladder becomes too difficult to reach. They learn to assess possible reasons for failing to reach their goal and to develop a rebounding plan. They are also asked to respond to simulated letters that depict individuals who have not reached their goals and to suggest strategies to help them be successful. Finally, they are asked to recognize their accomplishments to date and develop a plan to reward themselves for these accomplishments.

In the ninth workshop, "Identifying and Building on Your Strengths," participants identify their personal strengths, including those learned through the program, and identify how they learned these strengths. Then they are asked to identify an area in which they want to improve and list ways they can undertake this improvement based on their strengths and previous successes. This process is designed to help them transfer skills they have learned from one life domain to another.

In the 10th and final workshop, "Going for Your Goal," students play a game, "Know-It-All-Baseball," which provides an opportunity for them to integrate and apply the information covered in the nine other workshops, recite a rap which describes what they have learned, and take a pledge to continue working toward their goals and dreams.

Each workshop also includes a series of quotes appropriate to the workshop, an activity to be completed between workshops at home that often involves parents or other adults, and a choice of several closing activities that provides some review of the material learned.

DELIVERING LIFE SKILLS PROGRAMS

The program is delivered using what Seidman and Rappaport (1974) called an educational pyramid. At the Life Skills Center, we have begun to think of it as a leadership pyramid. The structural premise of the model we use is that life skills should be taught at all levels of participation. By teaching life skills at all levels, we maximize the positive effect that these skills can have for all the levels of participants involved in the program. Moreover, by involving various layers in a community, we are expanding community capacity through this radiating process.

The pyramid has four levels. At the top are staff from the Life Skills Center who know the program and are skilled in training others. The next level of the pyramid is composed of community or school personnel who coordinate the program in their respective settings. They participate in a 1- to 2-day condensed version of GOAL during which they perform all of the exercises that they will be teaching their students and practice teaching some of the workshops. If at all possible, college students are included at this level. We have found college students to be effective teachers and supervisors of the high school student-leaders. They also serve as role models for the high school student-leaders. Often these college students participate as part of a service-learning course.

The third level on the pyramid is the high school student-leaders, who are selected by their schools. We provide guidelines and a format for their selection, but the final decision about which students will be chosen is a local one. The student-leaders represent positive role models for the younger students they are teaching, who are the fourth level of the pyramid. Therefore, the student-leaders should have a good academic record, leadership qualities, involvement in extracurricular activities, and a history of exemplary conduct both in and out of school.

Peer leaders are especially effective at teaching skills because they are able to use their own experiences and successes as examples. If the role of the leader were to impart information, a more knowledgeable messenger such as the classroom teacher would be the most appropriate choice. However, because life skills are being taught, and the reasons for learning these skills are not obvious to the students, the more similar the teacher and student are in their life experiences and skill level, the more the student will learn. In other words, when teaching life skills to adolescents, a *coping* model is preferred over a *mastery* model. Because these high school students have grown up in the same neighborhoods, attended the same schools, and confronted similar roadblocks, they are in an ideal position to be effective teachers. As one of our leaders said, "It helps them [the students] because we are so reachable. They see us, can relate to us and can see themselves in our shoes in a couple of years. Also, it helps us learn to be more patient." A sixth-grade student, talking about having high school leaders, said, "They're fun and they're smart too. They want to make the right choices and help you make the right choices too."

The student-leaders are taught the program by the school and community personnel. A minimum of 2 days of training is necessary; 3 days is preferred. If college students are involved, they often become the primary teachers as they serve as role models for the high school students. The student-leaders learn the concepts taught in the program and how to apply them to their own lives. In fact, they are supposed to have a goal on which they are working as well as to be working on all the other skills they are teaching. In addition, they learn how to teach these skills to younger students, the program's ultimate audience. Leaders are also taught how to work with groups, organize a class or lecture, be a good listener, facilitate the transfer of skills, and work effectively with teams comprising both peers and adults. The content of the training is skills oriented.

The high school student-leaders also receive a detailed leader manual (Danish, 2002a) that provides information on how to teach skills, encourage discussion, communicate effectively and give feedback, and manage a group. For each workshop, the manual provides guidelines on what to say and how long each activity should take. Leaders are asked to complete all activities in the program. A critical program component is to share their personal experiences with the students.

As a middle layer of the pyramid, the high school student-leaders come to realize that they have been entrusted with influencing the future of students who are just a few years their junior. Not only do they have positive role models in the adults and college students who teach and supervise them, they also have an opportunity to take their first step in the direction of becoming community leaders themselves. We believe it is critical to prepare a new generation of leaders from today's adolescents. Our perspective on leadership is based on DePree's (1989) definition. Leaders are people who facilitate others (individuals, families, organizations, or communities) in reaching their potential by (a) helping them identify goals related to their potential, (b) instilling in them the confidence to reach these goals, (c) teaching them to develop and implement a plan to attain these goals, and (d) encouraging them to share with others in their community what they have learned. In other words, leaders have the requisite life skills necessary to succeed and the commitment and vision to use their skills and knowledge to help others succeed.

DISSEMINATING LIFE SKILLS PROGRAMS

GOAL started in Richmond in 1987. Since its inception, it has been taught to approximately 25,000 students in the United States and internationally. It has been taught in public and private schools and in inner city, suburban, and rural schools. It has been taught in Canada, Australia, and New Zealand, as well as in Greece and Portugal. The program has been both translated into other languages as well as adapted to be consistent with different countries' cultures.

Several additional programs have been developed based on GOAL. SUPER (Sports United to Promote Education and Recreation; Danish, 2002c) is a series of 18, thirty-minute modules based on GOAL developed to be taught like sports clinics for middle school and high school students either during or after school. College student-athletes are often the primary instructors. Participants are involved in three sets of activities: learning the physical skills related to a specific sport, learning life skills related to sports in general, and playing the sport. Goals for Health (GFH), a National Cancer Institute–supported intervention, is a 12-session program based on GOAL and taught by high school student-leaders to middle school students as part of their health class. GFH is designed to reduce fat intake, increase fiber intake, and reduce tobacco use. Living Free of Tobacco (LIFT) is a six-session program based on GOAL that is peer taught by high school students to middle school students during health classes. The intervention, supported by the Virginia Tobacco Settlement Foundation Board, is designed to help students become or remain tobacco-free. Finally, BRIDGE: Bridging the Gap to Better Health is a seven-session, National Cancer Institute–supported intervention that is genealogy based. High school students are taught by health education personnel to be their own health historians, to conduct self-breast and self-testicular examinations, and to set goals for their health.

For all but one of the programs (BRIDGE: Westerberg, Hoy, Danish, & Fries, 2001), there is a leader manual (GOAL: Danish, 2002a; SUPER: Danish, 2002c; GFH: Meyer et al., 1998a; LIFT: Life Skills Center, 2003a) and a student activity guide (GOAL: Danish, 2002b; SUPER: Danish, 2002d; GFH: Meyer et al., 1998b; LIFT: Life Skills Center, 2003b) for the participating student. For GOAL, an operations manual (Life Skills Center, 1999) has also been developed. We decided not to give or to sell the programs to communities but to work with the communities to implement them and to ask them to pay for training and the materials.

We recognize that there will need to be some adaptations of the program to accommodate differences in settings. However, the more an intervention becomes removed from those who designed it, the more likely it is to lose some (if not all) of its essence. By ensuring that new sites receive training and feel comfortable with our implementation processes, we hope to work with the site to maintain the much, if not all of the program's essence. When schools or community groups contact us, we ask that they identify local personnel to serve as a coordinating group for their community. It is helpful for this group to include someone from a local college, if one exists. With SUPER, participation by college students is even more critical. The community group should also include school liaisons at each participating school. When programs involve high schools and middle or junior high schools, liaisons from the high schools are responsible for the selection of the leaders and for some of their training, and liaisons from the junior high or middle school facilitate implementation in their schools. Involving all these groups enhances the commitment of the schools to the program. With such a commitment, there is a greater likelihood that the schools will involve themselves and their students more completely in the program and increases the chances that the program will be successful and ongoing.

We encourage local groups to find local, private sector support to implement the program. Having private sector support enhances the community's sense of local control. Furthermore, it is in the best interest of the private sector to be involved. They rely on well-trained, healthy, and motivated employees; intelligent and successful customers; and thriving communities. Businesses are beginning to realize that if they are to succeed in the long run, their involvement in such activities is necessary.

A BRIEF OVERVIEW OF THE RESEARCH FINDINGS

There have been numerous evaluations of the Life Skills Center programs, and these are summarized in the following. Initially, the impact of the program was assessed on samples of Hispanic, African American, and white middle school boys and girls, compared with controls. Participants learned the information the program taught, were able to achieve the goals they set, found the process easier than they expected, and thought they had learned quite a bit about how to set goals. They also had better school attendance, reported a decrease in violent behavior (boys only), and did not report the same increase in health-compromising behaviors including getting drunk, smoking cigarettes, drinking beer, and drinking liquor as was found in the control group (boys only). Finally, they thought the program was fun, useful, important, and something that would be helpful for their friends. Two subsequent studies of GOAL were conducted in California with mostly Hispanic students (O'Hearn & Gatz, 1999, 2002) that found skill acquisition in goal setting and problem solving.

In the GFH project, a randomized design at the school level was employed. Researchers assigned 23 schools to either intervention or control groups; behaviors, attitudes, and beliefs relevant to diet and tobacco use were assessed both prior to and following the intervention (immediately postintervention, and 1 and 2 years postintervention). Significant change patterns across the four assessment points in the predicted direction for fat and fiber knowledge and diet-related self-efficacy were found, although not for the 3rd year. No changes were found for tobacco use (Danish et al., 2003). Research also indicated that liking the program significantly predicted a number of program outcomes including self-efficacy to refuse tobacco, smoking attitudes, tobacco attitudes, self-efficacy to eat healthy, self-efficacy to switch to low-fat foods, increased GFH knowledge, total fiber intake, and total fruit and vegetable intake (Taylor, Fries, & Danish, 2003).

Abbreviated versions of SUPER have been evaluated in two studies. Positive results have been found on measures of social responsibility, emotional intelligence, interpersonal reactivity, goal-setting self-efficacy, goal knowledge, and social interest. In addition, participants who were involved in community service activities in the 6 months following the completion of the program had additional increases in social responsibility, emotional intelligence, interpersonal reactivity, and goal knowledge at follow-up (Brunelle, Danish, & Fazio, 2002; Danish, 2001; Danish, Brunelle, Fazio, & Hogan, 2001). In an evaluation of an abbreviated (eight-session) version of SUPER with Greek schoolchildren, ages 10 to 12 (Papacharisis, Goudas, Danish, & Theodorakis, in press), recipients, compared with controls, reported greater self-beliefs for personal goal setting, problem solving, and positive thinking and demonstrated greater improvement in their athletic skills.

In a pilot evaluation conducted on the BRIDGE program, 178 ninth and tenth graders were taught the program. At baseline, about 20% had never used sunscreen, and less than 15% had ever conducted a self-screening exam such as a breast self-exam or testicular examination. At the first follow-up testing, postintervention, about 80% of the students were sure they could conduct a breast self-exam or testicular self-exam. More than 60% were sure they could achieve their health goal, and more than 55% said that BRIDGE encouraged them to talk openly with their families about health.

LIFT was implemented and evaluated for the first time on 190 middle school students in 2003. The evaluation was conducted by the Youth Tobacco Evaluation Project. Included in the evaluation were 12 other prevention programs directed at middle school students and 11 other programs for high school students. Among the results were a small but significant increase in knowledge for middle school students at posttest, but a more significant change for high school student-leaders. Students exhibited little or no change in smoking intention from pretest to posttest (a positive effect). At least 50% of the participating middle school students responded very favorably to questions about the program's effectiveness and age appropriateness and favorably to whether they would recommend it to other students (Youth Tobacco Evaluation Project, 2003).

CONCLUSION

The life skills programs described provide opportunities to involve teachers so that they gain an understanding of the program and can build on the learning that has taken place for the students. For example, in several schools in which GOAL has been taught, teachers have assigned homework related to the GOAL material. In one school, the teachers had each student write a letter to the first author (they were learning how to write business letters) describing what they had learned from GOAL. In another school, teachers had the students discuss and analyze the meaning of the poems and quotes that appear at the beginning of each GOAL workshop. Some other possible activities include having the students place the academic goal they set on their desks or somewhere in the classroom so that the teacher can continually monitor the progress of the students. When students are having difficulty reaching their goals, teachers are able to help them overcome the obstacles they are facing.

The teachers familiar with GOAL will be able to help students use effective problem-solving strategies (STAR) and help-seeking behaviors (developing a Dream Team). The result is that teachers become part of students' Dream Teams and are better able to connect with the students at a social and emotional level when teaching academic subjects and other parts of the school day.

Authors' Note: Ongoing information about all aspects of the Life Skills Center and Going for the Goal and SUPER programs can be found at www.lifeskills.vcu.edu.

REFERENCES

Brunelle, J., Danish, S., & Fazio, R. (2002). *The impact of a sport-based life skills and community service program.* Unpublished paper.

Comer, J. (1988). Educating poor minority children. *Scientific American, 250*(5), 42–48.

Danish, S. (1997). Going for the GOAL: A life skills program for adolescents. In T. Gullotta & G. Albee (Eds.), *Primary prevention works* (pp. 291–312). Newbury Park, CA: Sage.

Danish, S. (2001). The First Tee: Teaching youth to succeed in golf and life. In P. R. Thomas (Ed.), *Optimising performance in golf* (pp. 67–74). Brisbane, Australia: Australian Academic Press.

Danish, S. (2002a). *Going for the GOAL: Leader manual* (4th ed.). Richmond, VA: Life Skills Associates.

Danish, S. (2002b). *Going for the GOAL: Student activity book* (4th ed.). Richmond, VA: Life Skills Associates.

Danish, S. (2002c). *SUPER (Sports United to Promote Education and Recreation) program: Leader manual* (3rd ed.). Richmond: Life Skills Center, Virginia Commonwealth University.

Danish, S. (2002d). *SUPER (Sports United to Promote Education and Recreation) program: Student activity book* (3rd ed.). Richmond: Life Skills Center, Virginia Commonwealth University.

Danish, S. J., Brunelle, J., Fazio, R., & Hogan, C. (2001). *The First Tee National Youth Golf and Leadership Academy: Final report.* Unpublished report.

Danish, S., D'Augelli, A., & Ginsberg, M. (1984). Life development intervention: Promotion of mental health through the development of competence. In S. Brown & R. Lent (Eds.), *Handbook of counseling psychology* (pp. 520–544). New York: John Wiley & Sons.

Danish, S., Fries, E., Westerberg, A., Hoy, K., Meyer, A., Ramakrishnan, R., et al. (2003). *Goals for Health final report to the National Cancer Institute.* Richmond: Life Skills Center, Virginia Commonwealth University.

DePree, M. (1989). *Leadership is an art.* New York: Doubleday.

Life Skills Center. (1999). *Operations manual.* Richmond: Department of Psychology, Virginia Commonwealth University.

Life Skills Center. (2003a). *LIFT (Living Free of Tobacco): Leader manual.* Richmond: Life Skills Center, Virginia Commonwealth University.

Life Skills Center. (2003b). *LIFT (Living Free of Tobacco): Student activity book.* Richmond: Life Skills Center, Virginia Commonwealth University.

Meyer, A., Danish, S., Brunelle, J., Figueiredo, M., Green, S., & Hogan, C. (1998a). *Goals for Health leader manual.* Richmond: Life Skills Center, Virginia Commonwealth University.

Meyer, A., Danish, S., Brunelle, J., Figueiredo, M., Green, S., & Hogan, C. (1998b). *Goals for Health student workshop book.* Richmond: Life Skills Center, Virginia Commonwealth University.

O'Hearn, T. C., & Gatz, M. (1999). Evaluating a psychosocial competence program for urban adolescents. *Journal of Prevention, 20,* 119–144.

O'Hearn, T. C., & Gatz, M. (2002). Going for the GOAL: Improving youth problem solving skills through a school-based intervention. *Journal of Community Psychology, 30,* 281–303.

Papacharisis, V., Goudas, M., Danish, S., & Theodorakis, Y. (in press). The effectiveness of teaching a life skills program in a school-based sport context. *Journal of Applied Sport Psychology.*

Seidman, E., & Rappaport, J. (1974). The educational pyramid: A paradigm for training, research, and manpower utilization in community psychology. *American Journal of Community Psychology, 2,* 119–130.

Taylor, T., Fries, E., Danish, S. (2003). *Youth perceptions of the Goals for Health program and their impact on program outcomes.* Unpublished manuscript.

Westerberg, A., Hoy, K., Danish, S., & Fries, E. (2001). *BRIDGE: Bridging the Gap to Better Health.* Richmond: Life Skills Center, Virginia Commonwealth University.

Youth Tobacco Evaluation Project. (2003, November). Outcome and process evaluation report for middle and high school youth: Result of Year 1 of VTSF-funding. Richmond: Virginia Commonwealth University.

20

Read and Serve

Student-Centered Service Learning and Literacy

Rose Reissman

With the renewed focus on citizenship and civics in the aftermath of September 11, 2001, it is not surprising that the public, school districts, and administrators are taking another look at service learning and school-based community service. Of course, in this current climate of enhanced worry about literacy accountability, standardized test scores, standards-based learning, and subject content mastery, service-learning programs not only serve needy sectors of the adult and childhood communities, but also include abundant opportunities for reading, writing, speaking, listening, discussing, and presenting.

It is ironic that although service learning is being restyled and reinvigorated in response to the heightened emphasis on citizenship and civics, the restyling often only gives lip service to standards-based models of student-centered learning (National Council of Social Studies, New York State Social Studies, National Council of Teachers of English, New York State English Language Arts, Balanced Literacy Workshop; see Web addresses in the Appendix). These standards-based models call for collaborative learning, which is both integral to a successful service-learning project and an excellent model for proactive community and workplace participation.

Because the designs of service-learning projects tend to be largely adult educator directed, these experiences are not owned or driven by student interests. This chapter describes a process by which teachers can enact and use social-emotional learning (SEL) to involve upper-elementary and middle school students in selecting and designing service-learning projects that truly reflect the students' input, talents, resources, and concerns.

A JOURNEY FROM DOING TO FACILITATING

As I and my colleagues conscientiously reached out to already-identified, community-based organizations, parents, and business people to develop service-learning projects, we never even considered including students in the process. This was not deliberate, but rather grew out of our never having considered how and why it would be advantageous to have students be the engineers of service-learning projects.

One evening as I was reading through my usual diet of four daily newspapers, I stumbled on student-friendly, easily accessible tools for engaging students in developing their own service-learning projects. These tools were newspapers, in print or online, and the use of any standard search engine.

Many articles described potential service-learning opportunities for students. One detailed the need for citizens to go to their local post offices to pick up letters addressed to Santa from impoverished children. Good Samaritans who picked up the letters were asked to select ones whose gift requests they could fill. Another article focused on a group of college students who traveled through the borough of Queens in New York City to help high school students fill out their college applications. Both of these newspaper articles struck me as offering potential service-learning projects that my Brooklyn (New York City) middle school seventh graders could adapt to suit their own strengths and needs. I knew the students had the financial resources to get and wrap simple toys for children in need. Furthermore, since they themselves were often from families living on public assistance, I knew that many of them would strongly identify and empathize with these children.

As far as helping with applications, my middle school students were skilled at preparing applications and essays for our own special middle school program. They had all successfully applied when they were sixth graders themselves. Therefore, it would be a perfect fit for them to travel around our district to help the students from the elementary feeder schools fill out their special middle school applications.

Given that my focus was to provide my students with actual service-learning leadership opportunities, I wanted to create formats that would allow them to lead in the projects' design. (It should be noted that demographically, the sixth- and seventh grade middle school students who participated in this project were reading just above grade level. They were from homes whose income level merited federal assistance and lunch subsidies. More than 85% of them were from English-language-learner backgrounds, and 15% lived in neighboring low-income public housing projects. A sizable minority, more than 8%, were from foster homes.) I began by modeling for the middle schoolers how I read through the newspaper and identified two potential service-learning options. I revisited and shared aloud how I had noticed that the letters to Santa and college student applications items in the print newspaper might well suit the needs, interests, talents, and emotional backgrounds of my students. I put the next step in personal terms and voiced my ideas about how I could go to our local post office to read through Santa letters that asked for simple, inexpensive gifts. Then I reasoned aloud about the connection between the special middle school program applications and the college applications discussed in the article. Finally, I speculated aloud about how my middle school students could use this service-learning project model to assist feeder-school elementary students with applications for our program.

SMALL-GROUP COOPERATIVE PEDAGOGY OF THE BALANCED LITERACY MODEL

I decided to use the cooperative pedagogy of the balanced literacy model as the basis for carrying out service-learning activities. First, I modeled reading, writing, and thinking out loud, which met the criterion of initiating lessons with a 10- to 15-minute whole-class instruction piece. Then, I followed that up with a 20- to 25-minute small-group, student-centered work piece. Specifically, I modeled for students how I had read the articles, formulated a response, wrote it down, and shared it (with them). I then challenged them to do the same by working in small groups on three issues taken from the newspaper (provided through our classroom Newspapers in Education program). In addition to providing each classroom team with their own individual newspaper (one per team), I also suggested that they could have the option of doing a search using the four classroom computers and print out their results.

As the groups of students divided up for their first 20- to 25-minute small-group work, I circulated around the room. Because preparation is a pivotal part of a deep service-learning experience, I requested that before they begin their searches through either print or electronic sources, they work together as small teams to brainstorm possible service-learning sites and resources in the school neighborhood and close-by areas. I was pleased to see that each group gathered information about local centers and public facilities, including our neighborhood senior center, the local hospital, and the precinct office to put on its experiential chart. I noticed that those groups who opted to use the computers were involved in Google and Yahoo searches using appropriate keywords and neighborhood sites. The small groups were asked to keep experiential charts that documented the process they used in doing their work and their unfolding findings and insights; I asked them to describe their search process and decision-making procedures for what they chose to follow up on or not, and include or not.

After the students had their small-group time to brainstorm and capture their learning in their group experiential charts, we returned for a whole-class discussion of our anticipated service-learning possibilities as captured in the small group charts. The range of potential neighborhood partners and sites for service learning identified by the student teams did not equal the broad spectrum I, their instructor, could have generated on my own. However, it was wonderful for me to note that their own ideas reflected their personal and family experiences and religious backgrounds and more than justified the approach of giving students much greater involvement in the design of the service-learning experience. For instance, from having visited a dying aunt at a neighborhood hospice, one student knew that some teens came by to assist the hospice participants with mail and bill paying. Another student knew that a local church collected, cleaned, and delivered used clothing and crocheted sweaters to a battered woman shelter. Another student mentioned what turned out to be a previous year's project of delivering Thanksgiving meals to neighborhood senior and disabled housing project residents that I had done with another class. It was rewarding to learn it had filtered down through family talk to my current students. Overall, it was touching and inspiring to hear how the students began considering the roles and support 11- and 12-year-olds might play in and give to these ongoing projects.

As the discussion came to a close, the teams' various anticipatory charts were posted and dated. The students were then given two full periods over a week's span, plus the weekend, to search through print newspapers and online resources for current service-learning opportunities and possible project ideas that matched resources they had identified. I also suggested that the students should be creative in their ongoing searches and investigations. Again, I modeled for them by telling them that I personally had found service-learning opportunities while reading flyers while I was in the Starbucks coffee line (collecting toys for the Holiday Angels Toy Drive and supporting the Starlight Children's Foundation).

With this in mind, I alerted them to the possibility that service-learning projects might be literally in front of their eyes or as close by as the counters of their everyday shopping hangouts. The students also reminded me of the fact that many of their families listened to Spanish news radio and bought Spanish print news resources that included stories and advertisements with service-learning possibilities. One student's mother worked as the custodian of a local church that served holiday meals to the homeless. Another student's relative worked for God's Love We Deliver, a nonprofit group that delivered food to the homebound and elderly. Several students asked if they could confine their investigations to going online to research various groups similar to God's Love We Deliver. They proposed developing a service-learning opportunity directory compiling the URLs and information they compiled from their online searches. Obviously, their work would be a rich resource of projects for our immediate class and other peers and was itself a kind of service project.

To inculcate students in habits of scholarly research and to familiarize them with ways to use different kinds of documents (both crucial literacy skills), I required that all students maintain a log of their findings. Their logs included the specific document type (advertisements, announcements, print material and electronic resources, digital photographs, charts, graphs), the source (newspaper, URL, broadcast), and the date it was identified. I further requested that they include a description of the document found, along with the potential service learning that students could envision. Placed in the context of being part of the method of service learning, the act of maintaining detailed records of their research involved students in critical reading, analysis, and descriptive and reflective writing.

Another literacy skill built into the project involved students interviewing local community neighbors and friends and family who were involved in ongoing community service initiatives. For the interviews, the students had to develop at least three questions and tape record or transcribe the interviewee's responses. They were further asked to summarize the responses in dialogue or paragraph format. Finally, they were required to share their write-ups with the interviewee and get a sign off of approval from the individual. When students did not know a local person to interview, they worked as a team with a classmate.

Over the assigned 1-week investigation period, many students approached me with supermarket flyers, lobby circulars, and local newspaper advertisements, all of which had always been right in front of their eyes. Now, through the service-learning lens of this project, they were beginning to grasp the rich number of opportunities in the community for students to play valuable, supportive roles.

STUDENT-GENERATED SERVICE-LEARNING OPPORTUNITIES

The outcome of this process represents a wonderful blend of service learning, academic skills development, and SEL. Among the specific projects that students designed are the following:

• Creation of flyers to share newspaper notices crucial to shut-ins and to impoverished individuals not accustomed to reading the newspapers or not fluent enough in English to read them. The students (and to some extent I, myself) realized in going through the newspapers that although they were filled with helpful announcements, those most in need of the information could not read them or did not have access to them.

• Development of Korean-, Chinese-, and Spanish-language flyers with multilingual flu shot resources and New York City Health Department phone numbers. The students clipped numerous articles on an impending flu epidemic and the problems of finding clinics where free flu shots were to be had.

• Collection of helpful illness and medical condition (e.g., asthma, flu, back pain, earache) pamphlets and hand distribution of them in buildings and local community centers or senior homes. We set up a classroom wellness information center that was quickly filled to the brim with circulars.

• Dry cleaning drop-off and pick-up services as well as laundry services for seniors and shut-ins.

• Collection of slightly used or child-outgrown toys for various seasonal toy drives (e.g., Christmas Starbucks Holiday Angels, Fleet Street Bank) and for regular distribution at the Montifiore Children's Hospital Ward and a local neighborhood soup kitchen. The students who suggested this project pointed out the fact that although many children and adults they knew were literally putting used toys on the sidewalk, few of them regularly stopped by the Starbucks or bank bins designated for these much needed donations. Therefore, the students conceptualized their project in terms of their serving as the outreach pick-up and delivery agents for the projects, sharing the information in neighborhood buildings and private houses and then picking up donated toys.

- Several project ideas were focused on breast cancer, which was far too familiar to these young students. Many of them wanted to not only participate in sponsored walks to make money to combat the disease, but also to translate into Spanish and Chinese key facts and treatment resources that were available but were not understood by Spanish- and Chinese-language speakers.

- Public health announcements, particularly those about the availability of free flu shots, in advance of predicted epidemics or health crises were particularly important to the students. Again, they realized how few of the key target populations who needed the shots (young infants, seniors, seriously ill individuals) could or did read the daily newspaper or went to public clinics. The students envisioned a squad of modern-day Paul Revere's going off on foot, scooter, bike, bus, or train to get the word out. Reality prevailed, and a small number of students made phone calls to place Access-a-Ride travel reservations to the public health clinics.

The Appendix at the end of this chapter contains Web sites, print resources, and resources that could inform a wide range of different projects.

A SAMPLE PROJECT

Here, with permission from a student and his parents, is an example of a sample project. An overview is followed by the summary of the student's presentation:

My name is Lance Troiano. I am 11 years old, and I am in sixth grade. I attend Louis M. Klein Middle School in Harrison, New York.

I am involved in a community activity, which I've named Lake Project 360.

This all began one day when my dad, my brother, and I were walking in the woods that surround our lake. We have often hiked the trails there over the years. In the summer of 2002, my brother and I realized that there was more and more garbage around the lake and decided that we should do something about it. We took bags to collect garbage and debris and decided it was too big a job for us to do alone. We sent a letter to our town's mayor and told him about the broken trees, destroyed trails, and garbage that were ruining our woods.

We finally visited the mayor in the fall of 2003 and talked about how we could make plans to restore our town's natural resources. Since then with the help of my mom, we have contacted the Harrison Environmental Committee, and the town's historian and other conservation groups. After we contacted everyone, we began to start a petition to gather people to help preserve our lake area. In the springtime we will continue this petition drive.

I feel excited that I'm helping my community and doing something good for our environment. It's been a kind of educational experience. I've learned a lot about the history of our town and how hard it is to organize the details to get a job done for the community.

The following document describes the story and events presented by Lance.

1. We live in a town called Silver Lake, in West Harrison, New York. In our town, there is a lake. The lake is surrounded by woods and a forest. This is where my parents played when they were young.

2. There are many trails paved with large rock and stone, and many steps that lead to the top of hiking trails were also fashioned with flat rocks. It is said that during the Great Depression, men were employed to build these paths.

3. There are trails behind the lake that date back 300 years. These trails can take you to more woods and streams for hiking, and they also lead to special places to see.

4. Between 1774 and the 1940s, Negro slaves who were freed resettled in the area behind our lake. They became independent framers and laborers. Their home foundations still remain!

5. Many of the dwellings are overgrown and destroyed by vandals but you can see here that some are in fact still well preserved.

6. There is also a dwelling where a hermit named "Old Pop" used to live. We believe he was a veteran. My grandfather knew of him and told us that he lived alone and walked to the town for supplies. He lived without plumbing or heat. His home still remains and is called "Old Pop's Cave."

7. People have destroyed it by removing the slate slab roof but if you crawl inside, there still stand his stone walls and fireplace.

8. George Washington's army used our woods in 1776. The battle of White Plains took place nearby on Merit Hill.

9. The lake itself is gorgeous, but today you can see that people have dumped barrels and picnic benches into it.

10. The paths around the lake are littered with garbage.

11. And trees are destroyed, broken, and cut down.

12. My brother and I wrote to the mayor of our town to try and find a way to preserve our natural resources and these historical sites.

13. We have met with Mr. Malfetano a couple of times and have organized ideas to find supporters interested in restoring the lake area.

14. We have contacted the Harrison Historical Society and various conservation groups and our schools to get everyone to help support our project, LAKE PROJECT 360. We will be distributing petitions to all, to help us find a way to keep our woods beautiful.

Table 20.1   Lake Project 360 Petition

We, the undersigned residents of the town of Harrison and the conservators of our lake's special places, persons, sites, trees, spaces, and history, do hereby call to the attention of concerned citizens within our town and surrounding areas the following civic, environmental, and historic challenges: West Harrison Lake cleanup.

Environmental and Geographical Challenges: replanting of trees, removal of fallen and destroyed trees, restoration of pathways, removal of garbage and dumping which prevents natural flow of brooks and streams. Removal of garbage and preventive measures for dumping garbage into the lake and destruction of the woods and all natural resources.

Historical Challenges: Restoration of historical spaces and artifacts. Redefining and remarking of historical trails, historical dwellings, stone pathways and steps, etc.

We respectfully request that the town provide manpower, seek grants, and sponsor community activities that will help address the challenges above and restore and protect the significant natural and historical resources of Silver Lake.

Date _____

Name _____

_____

_____

_____

_____

_____

(Student, occupation, status, other, address, phone number, e-mail)

You are also invited to contact us through e-mail: Lakeproject360@aol.com

CONCLUSION

In the wake of September 11, 2001, and in line with authentic efforts to connect literacy and community to school-mandated curricula themes, student-centered service learning can validate a broad array of academic, civic, political, and social goals. More important, it can engage students in constructing meaning, not only of words, but through proactive deeds that lay the foundation for caring, living communities. That is truly a learning service to students and society.

APPENDIX

Additional Web Resources

American Cancer Society
www.cancer.org
A key touchstone Web resource for identifying ongoing fundraising drives, runs, walkathons, and awareness activities that can seed student projects or network students with distanced or local peers.

Anti-Defamation League
www.adl.org
A wonderful resource for connecting service learning to teaching tolerance, increasing literacy, learning about banned books, and promoting intergeneration forums and dialogues. Student service-learning projects done in conjunction with this resource can easily address standards of literacy and social studies content.

Food Bank Organization
www.foodbank.org
Opportunities for students to collect and distribute food cans across the city. One of the options is serving in a kids' café.

KidsCare
kidscare.org
This site shares ideas, projects, and strategies that help students. Families and schools make their lives richer through compassion and community service. The site places these activities in international contexts through its global links.

King County Solid Waste Division Secondary School Programs
dnr.metrokc.gov/swd/schoolpr/second/second.htm
This site, developed by a school district in Seattle, nicely integrates civics, science, environment, writing workshops, and leadership. Students can use the *Kids Newsletter* as a model.

Learn and Serve America
www.cfda.gov/public/viewprog.asp?progid=1413
An excellent background resource for middle and secondary students and teachers outlining the purposes, goals, objectives, and academic learning connections of government-envisioned projects. This site served as a criterion-referenced touchstone for students as they developed their projects and built in assessments for them.

Missouri Teacher of the Year Named
dese.mo.gov/news/2003/toy.htm
This announcement article detailing the achievements of Missouri's Teacher of the Year for 2003 is notable because among her projects were a student civic freedoms oversight panel and an ongoing student-centered Web resource that publicizes civic issues challenging those unable to voice their views in person or online.

National Service Learning Clearinghouse
www.servicelearning.org
This site is the key resource and knowledge base for teacher educators and students. Its site map offers extensive curricula connections, model service-learning program designs, links for further information, and expert advice. In addition, the students hoped to eventually post their neighborhood projects on this site and exchange ideas and findings with other sites.

National Service Learning Cooperative Clearinghouse
www.nicsl.coled.umn.edu/links/k12.htm
This is an excellent resource for teacher educators and student/family service-learning design teams.

Opportunities for Service-Learning in the No Child Left Behind Act of 2001
www.servicelearning.org/filemanager/download/27/nochild.pdf
As part of our ongoing examination of the ways in which national legislation impacted the tests, requirements, and materials available for our classroom, the students had studied the text of the No Child Left Behind Act. Imagine the surprise of several when their Yahoo and Google searches turned up this article, which connected that piece of legislation with service learning. This truly validated the significance of this classroom investigation, which now turned out to have applicability for that initiative.

Service Learning—Program in Education—Duke University
www.duke.edu/web/education/service/
This site includes a section created by a graduate student that details various elementary and secondary student–run service-learning projects with contact e-mail addresses and also provides the section designer's e-mail address so that students can use her as an online expert. The site also has excellent guidelines and background information for teacher educators interested in starting to incorporate service learning into an ongoing curricula theme on various grade levels.

Starlight Children's Foundation
www.starlight.org
An excellent source of information about Starlight's initiatives to support impoverished and seriously ill children through toy drives and raising money for their care.

Standards and Workshop Web Resources

National Council of Social Studies Standards
www.ncss.org

National Council of Teachers of English Standards
www.ncte.org

New York City Department of Education
www.nycboe.net
Balanced literacy, workshop model approaches, and New York State English Language Arts and Social Studies Standards, with explanations of the workshop model plus theorists of that model

Print References

Barber, B. R. (1992). *From classroom to community service: A bridge to citizenship.* Los Angeles: National Youth Service Learning Network.

Berman, S. (1999). *Service learning for the multiple intelligences classroom.* Arlington Heights, IL: Skylight.

Furco, A., & Billing, S. H. (Eds.). (2002). *Service learning: The essence of pedagogy.* Greenwich, CT: Information Age.

Lewis, B., & Espeland, P. (1995). *The kids' guide to service projects: Ideas for young people who want to make a difference.* New York: Free Spirit.

Schine, J. (1997). *Service learning.* Chicago: Chicago University Press.

21

Heroes to the Rescue

Reaching the Roots of Learning

Eliot Rosenbloom and Ann Medlock

For all teachers, the pot of gold is seeing our students absorb what they have learned and integrate it into their lives; "transfer" is surely what teaching is about. But all too often, learning does not transfer at all. Instead, students just retain what they think we want to hear—until they are sure it will not be on the next test. The transfer of social-emotional learning (SEL) is, we think, even more valuable than that of other skills and of most information. In our work with the Giraffe Heroes Program, we have seen students integrate SEL into their lives, sparking a new interest in learning academic skills and acquiring information. We have also seen classroom management problems dramatically reduced.

To achieve those ends, we have found that material must work at the level of underlying motivation. It must touch students where they live and tap into their natural deep caring. Both anecdotes and formal studies tell us that the Giraffe Heroes Program is working. "I don't recognize these kids anymore," said one teacher who had used these materials. Said another, "I can't get my students out of the library." And a veteran inner-city teacher told us that each fall, her students arrive an every-which-way, self-absorbed bunch of individuals, many with serious behavior problems and most with stressed family lives. Year after year, she tried ways to manage them, to control them, to inspire them with the joy of learning, to get them to treat each other with civility. Some kids got it, some did not. Now getting it is no longer an issue. She begins each school year by letting Giraffe Heroes go straight into her new students' hearts, knowing their minds—and their actions—will follow.

USING THE POWER OF HEROES TO TEACH

Since 1982, the Giraffe Project has been finding and honoring people who "stick their necks out" for the common good. The project has a story bank of more than 950 such heroes, aged from 8 to 108, of all races, religions, and backgrounds, and from many countries. This story bank supplies the stories for the classroom programs. Here's an example from the Grades 3 to 5 guide:

Box 21.1   Touchdown for Tolerance

Ernesto Villareal

In the small Idaho town of Marsing, football was everything. On Friday nights, hundreds of people from the town and the farms around it would come to watch the Marsing Huskies play. Ernesto "Neto" Villareal was a star player on the high school team. Neto hoped that the team would win. That could earn him a college scholarship.

When the players did something good, everyone cheered. But when they made a mistake, something else happened—if the player was Latino, like Neto—people shouted insults like, "Stupid Mexican!" The shouters weren't even students. They were adults.

It happened a lot, and people seemed not to notice. Neto began to think about it and realized that it wasn't right.

He and the other players decided that they wouldn't play anymore unless the insults stopped. Their coach told them they would only make things worse by refusing to play. They couldn't win the state championship if they stopped playing. And Neto knew he could lose his chance at a football scholarship. But the insults had to stop.

Neto talked to the boy who was president of all the students. The president agreed to talk to the principal about the problem. The principal wouldn't listen. Then most of the players changed their minds and agreed to play.

It looked like it was up to Neto. He decided to go to the principal's bosses—the school board. He went alone and spoke before these adults. One of them had been seen shouting insults at the Latino players himself. It was difficult, but Neto told them why he was refusing to play. "Now," he said, "they can't say nobody told them."

The student president was inspired by Neto's courage. He wrote a letter on behalf of all the students, asking adults to stop the insults. It asked school officials to throw people out of the stadium if they made racist insults.

The next football game was to be a big one. It was homecoming, with a parade, music, and floats. The letter was to be read over the loudspeaker at the game so everyone could hear it. Then the four Latino players would play again.

But the principal refused to read the letter over the loudspeaker. The only person who had the power to let a student read the letter was the school superintendent. And he did give his permission.

Thousands of copies of the letter were printed. Students handed each car two copies of the letter in the parking lot. The stadium was full.

Over the loudspeaker, a student called for everyone' s attention. She read the letter. When she finished, there was silence. Then people stood up and applauded. They cheered. The team had won against racism. The insults stopped and Neto Villareal was back as their star player.

MATERIALS IN THE GIRAFFE HEROES PROGRAM

There are teachers' guides for Grades K to 2, 3 to 5, 6 to 9, and 10 to 12. The 10 to 12 guide also has individual student books. The teachers' guides include sequenced lesson plans, student handouts, overhead transparencies, and a video on people who have been commended as Giraffes.

In the K to 2 guide, there are also audiotapes of the program's mascot giraffes, Stan Tall and Bea Tall, who serve as storytellers, jesters, and stand-in learners for the children. They model social and emotional skills in their dialogues as they deal with disagreements, fears, questions, and concerns. The lesson plans provide questions in both the cognitive and affective domains.

The lesson plans suggest a range of multimedia activities to accommodate many learning styles, and reflection is a recurring theme so that students pause to understand and integrate what they have done and learned.

How Are the Stories Used?

The program weaves heroes' stories into lesson plans that progress in three stages: Hear the Story, Tell the Story, and Become the Story.

In Stage 1, Hear the Story, students learn about Giraffe Heroes and consider the qualities of character that make a Giraffe. The stories give students real heroes who lead exciting, meaningful lives. Students learn to distinguish such heroes from celebrities, who only have to be famous, not brave and caring.

In Stage 2, Tell the Story, the process becomes more active: Students launch their own search for Giraffes—in their studies, in the media, and in their community. They tell these stories to their class, to the school, and to the community, using oral presentations, skits, writing, and artwork. Many do articles for the school newspaper or for local media.

Searching for local Giraffes builds students' knowledge of challenges in their communities and of people who are taking them on. This awareness fosters hope and broadens the possibilities students see for their own lives. In this stage, students begin observing Giraffe qualities in each other and themselves. They begin asking how they can make a difference too.

The pump is now primed for Stage 3, Become the Story, which begins with exercises for observing the world around them and identifying the problems that concern them most. They then design and carry out a service project, using a planning process called the "Seven Neckbones." This is the most complex of the three stages to facilitate, and the most rewarding. It is here that students test themselves against real-world challenges. Here they experience the excitement and sense of meaning that come from service and from a job well done.

The Appendix contains an extended example of a Giraffe Heroes activity based on the guides.

THE SINE QUA NON: A STUDENT-CENTERED APPROACH

The make-or-break condition for success is that the service projects must be driven by the caring and concerns of the students, not by those of teachers or parents, however well meaning. This is true at every age level; even the youngest students can express their concerns and choose their projects, with some guidance. Only when students truly own their service projects will they make a full commitment to carrying them out. This is a sharp contrast to the reluctance of students who are told what to do.

The best illustration we know of this principle came from a high school teacher who described his first experience with school-mandated community service. He announced to his class that they were going to do a park cleanup. He provided gloves, trash bags, and a bus. The kids got off the bus and dispersed to all parts of the park, some sitting under trees smoking, some throwing dirt balls, and some disappearing totally. The next year, he tried something different: He asked his new class what *they* saw in the community that could use improving. To his surprise, they chose the same park. But this time, the kids decided they would need gloves and trash bags and raised the money to buy them. They arranged the transportation, and they even bought flowers to plant and dealt with city officials to get permission to plant them. When the kids left the park, it was not only clean, it was beautiful. And one teacher had learned a lesson he would never forget.

USING THE PROGRAM WITH HIGH-RISK KIDS

When the Giraffe Heroes program was being developed, some advisors thought it would work with suburban leadership classes, but not with high-risk students. That proved not to be a problem. Here is how the program took shape at one school considered a dumping ground for the district's "non-learners" and discipline problems:

The kids filled up on the stories of Giraffe Heroes in Stage 1, Hear the Story. They were sufficiently intrigued to be ready for Tell the Story: looking for real heroes themselves. The kids started looking at television with an agenda, instead of using it to "veg out." They got interested in the books, magazines, and newspapers in the library—were there Giraffes in them or not? Were there people they actually knew in their own neighborhoods or families who might be Giraffes? The world is a different place when you look for Giraffes in it. They entered Become the Story fully acquainted with lives made meaningful through caring, taking responsibility, being of service, rallying others to the cause, and not giving up when it got hard.

These were kids for whom "community service" had meant what a judge orders you to do because you are too young to lock up. But having been primed, they had a new view of service—it could even be exciting. Kids who had once barely acknowledged each other's presences brainstormed, discussed, and chose a problem they all cared about: A student had almost been hit by a car speeding past the school grounds; if something was not done, somebody was going to get hurt. They decided to present the county commissioners with a plan to lower the chance of someone being injured or killed. This was important, and they dug into the task with fervor, eager to learn the skills and gather the information they needed. They clocked passing vehicles, calculated average speeds, researched laws, wrote letters and reports, made presentation materials, and negotiated visits from state patrol officers and government officials.

These previously disengaged, high-risk kids succeeded in getting a traffic light, a crosswalk, and the awed admiration of every adult who witnessed their determination and dedication. They experienced the power of teamwork and of democratic processes, and the value of academic learning. They knew a lot about each other that created a new atmosphere of mutual respect—they were able people who could get an important job done.

TRAINING TEACHERS

The guides are designed to enable teachers to do the program successfully, without special training. Nevertheless, we have found that teachers appreciate the 1-day training sessions we do, telling us that they ignite a spark that might be called "Giraffe spirit." The training runs through each of the program's stages, imparting the spirit of each. Participants practice a key lesson from each stage, discuss implementation with the trainer and with each other, work out ways to integrate the material into their ongoing programs and, of course, ask any questions they may have.

Because we do not think programs taught by reluctant teachers work well, we recommend that teachers not be ordered to attend trainings or to use the program. When teachers who have chosen to do the program begin getting results, news spreads, and the next year, more teachers ask to use it.

When several teachers attend from a school, they find that their implementation of the program is synergistic, heightening the effect on their students and on the school as a whole.

WHOLE-SCHOOL PARTICIPATION

Research suggests that multifaceted initiatives often produce more attitude and behavior change than classroom study alone (Cameron, Mutter, & Hamilton, 1991; Cogdon & Belzer, 1991; Elias et al., 1997; Greenberg, Domitrovich, & Bumbarger, 2001). We find that the multiple approaches, activities, and venues in the program confirm that research.

When several classrooms or a whole school use the program, these benefits are multiplied. Classes have taken the program schoolwide by reading brief Giraffe stories on the P.A. system, by setting up Giraffe Halls of Fame, by putting on schoolwide assemblies, and by doing multiclass service projects. School counselors have been particularly effective in moving the program through entire schools, and faculties have collaborated on schoolwide uses of the materials. One elementary school launched a semester-long Giraffe Heroes theme with safari graphics all over the school and every teacher in pith helmet and safari shirt.

By alerting local media to the program, some schools have expanded beyond the school walls, letting the whole community know about local heroes and about student service projects. The community has also reached into the school, when local businesses and service groups have assisted students with their projects and their quest for heroes. Community volunteers have repeatedly expressed astonished admiration for the kids, for their teachers, and for the school as a community institution.

INVOLVING PARENTS

The guides provide letters sent home inviting parents to review the program and to consider providing classroom volunteer time. Parents have been excellent assistants to the students in searching for heroes and in carrying out their projects. In the younger grades, students take home Giraffe Sighting Reports that their parents (or guardians) help them complete. Interestingly enough, parents have reported being personally moved by the program, a most welcome, but unintended, consequence.

Because of the strongly student-centered nature of the program, involving parents can also be problematic. In pilot testing, we found that some parents influenced their children to choose projects that were of interest to the parents, rather than letting the children put forward their own concerns. Later editions were revised to minimize this problem and maintain the focus on the children's concerns.

TESTING AND EVALUATION OF THE PROGRAM

The program is the work of professional teachers and curriculum developers and was pilot tested in widely differing school settings. Based on feedback and suggestions received from more than a decade of research and development, the program has gone through extensive revision.

A third-party study by a team of evaluators from the University of Washington (Giraffe Heros Project, n.d.), funded by the W.K. Kellogg Foundation, reported the following:

- 100% of teachers surveyed stated that they observed some or many positive attitude and behavior changes in students as a result of using the program. They particularly noted an increase in self-esteem, caring, teamwork, and problem-solving skills.
- 92% rated the overall effectiveness of the program as excellent.
- 100% rated its user friendliness as excellent.
- 83% said they would encourage other teachers to use it.
- 75% said they observed positive changes in their own attitudes or behaviors.

STRENGTHS AND WEAKNESSES FOR SEL

Although Giraffe activities include many opportunities to exercise empathy, anger management, respect, conflict resolution, and impulse control, the program does not offer a multistep process for achieving those ends and is not a substitute for programs that do.

What the Giraffe Heroes program does do well, and which some of the more skill-based programs do to a lesser degree, is provide students with context and reasons to be socially and emotionally skillful. The context is living a meaningful life; the reason is students' own deep yearning for such a life. The program calls forth their own desire to be their own best selves. If that has not come forth—such as if, for instance, a young male still identifies with being the meanest, toughest kid on the block—he may learn and imitate conflict resolution skills to perfection, but when the teacher is not looking, he will not put them to constructive use. The challenge is to get the learning to the deepest levels, to the roots of students' identities.

CONCLUSION

Clearly, if we are concerned about kids' lives and not just their minds, this is the kind of change we are looking for. When students not only learn skills, but shift their reference group and shift their identity, their whole motivation system changes. When kids in the Giraffe Heroes program decide they want to be like the heroes whose stories they have heard and told, watch their behavior change. Now they gather information and learn skills because they want to; it helps them make a difference. They seek to understand others and their motivations because they want to; it helps them build consensus and have an impact. They work cooperatively because they want to; it helps them accomplish their mission, and they genuinely care for and want to support others.

When your students make this profound shift, the problem of "transfer" no longer exists. You have reached the roots of learning.

Authors' Note: Ongoing information about all aspects of the Giraffe Heroes program can be found at www.giraffe.org.

APPENDIX

A Giraffe Heroes Activity

Giraffe Spotting

Here is an exercise that works at all grade levels. Figure it will take at least 90 minutes, in at least two sessions.

1. Ask students who their heroes are. Write them all on the board without comment, and do not attach students' names to the heroes.
2. Tell the story of Neto Villareal.
3. Spark a class discussion about Neto, the risks he took, and the common good that his actions served. Tell them that Giraffe heroes stick their necks out for others.
4. Go through the list of heroes on the board, and ask what risks each of them has taken and who they helped by their actions. Without embarrassing the nominators, guide the class through a discussion that helps them see that being rich, talented, gorgeous, or bulletproof can make people celebrities, but not necessarily heroes. (For the bulletproof ones, remind them that it is not brave to do something courageous if you know you cannot get hurt.)
5. Divide the class into small teams. Ask each one to brainstorm several possible Giraffe Heroes and to select one to present to the class. Different teams could be asked to focus on heroes in the news, literature, history, movies, the community, and so forth.
6. Each group presents its hero's story using drama, art, narrative, or song—encourage them to be imaginative.
7. Ask the class to discuss each person whose story has been presented, focusing on the risks taken and the caring shown. Make a new list of class heroes, including all those who have indeed stuck their necks out for others. Do not forget to include anyone from the first list who turned out to be a real hero.
8. Students can present these heroes to the school in a Hall of Heroes display, at an assembly, or in P.A. announcements.

REFERENCES

Cameron, H., Mutter, G., & Hamilton, N. (1991). Comprehensive school health: Back to the basics in the 90s. *Health Promotion* (Special Issue on School Health), *29*(4), 2–5.

Cogdon, A., & Belzer, E. G. (1991). Dartmouth's Health Promotion Study: Testing the coordinated approach. *Health Promotion* (Special Issue on School Health), *29*(4), 6–10.

Elias, M. J., Zins, J. E., Weissberg, R. P., Frey, K. S., Greenberg, M. T., Haynes, N. M., et al. (1997). *Promoting social and emotional learning: Guidelines for educators.* Alexandria, VA: Association for Supervision and Curriculum Development.

Giraffe Heroes Project. (n.d.). *Programs for school & youth groups.* Retrieved September 13, 2005, from www.giraffe.org/ed_faqs.html

Greenberg, M. T., Domitrovich, C. E., & Bumbarger, B. (2001). The prevention of mental disorders in school-aged children: Current state of the field. *Prevention & Treatment*, *4*, Article 1. Retrieved September 7, 2005, from http://journals.apa.org/prevention/volume4/pre0040001a.html

22

The *Best Practices* in Prevention Curriculum

Foundational Life Skills for General and Special Education

Ellen Dietz, Joanne Glancy, and Mike Dobbins

Empathy is the foundation upon which life skills are built. As students gain empathy for each other, it sets the stage for a school climate of cooperation.

On any given day in Mrs. Arnold's seventh-grade class students learn important social skills in a variety of ways:

- Through one-on-one peer interviews, students learn communication skills and build awareness of how others feel about themselves.
- During group discussions, students learn to use brainstorming as a problem-solving technique.

- Individually, students complete worksheets to help them identify emotions. Then, as a group, they share and support each others' responses. Students learn to have empathy for each others' feelings.
- While learning anger management steps, students examine their self-talk as well as how the other person might feel in the situation.
- Small groups read scenarios together to decide if example situations pose reasonable or unreasonable risks. The class discusses risk taking as a group.
- Students role-play situations for the class to model assertive ways to deal with conflict. After each role play, the class discusses the assertiveness skills they used and how each person might have felt in the situation.

The common thread among life skills activities that Mrs. Arnold covers with her students is empathy.

EMPATHY: THE CORNERSTONE

Empathy, in the simplest sense, is identifying with the feelings or thoughts of another person. The word *empathy* comes from the Greek root for "affection," which helps us understand that empathy springs from the acts of kindness and respect one person shows for another when empathizing with that person. Empathy is the product of a nonjudgmental attitude and shows respect and concern for another person's emotions or plight. When taken in this larger context—affection, respect, openness, kindness, and sincere concern—we can easily see how empathy is the root for establishing a buildingwide climate of emotional learning. Students who can put themselves in others' shoes possess and promote this outlook of openness.

Empathy, shared and encouraged as normative behavior, is the very root of a peaceable climate. In Goleman's (1995) benchmark publication, *Emotional Intelligence*, he asserts that empathy is a key social ability. He describes empathy in terms of good listening skills, distinguishing between someone's action and your own reaction, respecting the differences in people's perspectives, negotiating compromise, building relationships, and cooperating. We would further assert that just as these skills promote empathetic responses, empathy, itself, is the foundation of social skills. Strengthening our personal emotional intelligence and fostering a climate for emotional learning can be a fun and rewarding experience.

Empathy can have several functions in developing social skills. Foremost, it provides an avenue for clear and effective communication. The person who can acknowledge the feelings and reactions of peers has just opened a channel of clear communication. By not overshadowing the other person's reactions with his or her own assumptions, perspectives, comments, or judgments, the student gains an insight into the true nature of the exchange.

Furthermore, empathy fosters skills that are useful in situations throughout life. For instance, when assessing the response of another person to a comment, situation, or other stimulus, we take into account their body language, vocabulary, the context of the exchange, and the person's actions, as well as his or her emotions. Therefore, it follows that empathy teaches us to be observant to verbal cues and emotional signals such as tone of voice, eye contact, and the pace and volume of speech. Consider the vast array of contexts in which these skills are necessary, from adolescence through adulthood: education, personal, business, relationships, social situations, volunteerism, politics, and so forth. For the fortunate few, the skills to succeed in these areas are a natural part of life, but most people must learn these social skills. In addition to teaching social skills, the activities in the *Best Practices in Prevention* curriculum can be catalysts for integrating them into a student's life and into the daily classroom environment.

BEST PRACTICES STRUCTURAL ADAPTATIONS

A curriculum designed for Grades 4 to 5 and 6 to 7, *Best Practices in Prevention* (Bilyk-Glancy, Carlton, Dobbins, Fisher, & Menkaus, 1994) is a comprehensive classroom tool that teaches life skills in conjunction with substance abuse and violence prevention. *Best Practices* has been written as an inclusive program, that is, appropriate for classrooms with a wide variety of learning abilities. This is the key to its success. A multitude of activities are included, addressing visual, auditory, tactile, and kinesthetic learners. This flexibility allows teachers to choose activities that fit the learning abilities of the class, rather than using a preset structure. Classrooms across the hall from each other will have as widely varied learning abilities as classes across the country. In addition to adapting to class needs, the curriculum adapts to the changing school climate.

This flexibility is especially important for students with special-education needs. Many students in special education rely on visual and tactile stimuli more so than their general education peers who work well under the widely used auditory (i.e., lecture) format. Activities in *Best Practices* use visual cues, kinesthetic classroom exercises, and repetition to reinforce important points and illustrate relationships in the materials. General-education students also respond well to the variety of activities, encouraging them to exercise other learning centers of the brain. You will find that as each student uses a wider variety of learning styles, they become more attuned to the needs of other students, encouraging them to seek and use more options for solving communication and other problems.

With a little time investment, teachers can apply some similar adaptations to their existing catalog of materials; other features of *Best Practices* have been specially designed to complement the curriculum. For instance, *Best Practices* relies heavily on guided notes, which are consistently mentioned by users as key teaching tools. Teachers have used these as homework assignments, as group assignments in the classroom, and as their original use as individuals' follow-along notes to lectures. Guided notes purposely reflect and reinforce key points throughout the chapters in *Best Practices*; with some imagination, teachers can create their own guided notes to use with other classroom lessons.

Another adaptation teachers can make to existing materials is to edit out verbiage and rewrite lesson pages with fewer words and in larger print. This adaptation is especially helpful to children with learning disabilities because it removes nonessential words that are more confusing than helpful, and the larger print aids physical reading ability. The main point of the material is intact; it is merely reformatted for use by more students. When increasing numbers of students can participate in the lessons, a climate for teaching social-emotional learning (SEL) is easier and faster to build. Further refinements, such as retooling primarily auditory-based lessons into visual, tactile, and other lessons are much more time consuming and come later in the process of integrating SEL into the environment.

BEST PRACTICES AS A TEACHING TOOL

As a teaching tool, *Best Practices* relies on cooperative learning as much as teacher lecture. The nonthreatening individual and group activities teach communication skills, anger management and conflict resolution skills, and the concepts of cooperation. These practices, in turn, help youngsters learn to teach each other, rather than relying solely on the teacher.

The curriculum can be applied in a variety of ways to be successful. Some teachers rely on curriculum trainers to provide 3 weeks of daily lessons. This usually takes place in a health education unit and is arranged ahead of time with the teacher and the principal. Other methods that have worked well are to use one class period each month to explore a specific topic. Another way is to use the lessons in response to a classroom or school situation, in the manner of a "teachable moment." Many teachers prefer this method to illustrate how a tense or inappropriate situation could have been handled with greater empathy. Other teachers have found additional ways of using the lessons, such as choosing lessons to fit into weekly 15- to 20-minute time slots.

Perhaps one of the greatest benefits of *Best Practices* is its ability to be used across the curriculum. In our informal, anonymous evaluation surveys, many teachers state that they "incorporate it across the curriculum," "use it in an advisor/advisee program," and "integrate it once a week, not as a lecture, but to encourage discussion." The activities develop skills that help students grow emotionally and socially. Within academic topics, these skills can be used to enhance the ability to listen to and understand their teachers and their peers, to support correct peer answers, and to suppress negative reactions to classmates' incorrect answers. These skills move far beyond a topic, reaching into how students build relationships, choose peer groups, react to situations and comments of their peers, and decrease verbal harassment of individuals perceived as different.

Students in special education are especially sensitive to peer influence, since many are already perceived as different from the majority of their classmates. Teachers can use the *Best Practices* adaptations to help students with special needs interact with their peers, such as using cooperative learning methods, using groupwork with guided notes, or incorporating more kinesthetic and visual activities into a predominantly auditory and tactile classroom style.

TEACHER PREPARATION

For those students who do not bring social skills with them to middle school or high school, adolescence is not too late to start empathy training. As young people grow emotionally during these formative years, they begin to define who they are in terms of their attitudes, choosing their peer groups, and deciding what is or is not important to them. As they grow to appreciate their feelings, abilities, and talents, they are also prepared emotionally to have compassion for others' feelings and situations. As their self-realization deepens, we can help them share this emotional awareness with their peers, that is, to move it from personal to interpersonal. One seventh-grade student wrote that "I learned a lot about stuff that will help me in the long run," which is, ultimately, what *Best Practices* intends to accomplish.

The *Best Practices in Prevention* curricula have several activities to help students understand and build empathy and social skills. In the chapter "Self-Concept and Empathy," the issues of experiencing and expressing one's emotions and allowing other students to express their own build both of these areas simultaneously. Using these activities in the class builds a feeling of emotional safety among students. Furthermore, it sets the tone for a climate of SEL and provides the opportunities to exercise the skills that will build this climate.

Back to Mrs. Arnold's Class

Let's return to Mrs. Arnold's seventh-grade class. She will lead the class in identifying emotions, perhaps as a scheduled activity, or perhaps in response to a recent situation the students faced. Using the "Feelings Survey" activity (see Appendix A at the end of this chapter), Mrs. Arnold will give her students a chance to vocalize emotions and compare them with other people's in a nonjudgmental and nonthreatening setting. First, her students independently complete the guided survey questions, like "I get angry when _____," "I am proud that _____," and "People hurt my feelings most by _____." Perhaps Mrs. Arnold will write responses on the board where the class can discuss them as a group, rather than putting students in a spotlight to voice their responses individually. As the list of responses on the board grows longer, each student learns that there is a vast range of emotional responses, and that none are correct or incorrect. They will learn there are some similarities in emotional triggers, and they will also find surprises in what can make their classmates feel happy or sad. For many children, these are revelations that are not discussed with family members and that are avoided in peer group situations in which fitting in (i.e., keeping quiet and following the leader) takes precedence over sensitive and truthful communication. Used in the classroom where there are rules of conduct and the setting is emotionally secure, students have the freedom to express true emotion without the threat of ridicule. Underlying this activity is the practice of empathy—that is, each student is open to others' emotional responses.

Using a variety of student-learning activities also promotes teacher preparation. Teachers often rely heavily on methods that address only one or two learning styles. By addressing a variety of learning styles, teachers learn new ways of presenting information, encouraging student participation, and increasing the amount of learning in the classroom.

TEACHING SOCIAL SKILLS

As educators, we can promote learning about emotions and responses in personal and interpersonal domains. Life skills activities in *Best Practices* teach students to identify and express emotions, and present options for dealing with them. This awareness of perspectives, cues, and reactions can give great insight into how and why people react the way they do.

An educator can begin at any time in a student's life to teach empathy. During early adolescence, children begin turning their attention from their families to their peers to deal with emotions, and relationships with friends take on more importance. The *Best Practices* curriculum reaches young adolescents at this critical point in their lives to teach social interaction skills that will help these youngsters build trusting relationships. No preliminary education or skills need to be in place prior to beginning empathy training. The skills that accompany empathy are best learned in a group situation that has been made safe by classroom rules and a teacher's social supervision, and where the rules are enforced socially by everyone in the class.

EMPATHY-BUILDING ACTIVITIES

Best Practices contains many different activities on building empathy. In the activity "Strengths and Weaknesses" (see Appendix B), students explore areas in which they can be successful and realize that everyone has weaknesses. Each student completes the student worksheet, and then the activity is opened for discussion. The curriculum recommends that teachers write worksheet responses on the board, without identifying individual students' responses. The teacher guides the discussion with a series of nonthreatening questions, such as "What do you do well?" "How do you use your strengths to help others?" and "What weaknesses did you have that were similar to other people?" In a foundational way, the exercise teaches students to be sensitive to others' weaknesses and to share a strength if it will help.

Students also get to role-play situations to teach empathy-building attitudes. For instance, in the "What's It Like?" activity (see Appendix C), students are given situations to react to and are given the opportunity to explain or defend their response. Situations might include being chosen last for a team sport, being singled out by a teacher for misbehavior, and receiving a compliment or an unexpected gift. When more than one student gets to react to the situation, other students can see that there is no correct response. Students are encouraged to react truthfully, and the audience is directed to be nonjudgmental and helpful in closing the situation with the least amount of turmoil, which teaches empathy building through cooperation, compassion, and a focus on positive outcomes.

Conflict resolution, refusal skills, anger management, and similar areas build on the foundations of empathy. Using topic-specific activities teaches the skill and also promotes a way for empathy to be integrated into typical situations. For example, *Best Practices* has several activities in anger management and conflict resolution. In class after class, teachers choose a learning assignment that illustrates to students how a parent or other adult coped with peer pressure. Although children gain ideas about useful refusal skills, the underlying message is that their parents can be resources and are excited about helping teach life skills to them. In "Thoughts on Peer Pressure," a refusal skills homework assignment, students interview a parent, guardian, or other adult using the following questions:

1. Did you feel peer pressure when you were in school?

2. Do you still feel some pressure to conform to a group? In what ways?

3. Did you ever want your parents to tell you that you could not do something so that you would have a reason to tell a friend no?

4. What do you think are the best ways for a person to resist peer pressure and be herself or himself?

In these and many other activities, students learn to interact in small groups and as part of the larger group to build personal skills and support their classmates. This climate of SEL can become the normative behavior in the classroom and beyond, when students internalize the empathy-building lessons. Amber, a seventh-grade student, wrote in her evaluation, "I would like Deb [the teacher] to come again because she was fun and gave us good tips for life."

An important benefit to be noted in empathy training is the decreased likelihood of problem behaviors, such as drug involvement, aggressiveness, and violence. Researchers have catalogued risk and protective factors, which are those characteristics, behaviors, skills, and situations that increase or decrease the chances, respectively, that a child will engage in destructive or delinquent behaviors. Empathy training is a protective factor that crosses individual, peer, and school domains. Empathy bolsters the protective factors of positive social attitudes, the ability to build close peer and social bonds, heightened school and community attachments, and decreased interpersonal conflict. When protective factors outweigh their risk counterparts, the likelihood of drug use, violence, and delinquency declines (Drug Strategies, 1998; Office of Juvenile Justice and Delinquency Prevention, 1995). Empathy-based skills can promote protection by teaching students to handle conflict nonviolently, use nondrug coping strategies, build and sustain close friendships, strengthen learning skills that bolster academic success, and more.

FOSTERING A PEACEABLE CLIMATE

The *Best Practices* curriculum has many benefits, some resulting from the curriculum's format, some from the topic content, and some from different styles of learning that occur with the curriculum. *Best Practices* uses a preventive approach, teaching skills that preclude or short circuit a student's involvement with violence or substance use. Among these skills are empathy training, anger management training, conflict resolution strategies, goal setting, and setting personal boundaries. When a student has the skills to avoid either entering or escalating a situation, then that student can remain a healthier and safer individual. Furthermore, the consistent use of healthy choices, particularly in public situations, acts as reinforcement of these as normative behaviors, rather than exceptions to the norm. Consequently, the use of these behaviors fosters a buildingwide climate of peace, cooperation, and mutual respect. Another benefit of using the curriculum is that it encourages diversity through acceptance and regard for people, traditions, races, and traits that are different from our own.

EVALUATING PROJECT OZ CURRICULA

Evidence-Based Structure

Best Practices was developed by educators and preventionists, and the curriculum uses many of the critical ingredients for a successful prevention program. Among these ingredients, identified in various research publications and reports (e.g., Collaborative for Academic, Social, and Emotional Learning, 2003), are life skills training based on a strong theoretical foundation; a multifaceted approach covering peer, family, and community domains; activities designed to promote a positive school climate or culture; introduction in primary grades and reinforcement across grade levels; interactive techniques such as cooperative learning, discussions, and role plays; ethnically and culturally sensitive material; teacher training to ensure that the program is delivered as intended; and incorporation of evaluation tools such as pretests and posttests. The skills specifically cited under life skills are anger management, empathy and social perspective taking, social problem solving, social resistance skills, active listening and effective communication, general social skills, and peace building skills. Best Practices uses all of these ingredients, offering teacher training as an added benefit but not a prerequisite to program use.

Information Derived From Data

Over the 2002–2003 school year, the Project Oz Best Practices Grades 6 to 8 curriculum was evaluated by University of Illinois' Center for Prevention Research and Development. The evaluation focused on students in the seventh grade. There were four schools participating in the evaluation—three schools receiving the education classes (intervention groups), and one control school (comparison group). With this evaluation process, the three intervention groups were administered a pre-survey at the beginning of the course. The post-survey was administered at the end of the semester instead of at the end of the 10-day course. The comparison school was administered the pre-survey at the beginning of the semester and the post-survey at the end of the semester. Positive results were found in terms of increased perception of personal choices in conflict situations and a decreased sense of frustration in a confrontation.

ASSESSMENT APPROACHES USED BY TEACHERS

The most often used method for evaluation has been a pretest given at the start of a unit followed by a posttest given at the conclusion of a unit. Questions can be derived from the lecture notes. Most questions relate to factual content of the lecture; others can relate to attitude shifts that might take place. A sample of the types of questions that have been used in the past are included in Table 22.1.

Another useful method of evaluation has been an attitude or behavior survey that is given at the beginning and end of a unit, similar to the factual pretest/posttest. On this type of survey, students can respond with "strongly agree," "agree," "disagree," or "strongly disagree" to various statements related to life skills materials. Some statements might relate to attitudes or perceptions they have, whereas others might relate to skills obtained over the course of the unit. Examples of some statements that might be used are listed in Table 22.2. Students' responses, which are typically anonymous, can be totaled collectively at the start of the unit and at the end to measure if the students' perceptions about their attitudes and behaviors changed after the material was presented.

Table 22.1   Sample Pretest/Posttest Evaluation Questions

Question	Choices
Which statement is true about stress?	Stress and health are not related.
	Some stress is OK.
	Stress comes mostly from negative events.
	Adults feel more stress than young people.
Which messages are helpful when trying to solve a conflict?	"We" messages
	"You" messages
	"I" messages
	"They" messages
Decisions that are made after thinking through all the choices and consequences are called what?	Snap decisions
	Habit decisions
	Logical decisions
	None of the above

Table 22.2   Sample Attitude Survey Questions

Statement	Choices
There is no harm in pushing or shoving another student to get your point across.	Strongly Agree
	Agree
	Disagree
	Strongly Disagree
It is usually easy for me to tell if something I say makes a classmate sad or upset.	Strongly Agree
	Agree
	Disagree
	Strongly Disagree
I can tell when I'm getting angry.	Strongly Agree
	Agree
	Disagree
	Strongly Disagree

Another means of evaluation involves the guided notes provided with most chapters. As stated earlier, these notes correspond with the lecture material and are designed to be used during the lecture. Some teachers have used these notes as quizzes or tests instead of during the lecture.

Lastly, student feedback can be used as a means of evaluation. This can be either written or oral or a combination of the two. We ask students things like which topic areas contained information that was new to them and which skills they feel would be useful in a real-life situation. If there are skills they remain uncertain about, this gives us an opportunity to reinforce those skills.

CONCLUSION

The sooner a social skill is taught to a child, the sooner that child can put the skill to use and integrate it into lifestyle choices. *Best Practices* begins introducing empathy concepts in Grade 4, and moves into comprehensive life skills teaching in Grade 6. As these skills are reinforced from year to year, the adolescent can draw on them during this high-growth phase.

The life lessons taught in the curriculum can counteract the availability of choices adolescents face as they move away from the security of the family and into forming and choosing peer groups and beginning to form close, one-on-one relationships. Their ability to distinguish between their self-perspective and what they will compromise to join a peer group will be severely tested. With the ability to empathize, the adolescent will build communication and other social skills that will help them successfully navigate the changing social situations in a safer, more responsible, and more goal-oriented manner than they could if they did not possess positive social skills. The habits, friendship qualities, strengths and weaknesses, and sincerity they cultivate through empathy building will be the foundation they will rely on for the choices they will make throughout life.

Give empathy building a workout in your classroom, and see how it can make a difference in the emotional climate. You can promote SEL by laying the foundation through empathy-building activities with your students. You will find that your students will begin to treat themselves, their peers, and the school staff with renewed kindness and greater respect, which in turn will promote a higher level of cooperation and satisfaction in every classroom day.

APPENDIX A

Feelings Survey

Objective:

To allow students to compare their own feelings with those of other students.

Directions:

1. Give each student a Feelings Survey worksheet and instruct them to complete the statements.

2. Collect the completed worksheets.

3. Give each student an extra worksheet and instruct him or her to use it to interview another person, recording the answers.

OR

Have another class fill out the Feelings Survey worksheet and allow your students to compare their own answers with those of the other class.

Discussion:

1. Did everyone complete the statements in exactly the same way?

2. Is it OK for different people to have different feelings? Why or why not?

3. Why is it important to know how you usually feel in certain situations?

Evaluation:

Guided discussion of the completed worksheet that allows students to compare their feelings with those of other students.

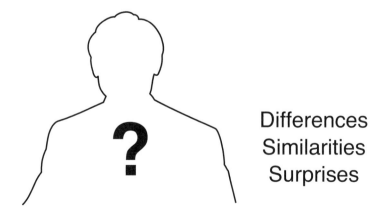

Differences
Similarities
Surprises

Feelings Survey

Complete the following statements:

1. I am best at _____

_____.

2. People hurt my feelings most by _____

_____.

3. I get angry when _____

_____.

4. In school, I do best when _____

_____.

5. People who know me well think I am _____

_____.

6. I need to improve most in _____

_____.

7. I have never liked _____

_____.

8. When my family gets together _____

_____.

9. I am proud that _____

_____.

APPENDIX B

Strengths and Weaknesses

Objective:

To enable students to explore areas in which they can be successful and realize that everyone has weaknesses.

Directions:

1. Have each student complete the Strengths and Weaknesses worksheet (which consists of a piece of paper with two columns, one for Strengths and one for Weaknesses, and lines on which to make multiple entries for each). Depending on the ability of the students, you may need to generate a list of strengths on the blackboard.

2. Have each student share their responses.

3. Hold a discussion.

Discussion:

1. What do you do well?

2. What do you have to do to improve your weaknesses?

3. How do you use your strengths to help others?

4. What are some strengths you admire in other people?

5. What strengths did you have that were similar to others?

6. What weaknesses did you have that were similar?

Evaluation:

Guided discussion to determine if students realize that everyone has weaknesses.

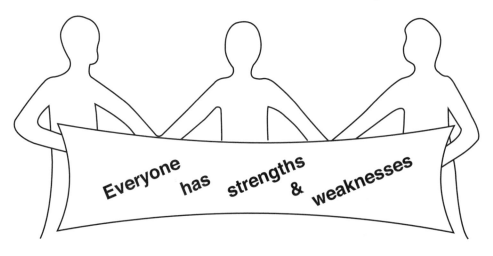

APPENDIX C

What's It Like?

Objective:

To express feelings and reactions to certain situations.

Directions:

1. Have the students discuss how it feels to be in the situations described on the What's It Like worksheet.
2. Instruct the students to focus on how they would feel in or react to the situations.
3. Have the students role-play the situations.
4. Have the students give suggestions to each other for more positive reactions.
5. Role-play the positive scenario.
6. You may want to write the suggestions on the board.

Evaluation:

Completed role play.

What's It Like? Worksheet

What's it like . . .

1. when you are the last one chosen for a game?

2. when people yell at you?

3. when someone doesn't do what he or she said he or she would?

4. when someone compliments you on a job well done?

5. when you get a gift you didn't expect?

6. when the teacher tells you to be quiet?

REFERENCES

Bilyk-Glancy, J., Carlton, C., Dobbins, E. M., Fisher, B., & Menkaus, L. (1994). *Best practices in prevention.* Bloomington, IL: Project Oz.

Collaborative for Academic, Social, and Emotional Learning (CASEL). (2003). *Safe and sound: An educational leader's guide to evidence-based social and emotional learning programs.* Chicago: Author.

Drug Strategies. (1998, July). *The methodology of safe schools: Safe students. A technical report.* Washington, DC: Author.

Goleman, D. (1995). *Emotional intelligence: Why it can matter more than IQ.* New York: Bantam Books.

Office of Juvenile Justice and Delinquency Prevention. (1995). *Delinquency prevention works.* Washington, DC: U.S. Department of Justice.

23

Teenage Health Teaching Modules

Social-Emotional Learning in the Context of Health Education

Christine Blaber

FEELINGS AND HEALTH

Understanding feelings is a prerequisite to leading a healthy life. As adults, we have had several decades to learn about ourselves and the spectrum of emotions through which we experience our lives. For the most part, we have learned to respond constructively to our feelings and to handle the stresses and strains of everyday and not-so-everyday events.

Adolescents are just beginning this learning process. They are experiencing new feelings, trying to sort out what they mean and how to respond to them. Adolescents experience life and their feelings with great intensity. They often have not had enough experience to know that intense feelings are natural parts of life and that feelings change and pass. One of the objectives of the Teenage Health Teaching Modules (THTM) is to empower students to make use of a variety of positive coping strategies that can help them cope during times of intense feelings and stress.

Consider the following situations from a THTM activity for Grades 9 and 10:

Derek stood on the line with the basketball in his hands. If he made these two free throws, his team would win the game. But both times the ball clanged around the rim and bounced out. His team lost the game. Derek was really mad at himself for messing up. He turned around and heaved the basketball into the bleachers as hard as he could. The basketball narrowly missed hitting someone in the face.

Kara was livid. For the second time this week her sister had borrowed clothes without asking and didn't even bother to return them. Kara searched through her sister's room and found her new sweater and skirt at the bottom of a pile on the floor. That did it! Kara emptied her sister's closet into a pile in the middle of the floor and stomped back to her room. Then she put a note on her door telling her sister that she couldn't borrow anything from her room. (Education Development Center, 1991a)

In analyzing these situations, students consider whether Derek's and Kara's methods of coping with anger were helpful or harmful and then brainstorm more positive ways to resolve each situation. Students suggest that Derek may be more embarrassed than angry, and that if he had been able to acknowledge his embarrassment, he might not have responded in such a violent manner, putting himself and others at risk for injury. The class then discusses how, in some situations, expressing anger can be harmful—especially (as in Derek's case) if it makes a stressful situation worse.

Students are quick to point out that Kara's actions illustrate that there may not always be a clear-cut distinction between helpful and harmful modes of expressing anger. Dumping her sister's clothes on the floor may help Kara's sister understand what it feels like to have clothes treated this way, but it also may escalate the situation if it prompts her sister to retaliate. Writing a note on the door is helpful, but it would probably be better for Kara to cool off and tell her sister directly how she feels about what her sister did.

The objective of the small-group exercise and the discussion that accompanies these situations is to help students understand that people cannot always control their feelings, but they can control how they respond to feelings by choosing how they act. Students learn the importance of "inserting a pause" between having a feeling and taking action. Whether the pause lasts a split second or much longer, it gives the person time to consider whether he or she wants to take action and which actions will lead to the most positive consequences for all involved.

THE THTM APPROACH

When young people can embrace their feelings as natural and helpful companions, they are well on their way to self-acceptance, a difficult but crucial task of adolescence. Self-acceptance is a cornerstone of THTM, a successful, nationally used, and independently evaluated comprehensive school health curriculum for Grades 6 to 12 (see www.thtm.org). The curriculum is composed of 25 modules, each of which consists of a teacher's guide with a detailed framework for conducting classroom activities and handouts designed to be duplicated for student use.

The overarching goal of THTM is an ambitious one: to provide adolescents with the knowledge, skills, and understanding necessary to act in ways that enhance their immediate and long-term health. Health, according to the THTM way of thinking, is "a condition that enables people to live fully, realizing their full potential. It involves the individual's total being: physical, mental, emotional, spiritual, and social" (Education Development Center, 1991b, p. 10). These factors are almost always interrelated. For example, THTM activities ask students to explore how personal beliefs and feelings, relationships, laws, and the ability to manage stress all affect their health—as well as the more obvious physical factors, such as exercise, diet, and use of tobacco. The adoption of a healthy lifestyle (a set of health-enhancing behaviors shaped by internally consistent values, attitudes, beliefs, and external social and cultural forces) is promoted as a way for adolescents to reach their full potential.

A FOCUS ON SKILLS

Why do some adolescents make the choices and take the risks they do? Consider the leading health problems and risk behaviors associated with adolescents: HIV/AIDS and other sexually transmitted diseases, alcohol and other drug use, unplanned pregnancy, motor vehicle crashes, violence, academic problems and school dropout, and eating disorders. These problems are symptoms of more profound, underlying issues such as low self-esteem, identity issues, a false sense of invulnerability, and peer pressure. As several research studies have established (Collins et al., 2002; Kirby et al., 1994), a school health curriculum with a strong skills-based focus helps young people build critical skills to address these underlying issues.

THTM emphasizes seven skills essential to adolescence: self-assessment, risk assessment, communication, decision making, goal setting, health advocacy, and healthy self-management. Focusing on this core set of skills throughout the curriculum enables students to learn and practice critical behaviors that will help keep them safe and healthy in a variety of situations. In addition, because of their significant relationship to health decisions and health behaviors, the themes of protection, responsibility, interdependence, and respect are reinforced in all of the modules.

EXPLORING THE LINKS BETWEEN PHYSICAL AND EMOTIONAL HEALTH

THTM strives to make explicit for adolescents the connections between their physical, mental, and emotional health. For example, the high school module titled "Living With Feelings and Handling Stress" explores how prolonged stress can lead to disease. When the body is exposed to a heightened level of stress over time, with no opportunity to relax and recover, body systems are overtaxed, immunity begins to decrease, and stress-related symptoms and diseases may develop. Not only does stress impact health, but health behaviors can increase stress. The class works in cooperative groups to analyze case studies of adolescents whose diet, exercise habits, and sleeping patterns create additional stress in their lives.

The following (abridged) case study features a high school student involved in binge-purge eating:

Melody is a tenth grader. After her father's death last fall, she avoided everyone by napping a lot and sleeping late. Finally, she decided that she had to do something active to feel better, so she got involved in an afterschool sports program. She found that she felt a lot less sad when she was physically active and with other people than when she went home to an empty house. Then Melody began to notice that the girls she hung around with were much more popular with boys than she was. She didn't understand, but it felt awful. Every Friday and Saturday night, Melody's friends went out while she sat home alone in front of the TV, munching on cookies, ice cream, and chips.

One night, while reading a popular magazine, Melody came on a story about several girls who found that after they slimmed down, they became more popular with boys. Starting that night, Melody began to diet. She soon discovered how hard it was because she had become accustomed to eating a lot of junk food. So she began eating less during the day and binge-ing on big dinners and after-dinner snacks. Before she went to sleep, she would force herself to throw up.

After several weeks, Melody began to get results. When anyone asked how she was getting slimmer, she told them that she was dieting. To back up this lie, Melody began eating less and less in public and hoarding all the food she could. When no one was around, she would binge on her stash of food until she felt sick and then force herself to throw up. After a few months, Melody felt disgusted by what she was doing and realized that she couldn't control her eating and bingeing cycles. She felt so badly about herself that she stopped participating in the school sports program. After school, she just ate and slept. She began to feel relieved that no one asked her out because she was tired of hiding the truth from everyone.

Students work in cooperative groups to analyze this case and two others using the following questions:

1. What are the stressors in this case?
2. What are the signs that the character is experiencing stress?
3. How did the character's diet create or reduce stress?
4. How did the character's exercise patterns create or reduce stress?
5. How did the character's sleeping habits create or reduce stress?
6. What does this character need to know about stress reduction, diet, exercise, and sleep?

The cooperative groups then present the results of their work to the entire class for general discussion.

Although activities like this often generate excitement in the classroom because they address issues that adolescents find compelling, many teachers find that they themselves lack the health knowledge (or easy access to accurate health information) to facilitate such discussions with confidence. To support teachers in this situation, THTM provides comprehensive resource information on key health topics. For example, the activities on stress and health include detailed background information for the teacher on the stress response, starve-purge eating disorders, and the links between diet, exercise, sleep, and stress. Background information in THTM typically includes a synthesis of research on the topic, an overview of how the issue impacts adolescents, warning signs, and the appropriate role for the classroom teacher.

INTEGRATION WITH OTHER DISCIPLINES

Research has shown that 50 or more hours per year of health instruction is necessary to produce desired student outcomes (Connell, Turner, & Mason, 1985). Since it is rare for schools to devote this much time to health education, it has become critical to integrate curricula like THTM into other content areas.

The middle grades provide an ideal setting for developing and implementing interdisciplinary units on a variety of health issues. Two of the newest THTM—"Building Foundations: Developing Skills for Life" and "Taking Action to Stop Bullying"—are designed to be co-taught by middle-grade English language arts teachers and health educators. These materials draw on the motivating power of literature to build students' reading, interpretation, and writing skills, as well as introduce them to positive skills for healthy living. Interdisciplinary teaching of THTM and other health curricula holds great promise, but it requires a high degree of commitment and coordination from teachers and administrators, ongoing teacher support, and opportunities for interdisciplinary staff development.

SERVICE LEARNING AND THTM

Opportunities exist throughout THTM for students to carry out community-based service-learning projects. These projects enable students to gather health information, act as health resources for others in the school or community, or learn about and experience how individuals in a community can work together to bring about positive changes. Community service projects encourage students to become involved in their community, working with peers and positive adult role models on issues that are important to them. Some researchers point out that such projects can protect against adolescent use of alcohol and other drugs. These kinds of long-term projects may require significant planning and ongoing management from the teacher.

As part of the high school THTM devoted to preventing alcohol and other drug use, students work in cooperative groups to design and carry out a community service project that actively expresses protection, a core theme of the curriculum. Students may focus on any age group in their school or community. Projects range from collecting and giving out information, to offering a needed service to the school or community, to writing a story for a local newspaper. The most successful projects are ones that are based on relevant local issues; these tend to both interest and excite students. For instance, after several teenage bicyclists were injured in one community, students advocated local regulations requiring the use of bicycle helmets. In other communities, episodes of violence have prompted students to work on gun control issues.

The goal of the project is for students to appreciate the protective links that can exist between themselves and others in the community. While helping their community, students can experience the intrinsic rewards of service and learn the power of a small group to make a difference. Helping the community also helps students explore the values of teamwork, planning, and follow-through outside the traditional classroom setting.

BUILDING A SUPPORTIVE SCHOOL CLIMATE

The physical and psychological atmosphere or climate of the school in which THTM is implemented has a tremendous impact on the overall success of the curriculum. At the most concrete level, the condition of the school's buildings and grounds significantly impact teaching and learning in THTM and all other classrooms (Henderson & Rowe, 1998). Additional factors that contribute to a schoolwide climate that is supportive of THTM include

- a school environment that is physically safe, that is smoke- and drug-free, and in which strategies for peaceful conflict resolution are practiced;
- school staff and faculty who understand—regardless of their discipline—that through their health-related behaviors they serve as role models for students (Haber, 1994);
- teachers who create a healthy, safe classroom environment for students by working with students to establish clear guidelines for behavior, employing fair and consistent classroom management techniques, establishing high expectations for all students, and interacting with students in a respectful, positive, and affirming manner;
- smaller classes in which students are able to work in cooperative groups; cooperative groupwork is used throughout THTM because it helps students develop the social skills of learning to lead, developing trusting relationships, making decisions, resolving conflicts, and communicating effectively;
- educators who honor the diversity of the student body and view adolescents as individuals with unique backgrounds, concerns, and needs, rather than stereotyping them according to particular groups (Haber & Blaber, 1995);
- school faculty and staff who are willing and able to identify and advocate for troubled students in need of additional health resources in the school or community. This is especially important in the context of a program like THTM, in which sensitive issues such as violence, sexuality, and alcohol and other drug use are explored.

INVOLVING PARENTS IN THTM

Because parents are the first and most significant health educators of their children, it is essential to involve them in the THTM program. Parents have the right as well as the responsibility to understand the teaching objectives of the class.

Inviting parents to class or asking them to be guest experts or to participate in a panel discussion of issues presented in THTM are a few methods of informing parents about what goes on in the THTM classroom. Teachers need to be especially sensitive to working parents who want to know about and be involved in health education issues affecting their children but have limited free time.

Another method of involving parents is through curriculum activities. All THTM include activities designed to be carried out at home to foster family-teen communication and mutual support. Some modules provide informational material on health issues that can be shared at home. Others provide activities that enable adolescents to initiate a discussion about health attitudes and practices. THTM teachers must be sensitive to students' and families' reactions to these activities and are advised not to press for details of family interaction. Teachers are encouraged to help students who are unable to rely on adult family members for support to identify other trusted adults with whom they can forge supportive relationships.

Additional ways that THTM teachers engage parents in the program include the following:

- Prior to teaching the curriculum, send home a letter describing THTM.
- Prior to teaching the curriculum, invite parents to an evening meeting to discuss THTM.
- Sponsor an evening meeting at which the teacher or students present THTM activities.
- Provide opportunities for parents to discuss their questions about THTM with the teacher privately.
- Encourage parents to ask their children about what was covered in class; encourage students to discuss with their parents what they have learned.

A new THTM, "Communicating With Caring: A Program for Early Adolescents and Caregivers of Adolescents," addresses parental involvement very directly. The module contains a series of 20 activities that are targeted to middle school students and their caregivers. "Communicating With Caring" aims to improve communication about sexuality between adults and the adolescents they are raising. Rather than advising parents and other caregivers what they should say to adolescents about sexuality, the module focuses on how to build respectful, two-way communication with young people to promote and protect their health.

TEACHER TRAINING

Teacher training is essential for THTM. From the evaluation of THTM (discussed further in the following section), we learned a few things:

- Teacher training was by far the most important factor affecting a teacher's self-reported preparedness to teach THTM.
- Teachers trained in THTM implemented the program with a significantly higher degree of fidelity than untrained teachers.
- THTM-trained teachers achieved more positive effects on student knowledge than teachers who did not receive training.

Implementing a new curriculum in the classroom is always challenging. This process can be greatly facilitated by teacher training in the program. Effective training enables teachers to become familiar with the philosophy and structure of the curriculum and teaching methods for the program and provides ample opportunity for teachers to practice skills and receive feedback. The Education Development Center has developed a cadre of certified trainers located in various regions of the country who are available to provide teacher training on THTM.

THE RESEARCH BASE FOR THTM

THTM is the first comprehensive secondary school health education curriculum to undergo a large-scale controlled evaluation. The study, conducted by Macro

Systems, Inc., involved almost 5,000 students, 150 teachers, and schools in seven states. The evaluation employed a quasiexperimental, pretest/posttest control group design to assess selected THTM in experimental and naturalistic settings. Highlights of the findings include the following points:

- THTM produced positive effects on the health-related knowledge and attitudes of middle school, junior high, and senior high school students.

- Senior high school students exposed to THTM reported positive changes in several health behaviors, including a reduction in tobacco, alcohol, and other drug use. No significant effects on the self-reported behaviors of middle school or junior high students were observed. (Some possible explanations are: Middle-grade students are going through changes so quickly that it is difficult to have or capture an effect, or students at this grade level have just begun to engage in certain health risk behaviors, the incidence of which remains low.)

- Teachers who received THTM training felt more prepared to teach the curriculum, were less apt to modify it, and achieved more positive effects on student knowledge than teachers who did not receive training.

Schools today experience increasing pressure from the federal, state, and local levels to implement programs that have been rigorously evaluated and shown to be effective. As the only comprehensive health program at the middle school and senior high school level that has undergone an intense, controlled evaluation, THTM is included in the lists of model and promising programs compiled by federal agencies and national initiatives such as the U.S. Department of Education, the Substance Abuse and Mental Health Services Administration, and the Collaborative for Academic, Social, and Emotional Learning.

ASSESSMENT OF STUDENT LEARNING

THTM incorporates multiple assessment strategies designed to help educators measure what students know and what they can do. The large-scale controlled evaluation of THTM (described previously) incorporated two student assessment instruments, one targeted to Grades 7 and 8, and the other for Grades 9 to 12. Each instrument contained 105 items and gathered demographic information from students as well as information about their health-related knowledge, attitudes, and practices. THTM staff have introduced minor changes to the high school instrument to reflect the content of new and revised modules. The new instrument is available by contacting THTM staff: Education Development Center, Inc., 55 Chapel St., Newton, MA 02458; phone: 617/618-2737.

In addition to the outcome evaluation instrument, the curriculum itself offers many opportunities for formal and informal assessment of student learning. The nature of the curriculum encourages students to become active participants in every class. The teacher may elect to keep records of student progress from day to day and provide students with an opportunity to discuss what they learned. In addition, the final session of each module is designed as a tool to evaluate student learning. Some provide both short-answer and essay questions, whereas others are entirely essay questions. These instruments prompt students to practice skills, analyze information, and synthesize ideas. Furthermore, every THTM session (except the last one in a module) includes a homework assignment, and most sessions feature student hand-outs that can be collected and graded. The teacher may decide to use some of these assignments as in-class assessments.

One of the goals of the national health education standards (and the related student performance indicators for Grades 4, 8, and 11) created by the Joint Health Education Standards Committee (1995) is to provide a basis for assessing student performance in health education. THTM developed since the release of the national standards are aligned with these standards.

CONCLUSION

As the evaluation of THTM demonstrates, the teacher plays a critical role in the success of the program. He or she knows the needs, strengths, and limitations of the students, as well as the community the school serves and the internal environment of the school. THTM is simply a written curriculum. What is delivered in the class-room depends on how the teacher delivers it, which in turn rests on the teacher's training, motivation, and skill in making the program his or her own. THTM aims to provide teachers with many opportunities to influence their students' lives, health, and futures in important and positive ways.

REFERENCES

Collins, J., Robin, L., Wooley, S., Fenley, D., Hunt, P., Taylor, J., et al. (2002). Programs that work: CDC's guide to effective programs that reduce health risk behavior of youth. *Journal of School Health, 72*(3), 93–99.

Connell, D. B., Turner, R. R., & Mason, E. F. (1985). Summary of findings of the School Health Education Evaluation: Health promotion effectiveness, implementation, and costs. *Journal of School Health, 55*, 316–321.

Education Development Center, Inc. (1991a). *Teenage Health Teaching Modules: Living with feelings and handling stress.* Newton, MA: Author.

Education Development Center, Inc. (1991b). *Teenage Health Teaching Modules: Teacher's guide for grades 9 and 10.* Newton, MA: Author.

Haber, D. (1994). Health education: A role for all. *ASCD Curriculum/Technology Quarterly, 3*(4), 1–3.

Haber, D., & Blaber, C. (1995). Health education: A foundation for learning. In A. Glatthorn (Ed.), *Content of the curriculum* (2nd ed., pp. 99–129). Alexandria, VA: Association for Supervision and Curriculum Development.

Henderson, A., & Rowe, D. E. (1998). A healthy school environment. In E. Marx, S. Wooley, & D. Northrop (Eds.), *Health is academic: A guide to coordinated school health programs* (pp. 96–115). New York: Teachers College Press.

Joint Health Education Standards Committee. (1995). *National health education standards: Achieving health literacy.* Atlanta, GA: American Cancer Society.

Kirby, D., Short, L., Collins, J., Rugg, D., Kolbe, L., Howard, M., et al. (1994). School-based programs to reduce sexual risk behaviors: A review of effectiveness. *Public Health Reports, 109*, 339–360.

24

Facing History and Ourselves

Martin E. Sleeper and Margot Stern Strom

I found my voice, my moral voice, because of our class. I had been so quiet when others were loud and I never felt like I had the right to speak or that I had anything to say, especially about things other people felt strongly about. That's all changed now. I am a different person. I know a lot about something and that something is connected to social justice. And a lot of this I discovered myself. It wasn't fed to me or laid out for me to memorize. The questions we took on helped to hear other voices and to learn from history and from ourselves.

—Anonymous high school student

The class to which this high school student was referring was part of a course called Facing History and Ourselves. In Facing History classrooms, middle and high school students learn to think about individual decision making and to exercise the faculty of making judgments. By illuminating common themes of justice, law, and morality in the past and present, Facing History offers students a framework and a vocabulary for examining the meaning and responsibility of citizenship and the tools to recognize bigotry and indifference in their own worlds. Through a rigorous examination of the failure of democracy in Germany and the steps and events that led to the Holocaust, along with other case studies of hatred and collective violence in the past century, Facing History teaches one of the most significant and necessary lessons for adolescents to understand: Situations that led to mass violence and genocide in the past were not inevitable but rather shaped by choices made by individuals and groups—choices that at the time may have seemed ordinary and unimportant, but which, taken together, led to extraordinary, unimaginable consequences.

Facing History encourages adolescents to draw connections among events in the past, choices in the present, and possibilities of the future. It is rooted in a pedagogy that identifies concerns and choices that adolescents confront each day about issues of identity, group membership, conformity, loyalty, labeling, ostracism, obeying, or speaking out and uses them as connections for students to move back and forth between understanding choices of the past and the present—between the history and ourselves. The opening component of a Facing History course begins with an examination of individual and group identity. A typical lesson might ask students to make identity charts of themselves:

Figure 24.1   Charting Identity

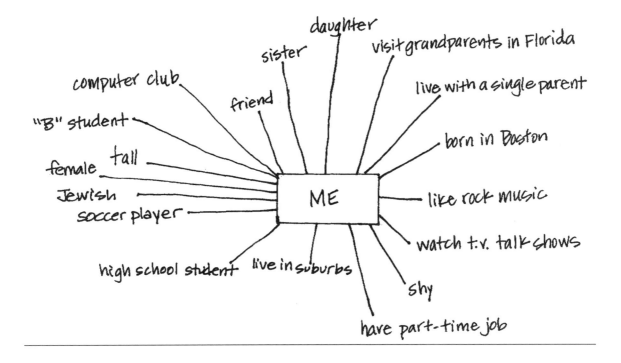

Create an identity chart for yourself, similar to the example in the figure. Begin with the words or phrases that describe the way you see yourself. Add those words and phrases to your chart. Most people define themselves using categories important to their culture. They include not only gender, age, and physical characteristics, but also ties to a particular religion, class, neighborhood, school, and nation. Compare your chart with those of your classmates. Which categories are included on every chart? Which appeared only on a few charts? As you look at other charts, your perspective may change. You may wish to add new categories to the one you created. This activity allows you to see the world through multiple perspectives. What labels would others attach to you? Do they see you as a leader or a follower? A conformist or a rebel? Are you a peacemaker, a bully, or a bystander? How do society's labels influence the way you see yourself? The kinds of choices you and others make each day? For example, if a person is known as a bully, how likely is he or she to live up to that label?

Students add categories to their identity charts of people or experiences that have influenced who they are and how they think others see them. In most Facing History classes, students keep journals in which they reflect on materials they read, videos they watch, speakers they hear, and discussions in which they participate during their study. One student noted in her journal that for her, the category of people and experiences that influenced her identity included

> the foster children that my mother took in. They were from all races and from all different countries. So now when I hear racial slurs or something like that, it really hurts me because I think of them—I know they are part of who I am.

The class then examines the meaning of group identity, issues of membership, and how people define who is identified as "us" and who becomes "them." Vocabulary lists are developed with working definitions of new words like *stereotype*. Student journals reflect the meaning of such terms in their lives. One student wrote about people

> here and everywhere who base their expectations on what they see when you first come in their room. And when they look at me, they see an African-American girl with an attitude and sometimes the game is over before it begins.

Concepts like inclusion and exclusion in groups take on deeper meaning when students learn they have sometimes been the basis of determining who belongs to a nation, who is accorded basic rights of citizenship, and which groups have been defined as "the other."

Facing History classes employ a carefully structured method that continually provokes thinking about complex questions of citizenship and human behavior. The primary case study examines the failure of democracy in Germany, the systematic process of dehumanization of a group of people, the rise and domination of Nazism, and the steps that led to genocide and the events of the Holocaust. To study and teach about this history is to investigate the deepest questions and issues of human behavior; to wrestle with the fullest range of moral and ethical choices and judgments, and to examine a history that engaged all of the political, economic, cultural, religious, and educational institutions of a society. In no other history have the steps that resulted in totalitarianism and ultimately genocide been so carefully documented by the perpetrators, victims, and bystanders. It is also a history that reveals the fragility of democracy and the critical role that choices made by all citizens play in building and preserving democratic institutions.

Much of the program's content is laid out in the Facing History and Ourselves primary resource book, *Holocaust and Human Behavior,* available in print and online through the Facing History Web site (www.Facinghistory.org) After the opening chapters on identity and membership, the program explores the history of the Weimar Republic in post–World War I Germany and the rise of the Nazis. Students examine the societal conditions that put democracy at risk and learn how messages of hatred, racism, and anti-Semitism that were initially put forth by fringe groups penetrated and eventually dominated mainstream thinking. They also encounter the range of responses to Nazi ideology and confront the power of propaganda and indoctrination. They think about the choices that people had for making a difference and learn that the available choices during the decades of the 1920s and 1930s were very different from those in later years. They read about the decisions that German citizens had to make about whether to take an oath of allegiance, befriend a classmate singled out for official ridicule, or speak out in favor of a colleague in danger of being dismissed from a job or position. They confront the small steps that led to the total transformation of a society.

Facing History materials draw on resources from history, literature, art, and science. One document used in classrooms to study the rise of Hitler and the Nazi Party is an excerpt from the 25 Point Nazi Party Platform issued in 1920. As students read the document, they refer to underlying factors like 19th-century notions of race, anti-Semitism, and World War I and its legacies in the Versailles Peace Treaty. Students are asked how this party platform was used and why many Germans found the points of the platform so appealing. They examine other historical resources, such as propaganda posters that demonstrate the power of labeling and the use of words to turn neighbor against neighbor. Examples of actual lesson plans that taught anti-Semitism and racism that were used in schools in Germany provoke thinking about the roots of hatred and the type of education that is necessary to counteract prejudice and racism in a society. Throughout the unit, students learn and practice the skills of in-depth historical thinking and understanding, including knowing about chronology, analyzing historical context, evaluating evidence, determining causality, and confronting multiple perspectives.

Students learn that violence and injustice begin with small steps of indifference, conformity, acceptance, and not thinking about what is happening. They discuss what words like *perpetrator*, *victim*, and *bystander* can mean in the context of both everyday and extreme situations. First-person narratives, as expressed in writings, video testimonies, and guest speakers, constitute a compelling core to the program. Holocaust survivors discuss their experiences and talk about the need to confront and to bear witness to this history. Personal testimonies further allow students to consider their own life stories in relation to history. In journals, poetry, artwork, and musical compositions, as well as in writing assignments, students reveal their connections between the past and their own lives. They identify incidents in their world such as the teasing of a newly arrived immigrant whose English is faulty, the jokes about individuals with physical handicaps, and the bullying of a child on the playground. They think about individual and group responsibility in these situations and the difference that someone speaking out could have made. "I know it is true," wrote a student after studying how the Jews were systematically dehumanized in Nazi Germany. "I have done it myself. I have marginalized people because of their looks or their race. I have been scared of people because someone taught me to be scared of them. I have treated people badly because they are different or not popular. The question we are raising is why do I do that when I know it isn't right? Can I break the cycle?"

Students think about the question of legacy and how history is preserved, interpreted, and taught to future generations. One of the ways in which Facing History classes often complete their study is to examine the role of monuments and memorials in a society. "They are the signposts of past wrongs we don't want to repeat in the next generation," wrote one student about the role of monuments in promoting historical memory. "We need to know what happened in the past to clearly understand what we face in the future."

Connections between the history and choices that are faced today take on deeper meaning as students move from thinking about history to confronting issues of responsibility and judgment. They ask,

> Who knew? Who was responsible? How do we judge the actions and inactions of people in another time? What is the difference between being held guilty, as were the defendants at the Nuremburg Trials, and being responsible, as when someone knows about something wrong that is happening and does nothing about it?

Many classes take the time to examine other ways in which countries like South Africa or Rwanda that have experienced collective violence are now attempting to promote healing and renewal through truth and reconciliation commissions and organizations to achieve transitional justice for past wrongs.

The concluding sections of the program examine the issue of participation in ways that can make a difference. Students are asked to think about individuals and groups who have taken small steps to build just and inclusive communities. Some take action, like the student who chose to do community service work in a shelter for battered women. "I have decided to volunteer as a baby sitter there because the victimization of these women by their men is not so different from the subject we are studying," she wrote in her journal. "Options seemed to disappear from them little by little. The Holocaust victims and these women probably both thought to themselves, step by step, 'How can it get any worse? It has got to get better.' Because of the things we are talking about in class and writing about, I can see all this much more clearly." Another student joined in a "ride against hate" protesting against an attack on a young Moroccan girl who was thought to be gay. "I learned that once you take the initiative to do something right, other people will join in. . . . Instead of just watching bad things happen around you and realizing that they are bad, you can actually have an effect on the world by taking a stand and taking some action."

Facing History classes have been shown to be successful in expanding adolescents' capacity for interpersonal understanding, in enhancing their ability to take the perspective of another, and in increasing their inclination to reflect on the personal meaning of issues of social justice. The history that the program teaches engages students because of its "realness" and the fact that they are studying, as one put it, "what actually happened." That study is connected to the developmental concerns of adolescence—peer relationships, identity, loyalty, belonging, isolation—so that history is seen, in John Dewey's (1916) terms, as connected to students' experiences and the choices and responsibilities that they confront in their current world.

For its ever-expanding network of classroom teachers and educators, Facing History is a continual source of inspiration, in-depth knowledge, and ongoing support. One participant wrote,

Facing History has helped shape my moral guidepost as a classroom teacher in an urban high school. I am able to teach a rigorous academic curriculum that deals with issues of fear, hatred, ostracism, war, and the choices we all face.... Facing History can't change the conditions in which my kids live, but [it] continually [pushes] me past my doubts so that I can teach my kids about power and choices.

Teachers are introduced to the program through workshops that are offered in school and community settings or online. Professional development institutes, all of which include face-to-face interaction and online components, provide intensive sessions in the latest scholarship and in the method of teaching sensitive issues in the classroom. Content is interwoven with pedagogy to engage institute participants in fundamental issues of teaching: how to come to grips with the prejudices and preconceptions teachers and students bring to difficult and controversial subject matter; how to address moral decisions with students without preaching or evasion; how to build a classroom environment of trust and respect for diverse opinions; how to orchestrate discussion in which students truly talk and listen to one another; how to use journals, personal writing, and reflection; how to ask the additional question that complicates the simple answer and provokes critical thinking; and how to assess learning about citizenship, judgment, and participation. Once part of the Facing History educator network, teachers continue to receive follow-up support through an interactive campus on the Web site that offers new resources, lesson plans, and modules for in-depth examination of particular topics related to the Facing History program, such as the history of Weimar, the nature of transitional justice, the role of memory and memorials, and the history of notions of race and eugenics.

By studying the steps leading to the Holocaust and other examples of collective violence in the 20th century and human behavior, Facing History gave students a lens to examine the past that would enable them to recognize bigotry and indifference in their own present and future worlds. The 20th century provided extraordinary evidence of how leaders could use ancient myths and misinformation in conjunction with propaganda techniques to unleash ethnic hatred and cause neighbor to turn against neighbor and to see "difference" as alien and threatening. Its legacies—humiliation, dehumanization, discrimination, and mass murder—fuel confrontations among people all over the world, just as other pieces of those legacies, embodying courage, compassion, dissent, and resilience, offer hope for cooperation and understanding. As the 21st century unfolds, the international context, in which programs like Facing History educate, is critical. Facing History's newest materials are framed in that context. Its recent online forums brought together scholars and educators from more than 50 countries to discuss such issues as the role of religion in identity and the nature of transitional justice in societies that have undergone mass violence. Its most recent publication, *The Crimes Against Humanity and Civilization: The Genocide of the Armenians*, explores a history that is often denied or revised beyond the recognition of its survivors and also examines how that history has informed the growing international human rights movement. Other new materials deepen program themes in the context of American history. The resource guide *Race and Membership in American History: The Eugenics Movement* and a study guide on *Becoming American: The Chinese Experience in America* look at issues of identity and membership and examine how social and scientific constructions of race influenced America's struggle to define membership in the late 19th and 20th centuries.

CONCLUSION

Through its power to engage teachers from different disciplines, along with specialists, librarians, counselors, and administrators, Facing History can facilitate thoughtful and positive change in a school community. "Students can make a difference to themselves and the world around them," concluded one Facing History teacher. "And the world doesn't have to be all that far away; it can be as close as the lunchroom or the playground. I share with the kids how this is hard work but it has to be done." For adolescents as well as adults, the connections between thinking and responsibility, between knowledge and participation, and between conformity and democratic citizenship are the overarching connections between history and ourselves.

Authors' Note: Ongoing information about all aspects of Facing History and Ourselves can be found at www.Facinghistory.org.

REFERENCE

Dewey, J. (1916). *Democracy and experience*. New York: Macmillan.

25

The "Senior Passage" Course

Rachael Kessler

What am I going to do with my life?

Who am I?

Will I marry?

Will I be successful in life?

What is it I'm looking for? Will I find it? Does it matter?

What, of all I feel and believe, is truly my own? Is there anything left beyond that which others have implanted in me?

Why do my parents fight so much?

Why do people suspect our generation?

Why do I worry?

What is my purpose in life?

Is there a God?

Why are some people so mean?

What is there after death?

Where did life really start?

Why do I let people step over me?

Will I ever find someone to love?

Why do I hate people so easily?

Will I get AIDS?

Why do I get so angry?

Why do I feel scared and confused about becoming an adult? What does it mean to accept that this is my life and I have responsibility for it?

Why do I use drugs?

Will a bullet come in my window and kill me?

Do I believe in anything?

Am I normal?

Will there ever be peace?

Will blacks and whites make peace?

What do others think of me?

Is racism ever going to end?

When will kids stop shooting kids?

Why is it so hard for people to forgive?

Is there anyone out in the world like me?

How do people who love you hurt you? Why?

What is God? Man or woman?

Why does violence have to be the answer to everything?

Why do people hate others—black, white, Hispanic, etc.?

I wonder about nature—are we doing irreparable damage with our lack of concern?

These are some of the questions written by high school seniors from around the country when asked to write anonymously their personal mysteries about themselves, others, and life. Capturing their wonder, worry, curiosity, fear, and excitement at this moment in their lives, these questions are central to the curriculum of the Senior Passage course. This curriculum provides a structure for addressing the common challenges faced by high school seniors, as well as parents and teachers grappling with "senioritis." Opportunities for social-emotional learning (SEL) are relatively rare for the older adolescent. The Senior Passage course provides one example of how we can offer young people the skills and experiences that support them in their leap from adolescence to adulthood.

THE NEED

The senior year of high school is an enormous transition—for students, family, and faculty. Students must cope with the pressure of crucial decisions at a time when their identity is just beginning to form. Some anticipate the emotional shock of leaving behind nurturing relationships at every level—parents, siblings, teachers, or friends. Others, who missed this sense of connection during their childhood, feel an urgent need to belong before they can let go of childhood. On the threshold of the unknown, seniors say good-bye not only to others—they must let go of their own childhood and adolescent identity.

Anxiety and mood swings are common for both students and parents who feel the shock of letting go. Family relationships may become volatile—familiar patterns between parent and child often change and even reverse, bringing much confusion in their wake. Even disciplined students may lose their capacity for focus at this time—senioritis threatens both the quality of learning and the harmonious climate between student and faculty.

An exciting awakening is also occurring for seniors. Students glimpse the possibility of larger purpose and deeper meaning in their lives and in life itself. They reflect on the larger existential questions. They begin to have the adult's acuity of mind while still bubbling with the vitality and playfulness of the child. Given the opportunity to explore these depths with adult guidance and peer wisdom, seniors access strengths of character that help them meet with grace the challenges described here.

Designed to guide students through the turbulent waters of this major transition, the Senior Passage course provides a structure in which to address these concerns and allow students to see their normality. The curriculum guides them to recognize and honor the change that is taking place. Students prepare for loss and learn tools for healing grief from previous losses that is reactivated by this letting-go stage in their development. Initially called "Senior Mysteries," by founder Jack Zimmerman, this curriculum was developed as a required one-semester course for all seniors at the Crossroads School for Arts and Sciences, a private school in Santa Monica, California, where it has served seniors more than 20 years. It was adapted in 1993 by educators at University Heights High School, a New York inner-city public school, and in 1996 by a veteran science teacher in a public high school in Oregon. In recent years, educators in Washington, Nebraska, Colorado, and Michigan have also adapted this curriculum for use in public schools. As one of the original team that developed and codified the course at Crossroads, I have supported these educators as a trainer and coach and have continued to lead Senior Passages as an afterschool program to public and private school students in Colorado.

Although this curriculum has been most often used for a class dedicated specifically to SEL, methods and themes can be easily integrated into an academic classroom. Doug Eaton, science teacher, integrates the Senior Passage curriculum into a course called Society and Nature, which not only gives a science credit but also meets the current district character education standards. Dana Knox, an English teacher in Seattle, Washington, offers Senior Passages as a general elective. In Colorado, teacher Marc Small and counselor Susan Spoon have collaborated to integrate the curriculum into a senior psychology elective. And some schools may, like the Alexander Dawson School in Colorado, have used core elements from this curriculum to design a senior retreat. The Appendix contains additional background information about the curriculum.

OVERALL STRUCTURE OF THE SENIOR PASSAGE COURSE

In its most complete implementation of the curriculum, this course is designed to meet once a week for a 1.5- to 2-hour session for one semester. In Washington, the Senior Seminar meets for an hour on one day and then for 100-minute blocks on two other days. In Oregon, students sign up for an elective called "Society and Nature," which meets every other day for 1.5 hours for 18 weeks. Approximately 20 lessons from the Senior Passage curriculum are interwoven thematically with science lessons.

Each class dedicated to Senior Passages follows a similar structure and rhythm: For the first 15 minutes, there is a warm-up activity to help individuals become fully present and to bring the group together. Then the group sits in a circle, sharing stories or reflections on a theme set by the teacher. After each student and teacher has had one opportunity to speak, 10 to 20 minutes are taken for responses—to an individual or to the experience of witnessing or being witnessed in this way. The class ends with a closing exercise designed to help students make their transition out of this intimacy and vulnerability to feel ready for what greets them outside our door.

GETTING STARTED

Play is an important element at the opening of many sessions—many warm-ups are theater or adventure-based learning games. Games are designed to foster alertness, focus, cooperation, and laughter. Students learn about "presence," the concept that unless we are fully present, we cannot learn, listen, or give or receive love. The games help us all become present so we can be ready for something new to happen.

Art activities may be an alternative to playful games. Drawing or sculpting encourage expression through metaphor and symbol. Students might be given crayons to draw a symbol of their past week or a lump of clay to sculpt a symbol of how they are feeling right now. Later in the course, the clay could be used for a symbol of a deeper theme, such as "intimacy" or "letting go."

In the early weeks, we ask everyone to bring an object that symbolizes something that they feel is important in their life right now.

"Does the object have to be valuable?" a student asks. "No, the object is just a symbol—it could be something you cherish, but it can also be a trivial object that symbolizes something very important to you right now."

The students cover their objects so no one will know from whom they come. They leave the room so I can lay out the objects on a beautiful cloth in the center of the room. No one knows who brought the ring, the book, the cupcake, the exquisitely delicate small box, the stone, the set of keys, the painting, the locket, and so forth. Each student and teacher has an opportunity to share the meaning of this symbol.

Some students, when their objects are chosen, talk about surprising gains and disturbing losses in the stories of their families. One feels blessed and surprised by a rose given her by her stepgrandparents. The next student, holding up a thick gold band, tells a more typical tale from the divorce wars.

"This is my Dad's wedding ring," says Jen, holding up a thick gold band. "I wear it now, since they divorced. He travels a lot and I worry about him. Wearing the ring on a chain around my neck keeps him close to me. And it reminds me of how precious relationships are and how quickly they can be gone."

Petra has brought a picture of her family and laid a cross on top of it—a cross she had made herself, carved out of wood. She has glued a lifesaver in the center of the cross. "I became a Christian a few years back. It's been the most wonderful thing in my life. I can't tell you what it feels like to know that I'm loved like that. Always loved and guided. By Jesus. And it's brought our family much closer. Guys—it's amazing."

I wonder how the other students will react to religious fervor in the classroom. I relax as I see how easy and natural it is for everyone when this young woman shares her faith with her peers.

Because each story comes straight from the heart, these students are quickly engaged, eager to listen. Many of them are surprised to feel respect for classmates they never knew or wanted to know. Many notice more similarities than they expected. The students begin to exude calm when they discover how easy it is to enter the circle and be heard.

Telling their stories about the symbols they brought with them, these seniors introduce themselves to each other through what they value most in life. Whether it is the clay they mold into a symbol of their feelings or the objects they bring to represent what is most important in their lives, symbols allow students to reveal their emotions indirectly. Through the use of such exercises, they have the freedom to explore and express feelings that might otherwise be too private or uncomfortable to put into words this early in the semester.

We end each session with an activity to bring closure and transition from this very open, connected place to the pace and style of modern life. Students may reflect silently on what they have heard and felt. Or we may all rise, stand shoulder to shoulder and call out one word that describes how we each feel right now. In the later weeks, we are more likely to close by holding hands and looking into each others' faces for a moment of silence. Or the group invents its own closure. Teachers in the Bronx found that having the students write in their journals for the last 20 minutes both consolidates learning and is an excellent prompt for developing writing skills. (For a full exploration of deep connection, silence, meaning, and several other gateways to the souls of students, a more detailed description of the themes in the Senior Passage curriculum, and an example of an eighth-grade rite of passage program, see Kessler, 2000.)

SACRED CIRCLES

Each session includes speaking and listening from the heart in a circle. At first, this circle is introduced as a time to listen and let people speak without interruption or immediate reactions. Each group is guided through an "agreements for safety" process: What do they need to be able to speak authentically here about things that matter deeply to them? Their list resembles those created by most classrooms that use the SEL approach to collaborative ground rules: respect, listening without interruption, honesty, no put-downs, fairness, openness, the right to pass, and so forth. Then we are ready to speak in the circle.

After the first 2 weeks of students meeting in the circle format mentioned previously, lesson plans for the next several weeks are set by the teachers or guides with a focus on looking back to childhood, to origins and ancestors. To fully celebrate childhood before beginning the journey of letting go, we evoke early memories: We ask them to review childhood photos and bring in a baby picture; we encourage interviews with parents to learn about pregnancy and birth stories as well as pivotal moments in the lives of their parents and grandparents. At the end of the second week, we ask students to research their names—first and last. Where did these names come from? How was their name chosen? Does it have a particular meaning? How do they feel about their name?

I begin the circle about our roots with my story. They often express amazement that a single name can carry so much history: immigration, assimilation, feminism, anti-Semitism, and World War II. Powerful forces in the American story are evoked in the story of my name. My students are inspired to look deeply into the strands of connection and meaning flowing in their own names. As they each tell their own story, we weave a tapestry rich with the many colors and textures of American life.

> Our name was O'Connell but they changed it to Castle—an English name—to hide our Irish roots. The Irish were looked down on in this country when my people came here. But I cannot wait to visit my real home. I found this lady on the Internet this year that speaks Gaelic—she's teaching me and she invites me to cultural events. When I began to learn Gaelic this year, I felt this incredible connection to my people.

A flood of feeling rushed through this young man's face and voice.

> My first name comes from my father, and his father, and probably his father before him. But our last name—Walker—well, that's a slave name. I mean, some slave-owner probably gave my people that name. I have no way to know what our real name was.

Around the fifth week, we do the "Mysteries Questions." These questions, like the ones you read at the beginning of this chapter, are elicited anonymously in a reflective process in which students are asked to write their personal mysteries about themselves, about others, and about life or the universe. "What are you worried about, curious about, afraid of, excited by? What do you wonder about when you cannot sleep or find yourself walking alone, lost in thought?" The guides collect all these questions, type them up verbatim by category, and then read them back the following week to the group in a ceremonial tone. The reading of the Mysteries Questions is a turning point in the course: Students feel honored to hear their own words read aloud, amazed at the wisdom and depth in the questions of their peers, surprised at the repetition of certain themes, and profoundly connected as they realize that they are not alone in their deepest yearnings and concerns.

At this time, we introduce "Council"—shifting the quality of the circle from the secular to the sacred. Council, we explain, is adapted from indigenous peoples all around the world who built community through speaking from the heart, sitting in circles close to the earth. In Africa, in Hawaii, among the Native Americans, and in ancient Greece, people passed a special object to empower the speaker to speak without interruption. In Council, we often create a hearth at the center of our circle—a beautiful cloth, some objects that are special to the students, and a candle or lovely bowl that is filled with water. Then we call for one or several dedications for our Council:

- I dedicate this Council to friendship.
- I dedicate this Council to my uncle, who is dying now.
- I dedicate this Council to our soccer team—we just won the state championship!
- I dedicate this Council to my sister's new baby.
- I dedicate this Council to ending the war.

With these dedications, we use the bowl of water. Students making a dedication choose a stone from the center and place it in the water as they speak. Each class can create their own way to create beauty, natural elements, and focus at the center of the circle.

The themes of Council are often linked to what students have posed in their Mysteries Questions. In this way, the curriculum becomes student centered, re-created by each new group. Of course, certain themes persist. Lesson plans address issues such as

- managing stress;
- personally defining success and setting goals;
- searching meaning and purpose;
- learning to live with regrets and disappointments;
- working with fear, excitement, and decision making about this next crucial step in their lives;
- taking responsibility for self and supporting others;
- exploring gender similarities and differences;
- beginning to discover forgiveness;
- understanding intimacy;
- exploring spiritual development; and
- preparing for loss and learning about grief.

A question sets the theme at the beginning of the Council. For example, what is causing stress in your life right now, and what do you find helps in dealing with that stress? Students have 2.5 minutes each to share a story or express their thoughts or feelings on the theme. Silence is also considered a worthy statement. Following the first round, student who passed are given another opportunity to speak or choose silence. Then the teacher invites "connections": "Let someone know if their story or statement was moving to you, and why." A brief open dialogue follows the 5 or 10 minutes of connections. In some cases, the theme may also be explored through art or language arts on another day: Students in the Bronx collaborate on a mural on the theme "where I'd like to be in the future."

Society and Nature interweaves science themes such as ecology, dendrology, wilderness ethics and cartography, nature writing, Native American studies, environmental issues, and outdoor trip planning. For example, a Council exploring their Mysteries Questions about nature and the universe is included in a field trip.

Around the 10th week, we begin to prepare for the retreat. We give students a brief conceptual framework about rites of passage. Then, through exercises and themes in class and between classes as homework, we begin the journey.

THE RETREAT

Embedded in this course is a retreat designed to be a rite of passage from adolescence to adulthood. The absence of such adult-guided and sanctioned experiences in our present culture has led many students to seek self-destructive badges of adulthood. For many girls, losing virginity or actually bearing a child has become a self-determined rite of passage; for boys, going to the furthest edge with alcohol or the speed of a car, or even a first murder, have become emblematic of their passage. There is ample reason to believe that, in the absence of adult-led, constructive rites of passage, students will initiate themselves and each other with often dangerous results. "If the fires that innately burn inside youths are not intentionally and lovingly added to the hearth of community," writes poet Michael Meade (1993), "they will burn down the structures of culture, just to feel the warmth" (p. 19).

Young people need at this time to face challenges that stretch them to their larger capacities—the courage, stamina, and responsibility that defines genuinely adult character—and then to be honored and welcomed into the adult community.

Retreats range from 1 to 5 days in length. Each of these journeys use periods of solitude and reflection as well as group activities that build to a pitch of intensity in releasing childhood. The retreat and the weeks of follow up with students, parents, and faculty provide a ceremonial experience of the transit that the course itself nourishes over a longer period.

Returning from the retreat, the last three or four sessions of the class focus on learning to say good-bye in ways that foster completion and wholeness. Lesson plans on closure not only help the group complete their relationships with each other but also become a model of how to approach good-byes in other spheres of their lives.

INVOLVING PARENTS AND FACULTY

In Colorado, we have hosted an informational evening for parents and students before they sign up or early in the semester. Staff speak about the needs we are addressing, reviewing themes discussed earlier in this chapter. Past participants—students and parents—speak about what was significant for them.

"We have always been such a tight family," says one mother. "But we just didn't know how to do this good-bye thing. I don't know what we would have done without the course. It really helped us see that we could let go and still remain loving. And for my daughter, the most amazing thing was the way she got so close to students she had judged so harshly those first weeks of the course. She started college with such an open mind, and so much more resilience."

"As weeks passed, I started to trust people for the first time in years," says Leah, who has taken the first semester after high school off to earn money for college. "I was comfortable with them and I looked forward to seeing them in school every day. I used to say I hated everyone at my high school and that none of them were worth my time. Well, suddenly, I didn't hate anyone anymore. That's one of the things I learned has impacted me the most—that we are all the same. We all have fears and pains and some good sides and some bad sides. I judged people so easily before; Senior Passage showed me a whole new way to look at people. I discovered the beauty of an open mind."

"This class has provided me with an environment that allows me to clear my head, slow down, and make healthy choices for me," says Juan. "It makes me realize just how unique each individual's experience is, and the importance of listening. A senior in high school must make colossal decisions whether he or she is ready or not. The more people can be honest about and aware of their own needs when making these decisions, the healthier the decisions will be."

After the opening presentations, parents and students have time for questions and dialogue. Parents receive a two-page written summary to take home with them, and later in the semester, receive a letter about the upcoming retreat and parent evening. Students receive a one-page description addressed to them.

Two weeks before the retreat, parents participate in a special session of the class. We begin with a brief introduction and playful warm-up. Then we hold a "Witness Council." Each generation has a turn to be in the center, holding a Council on how they feel about the impending leave taking. The parents listen to the students first, and then two or three have a chance to comment about how they feel bearing witness to these young people: "I feel hope for the future for the first time," says one father jumping up to speak. "I'm a coach, I work with young people all the time, but I never get to hear their innermost thoughts. I can't believe how articulate and wise these kids are!"

"I knew my son was dealing with these feelings, even though he's reluctant to tell us sometimes," says a mother. "But listening to the same feelings coming from so many students, it helps me understand and appreciate my own son so much better."

Now parents come into the center circle. They speak about how they feel about this leave taking. And we encourage them to look at the baby picture they brought with them and at their child today, and to speak about the growth they see today.

The tears always flow on this evening, with many parents and students moved by the depth of feeling and healing as parents seize this rare opportunity to publicly honor their own child. When the students are asked to speak about what it is like to witness this, they share the new respect they feel for adults as they witness their honesty, their caring, and the struggle to be a good parent and to let go.

For faculty, there is another ceremony that helps bring closure and unites the community around giving a new level of strength to seniors before they make their challenging leap. A list of seniors goes out to the faculty weeks before the ceremony so they can volunteer to be the teacher who takes responsibility for that particular student. On the evening of the event, students are gathered along with their parents, some faculty, and administrators. In the center of the circle is a bucket filled with a variety of long-stemmed flowers. After a brief introduction by the principal, the ritual begins. A teacher rises, selects a flower, and addresses the student, honoring him or her for the particular gifts that student has given to the school community. Unlike the awards ceremonies for athletics or academics, this ceremony publicly honors all the students for the quality of their characters—for their social and emotional growth.

And, in Washington, parents were invited to an evening class for culminating exhibitions.

In addition, other faculty are encouraged to join a Senior Passage class on a voluntary basis as an ongoing participant who has no responsibility for planning or facilitation. The added adult perspective enriches the Councils, and the teachers feel rewarded by developing a different quality of relationship with seniors than they have had in academic classes. Some faculty, who cannot attend regularly, will join the retreat.

IMPACT

We have already heard some students and parents in Colorado with whom I worked personally in an afterschool program describe the impact of this course on their lives. Here are some student responses from some of the public school–based programs:

> I got to know my friends way deeper, and I learned about where I was coming from in life. The class allowed me to see why I felt the way I felt, and how that was not different from many of the people in the group. It was such a safe place to be real about how this time of change was affecting us. I spent the entire summer with the friends I made in this group, and I think that is because we developed a deeper truer friendship. This class fit so well into the final semester of my senior year.
>
> —Society and Nature student, Albany, Oregon

> Senior seminar was a place where I felt safe. I was treated like a human being, not a container to be filled. The class was the voicing, the materializing of what we all really think about during school. We didn't discuss concepts that were up to us to apply to our lives, we discussed real life, itself.
>
> —Senior Seminar student, Seattle, Washington

Here is how some counselors and teachers saw the results at University Heights High School in the Bronx, where seniors had for years sabotaged themselves so they would not have to graduate and leave the sanctuary of caring and safety created in this alternative public school:

"They were such a team," said school social worker Risa Marlin. "Our seniors had never had such a spirit of mutual support and empowerment. And the self-sabotaging had stopped. We just weren't seeing it anymore. Having a place and a formal way to work through the emotional challenges they were all facing allowed them to focus on their work. They were determined to graduate and they had the confidence and concentration to do so."

"They want to work for us in a way I've never seen before," said English teacher Marion Fuller. "They believe us now when we say the academic work is for their own good. We've listened to what is in their hearts. They have felt our compassion for and encouragement with the larger issues in their lives. So they trust that when we doing academics together, we can be also be trusted as guides."

The course has a profound impact on the teachers as well.

"I learned a lot from guiding my first 28 seniors," says science teacher Doug Eaton. "The culminating wilderness rite of passage weekend and the parent leaving/honoring ceremony were milestones in my career. It was not hard to let go of the seniors. They were ready to move on and so was I. When I started my second senior passage group at the beginning of 1998, I was able to bring this work to the forefront in the district and community. Meeting recently with the school superintendent and three other administrators over the uniqueness of this class, I found myself speaking from my heart and with a new confidence. My commitment and passion to the work was recognized and I have new allies . . . at the top!"

CONCLUSION

Fresh from the terrain of childhood and now perched on the brink of adulthood, my seniors have inspired me, moved me, and enriched my heart and soul more than any age group I have been privileged to work with. Young people who are given a safe space for authenticity at this particular moment in the life cycle bring a vulnerability, passion, playfulness, and intensity of aliveness that makes this work deeply nourishing to my soul.

I began this work with a deep concern about the spiritual void in the lives of many adolescents today. I came with a sense of wonder and mystery about whether it was possible to nourish the spirits of young people in secular settings. It was the seniors, through their stories, who taught me that spiritual development may be addressed in many ways. They taught me that connection—deep connection to the self, to another, to a group, to nature, or to a higher power—was the most pervasive longing of the human spirit. I saw a longing for solitude and silence, despite the initial resistance to both that would rise in many of them after living in a culture that suppressed both so thoroughly. And their Mysteries Questions revealed a great need to explore or at least name the search for meaning and purpose, and the mystery of origins and endings in life.

A generation of young people is yearning for adults and elders who are willing to give as much importance and care to their hearts and souls as their academic success and athletic prowess. Although it is not always easy to incorporate such courses into schools, it is deeply rewarding to do so. I believe that the health of future generations, as well as the health of our democracy, depends on a new commitment to our young as they strive to join us as adults—a commitment to listen, to learn, and to teach what we have learned about the journey to personal wholeness and caring community.

APPENDIX

Background Information

A Senior Mysteries course was introduced to the Crossroads School for Arts and Sciences in 1984 by Jack Zimmerman, President of the Ojai Foundation, with the help of Ruthann Saphier and Maureen Murdock. The following year, under the visionary leadership of Paul Cummins, Crossroads created a Department of Human Development to coordinate existing programs in ethics and community service and to develop a Mysteries program to serve students in Grades 7 through 12. I was hired to chair that department and teach Mysteries at all grade levels. Working as a team with Zimmerman, Saphier, Murdock, Peggy O'Brien, and Tom Nolan, we refined and expanded the senior course over the 7 years of my tenure as chair. The rich curriculum of the Senior Passage course reflects the unique gifts and creativity of each of these educators, as well as new contributions from the University Heights faculty adapting it for their inner-city population and my partner Jeffrey Duvall in a 7-year afterschool Senior Passage program in Boulder, Colorado. The Senior Passage program is now available to educators who have attended the Foundation Course of the PassageWays Institute. The program includes a detailed curriculum and 10 coaching sessions. The PassageWays Institute is also developing rites of passage curriculum for students navigating the vulnerable transitions at the end of elementary school and middle school as well as for students entering the cultures of middle and high school. Currently available are the fifth- and sixth-grade programs.

REFERENCES

Kessler, R. (2000). *The soul of education: Helping students find connection, compassion and character at school*. Alexandria, VA: Association for Supervision and Curriculum Development.

Meade, M. (1993). *Men and the water of life*. San Francisco: Harper.

Epilogue

You cannot acquire experience by making experiments. You cannot create experience. You must undergo it.

—Albert Camus (1965)

This book reflects a journey for the reader through emotional intelligence (EI), social-emotional learning (SEL), professional development, and thoughtful insights into each of these topics that are so important to the future of our children. It has been more than a decade since Daniel Goleman (1995) published his groundbreaking book, *Emotional Intelligence*. This publication redefined America's view (and that of people around the world) of what it means to be smart. At the heart of this book was an explication of why EQ matters more than cognitively defined intelligence (IQ) for success in life.

In our earlier text, *EQ + IQ = Best Leadership Practices for Caring and Successful Schools,* we posit that our schools must address EQ *and* IQ to be successful in the development of our children (Elias, Arnold, & Hussey, 2003). We must believe deeply and strongly that we must develop the whole child. There are significant linkages between academic learning and performance and social and emotional skill development. Those skills are essential in the development of citizens for a democracy that thrives in our schools, families, workplaces, and communities. Those who promote EQ plus IQ know that this is an essential combination in the growth and development of educational leaders of our school and our world.

Although the EQ journey began in 1995 for many educators, it started much earlier for some of the project and program leaders highlighted in this text. Our travels for this publication began in Part I, which was aimed at illustrating the importance of teachers being prepared to understand and become aware of the social and emotional needs of their students in a classroom setting.

We wanted Part I to assist teachers and administrators in their search to seek out instructional strategies that will be successful in their local school communities. We issued a challenge regarding the importance of school administrators supporting and sharing leadership through dissemination of SEL messages to make a marked difference in the improvement of academic achievement in their schools. As travelers on this journey of SEL, we all come face to face with the necessity of giving our students essential academic competencies and also preparing them to be citizens of the world. Teachers and administrators must seek to prepare students to become world-class people and citizens of a planet that continues to be in need of better and better citizens who read, write, compute, think, and feel.

The road to SEL will often seem smooth, then crooked, and then straight. There are hills and mountains with high peaks and very low valleys. We see ourselves on that long trip that seems to span a continent. Part II of this text crosses the bridge from the fundamentals and examines the contexts of how SEL enhances key areas of concern for all educators.

Part II was designed to ground readers in the research and theory showing the powerful connections between SEL, character, and academic success. The presentation of the brief essays in Part II link SEL to key program areas found in urban, suburban, and rural school districts. These essays were designed to have thought-provoking implications that can be derived for students in differing developmental periods of their lives. Some are age related, whereas others demonstrate the connections of SEL to service, citizenship and the school-to-work transition, comprehensive student health, teacher preparation, and continuing professional development.

Our travels began with fascination and a high level of anticipation, perhaps with an idyllic vision. We are, after all, on this long trip with dreams of what we will learn about our children, ourselves, and the communities in which we work. It is in Part III of this text that the connections are made to the practitioner in the field. On our journey, we hear the voices of the conductor or the driver who has had extensive knowledge and experience. These are the people who know "what to do on Monday morning." These are the voices of mentors, coaches, and guides. The programs that they serve are the backbone of SEL. It is their stories and voices that move us to try SEL approaches, read more, contact them electronically, or just pick up the telephone and make personal contact.

In Part III, we address the questions, "What can happen if I try this approach at my school?" and "Why not try this program?" Teachers who are at different developmental stages of their careers share their voices and hearts through anecdotes drawn from their lives, perceptions, and experiences. Through this, we wanted readers to understand the importance of SEL in their classrooms and school communities. The sample materials and the instructional strategies were prepared so that classroom teachers, school support professionals, staff developers, teacher leaders, department heads, and local school leaders can implement the programs in their own school communities. The stories in Part III were prepared by master teachers who have worked with SEL for many years in their own classrooms; they know the value of success with their children. The contributors to Part III will be successful if they have inspired you to give SEL approaches an opportunity in your schools and in your classrooms and, if you have already begun the journey, to continue and perhaps to take bolder steps.

FINAL WORDS

This text offers a comprehensive look at SEL in our schools today. The need to educate and prepare the whole child is important in our society and cannot continue to be overlooked as we continue in this second millennium. What seems like an increasing flow of research findings indicates the need for academic and social-emotional balance in our schools; these can best be accessed and monitored in an ongoing way through the Web site of the Collaborative for Academic, Social, and Emotional Learning (www.CASEL.org).

Academic preparation is simply not enough; education must support students who are also emotionally prepared for the 21st century. Providing this preparation for children will not come from clicking one's heels three times and wishing it to be so, nor can we rely on determination alone, of the kind "I think I can, I think I can. . . ." We need to keep in mind that "we can't teach what we don't understand." This simple statement, although self-evident, is well documented by research examining the relationships between what teachers know and how they teach (Shulman, 1986, 1987). This book was designed to allow readers to both understand and "see," and, therefore, to implement.

The genesis of a learning community for all of the members of our schools begins with knowledge, and this text offers an opportunity to learn, experience, and grow. We envision a community in which support is highly valued and fosters and facilitates professional growth and development.

The stories, essays, research, and practice of this text send a powerful message that we must connect the mind and the heart. As educators, we know the importance of building professional learning communities. It is in the context of SEL that we are able to view the key elements of a professional learning community such as collective creativity, shared values and vision, supportive conditions, shared personal practice, and supportive and shared leadership. Those powerful connections are vital to educating the whole child in our society today. Our journey does not come to a close but continues as we cross the bridge of transformation. It is through our connection to children that we link our knowledge, experiences, feelings, and understanding of our future.

REFERENCES

Camus, A. (1965). *Notebooks, 1935–1942.* New York: Modern Library.

Elias, M., Arnold, H., & Hussey, C. (2003). *EQ + IQ = Best leadership practices for caring and successful schools.* Thousand Oaks, CA: Corwin.

Goleman, D. (1995). *Emotional intelligence: Why it can matter more than IQ.* New York: Bantam Books.

Shulman, L. S. (1986). Those who understand: Knowledge growth in teaching. *Educational Researcher, 15*(2), 4–14.

Shulman, L. S. (1987). Knowledge and teaching: Foundations of the new reform. *Harvard Educational Review, 57*(1), 1–22.

Index

Page references followed by *fig* indicates an illustrated figure; followed by *t* indicates a table; followed by *b* indicates a box.

CORWIN
PRESS

The Corwin Press logo—a raven striding across an open book—represents the union of courage and learning. Corwin Press is committed to improving education for all learners by publishing books and other professional development resources for those serving the field of PreK–12 education. By providing practical, hands-on materials, Corwin Press continues to carry out the promise of its motto: **"Helping Educators Do Their Work Better."**